SCHOLARSHIP IN WOMEN'S HISTORY: REDISCOVERED AND NEW

Editor

GERDA LERNER

A CARLSON PUBLISHING SERIES

For a complete listing of the titles in this series,
please see the back of this book.

Matronage

PATTERNS IN WOMEN'S ORGANIZATIONS, ATLANTA, GEORGIA, 1890-1940

Darlene Rebecca Roth

CARLSON
Publishing Inc

BROOKLYN, NEW YORK, 1994

Please see the end of this volume for a listing of all the titles in the Carlson Publishing Series *Scholarship in Women's History: Rediscovered and New*, edited by Gerda Lerner, of which this is Volume 9.

Copyright © 1994 by Darlene Rebecca Roth

HQ1906
.A7
R67
1994

Library of Congress Cataloging-in-Publication Data

Roth, Darlene Rebecca
    Matronage : patterns in women's organizations, Atlanta, Georgia
1890-1940 / by Darlene Rebecca Roth.
        p.   cm. — (Scholarship in women's history ; 9)
    Includes bibliographical references and index.
    ISBN 0-926019-70-8
    1. Women—Georgia—Atlanta—Societies and clubs—History.
I. Title. II. Series: Scholarship in Women's History ; 9.
HQ1906.A7R67   1994
305.4'06'0758231—dc20   94-18184

Typographic design: Julian Waters

Typeface: Bitstream ITC Galliard

Jacket and Case design: Alison Lew

Index prepared by Scholars Editorial Services, Inc., Madison, Wisconsin.

Printed on acid-free, 250-year-life paper.

Manufactured in the United States of America.

Contents

Editor's Introduction
to the Series

An important aspect of the development of modern scholarship in Women's History has been the recovery of lost, forgotten or neglected sources. In the 1960s, when the practitioners of Women's History were so few as to be virtually invisible to the general profession, one of the commonly heard answers to the question, why is there nothing about women in your text? was that, unfortunately, women until the most recent past, had to be counted among the illiterate and had therefore not left many sources. It was common then to refer to women as among the "anonymous"—a group that included members of minority racial and ethnic groups of both sexes, most working-class people, colonials, Native Americans and women. In short, most of the populations of the past. These ignorant and erroneous answers satisfied only those who wished to stifle discussion, but they did make the issue of "sources" an urgent concern to practitioners of Women's History.

To historians who had done work in primary sources regarding women, it was obvious that the alleged dearth of sources did not exist, but it was true that the sources were not readily available. In archives and finding guides, women disappeared under the names of male family members. The voluminous records of their organizational work were disorganized, uncatalogued, and not infrequently rotting in file boxes in basement storage rooms. Since few if any researchers were interested in them, there seemed to be little purpose in making them accessible or even maintaining them. There were no archival projects to preserve the primary sources of American women comparable to the well-supported archival projects concerning Presidents and male political leaders. There were only a few and quite partial bibliographies of American women, while the encyclopedic reference works, such as the *DAB* (*Dictionary of American Biography*) or similar sources traditionally neglected to include all but a small number of women notables.

When the three-volume *Notable American Women: 1607—1950: A Biographical Dictionary* appeared in 1971, (to be followed by a fourth volume in 1980), it marked an important contribution to sources on women.[1] This comprehensive scholarly work consisted of 1,801 entries, with a biographical essay and a bibliography of works by and about each woman under discussion. It readily became obvious to even the casual user of these volumes how few modern biographies of these notable women existed, despite the availability of sources.

The real breakthrough regarding "sources" was made by a "grand manuscript search," begun in 1971, which aimed to survey historical archives in every state and identify their holdings pertaining to women. This project was started by a small committee—Clarke Chambers, Carl Degler, Janet James, Anne Firor Scott and myself. After a mail questionnaire survey of 11,000 repositories in every state, to which more than 7,000 repositories responded, it was clear that the sources on women were far wider and deeper than anyone had suspected. Ultimately, the survey resulted in a two-volume reference tool, Andrea Hinding, ed., *Women's History Sources: A Guide to Archives and Manuscript Collections in the United States.*[2]

The project proved that there were unused and neglected sources of Women's History to be found literally in every archive in the country. Participation in the survey convinced many archivists to reorganize and reclassify their holdings, so that materials about women could be more readily identified.

The arguments about "illiterate women" and absence of sources are no longer heard, but the problem of having accessible sources for Women's History continued. Even after archives and libraries reorganized and reclassified their source holding on the subject, most of the pertinent materials were not available in print. Many of the early developers of Women's History worked on source collections, reprint edition projects and, of course, bibliographies. The rapid and quite spectacular expansion of the field brought with it such great demand for sources that publishers at last responded. The past twenty years have seen a virtual flood of publications in Women's History, so that the previous dearth of material seems almost inconceivable to today's students.

For myself, having put a good many years of my professional life into the development of "source books" and bibliographies, it did not seem particularly urgent to continue the effort under the present conditions. But I was awakened to the fact that there might still be a problem of neglected and forgotten sources in Women's History as a result of a conference, which Kathryn Sklar and I organized in 1988. The Wingspread Conference "Graduate Training in U.S. Women's History" brought together 63 representatives of 57 institutions of higher education who each represented a graduate program in Women's History. As part of our preparation for the conference, we asked each person invited to list all the dissertations in Women's History she had directed or was then directing. The result was staggering: it appeared that there were 99 completed dissertations and 236 then underway. This was by no means the entire national output, since we surveyed only the 63 participants at the conference and did not survey the many faculty persons not represented, who had directed such dissertations. The questions arose—What happened to all these dissertations? Why did so many of them not get published?

When Ralph Carlson approached me at about that time with the idea of publishing "lost sources" in Women's History, I was more ready than I would have been without benefit of the Wingspread survey to believe that, indeed, there still were some such neglected sources out there, and to undertake such a project.

We used the dissertation list from the Wingspread Conference as a starting point. A researcher then went through all the reference works listing dissertations in history and other fields in the English language from 1870 to the present. Among these she identified 1,235 titles in what we now call Women's History. We then cross-checked these titles against the electronic catalog of the Library of Congress, which represents every book owned by the LC (or to define it differently, every book copyrighted and published in the U.S.). This cross-check revealed that of the 1,235 dissertations, 314 had been published, which is more than 25 percent. That represents an unusually high publication ratio, which may be a reflection of the growth and quality of the field.

A further selection based on abstracts of the 921 unpublished dissertations narrowed the field to 101. Of these we could not locate 33 authors or the authors were not interested in publication. Out of the 68 remaining dissertations we selected the eleven we considered best in both scholarship and writing. These are first-rate books that should have been published earlier and that for one reason or another fell between the cracks.

Why did they not get published earlier? In the case of the Boatwright manuscript, an unusually brilliant Master's thesis done in 1939, undoubtedly the neglect of Women's History at that time made the topic seem unsuitable for publication. Similar considerations may have worked against publication of several other earlier dissertations. In other cases, lack of mentorship and inexperience discouraged the writers from pursuing publication in the face of one or two rejections of their manuscripts. Several of the most valuable books in the series required considerable rewriting under editorial supervision, which, apparently, had not earlier been available to the authors. There are also several authors who became members of what we call "the lost generation," historians getting their degrees in the 1980s when there were few jobs available. This group of historians, which disproportionately consisted of women, retooled and went into different fields. Three of the books in this series are the work of these historians, who needed considerable persuasion to do the necessary revisions and editing. We are pleased to have found their works and to have persisted in the effort of making them available to a wider readership, since they have a distinct contribution to make.

The books in this series cover a wide range of topics. Two of them are detailed studies in the status of women, one in Georgia, 1783-1860, the other in Russia in the early 1900s. Two are valuable additions to the literature on the anti-woman's suffrage campaigns in the U.S. Of the four books dealing with the history of women's organizations, three are detailed regional studies and one is a comparative history of the British and American Women's Trade Union League. Finally, the three biographical studies of eighteenth- and nineteenth-century women offer either new information or new interpretations of their subjects.

Eleanor Miot Boatwright, *Status of Women in Georgia, 1783—1860*, was discovered by Professor Anne Firor Scott in the Duke University archives and represents, in her words "a buried treasure." An M.A. thesis written by a high school teacher in Augusta, Georgia, its level of scholarship and the depth of its research are of the quality expected of a dissertation. The author has drawn on a vast range of primary sources, including legal sources that were then commonly used for social history, to document and analyze the social customs, class differences, work and religion of white women in Georgia. While her treatment of race relations reflects the limitations of scholarship on that subject in the 1930s, she gives careful attention to the impact of race relations on white women. Her analysis of the linkage made by Southern male apologists for slavery between the subordination ("protection") of women and the subordination of slaves (also rationalized as their "protection") is particularly insightful. The work has much information to offer the contemporary scholar and can be compared in its scholarship and its general approach to the work of Julia Spruill and Elizabeth Massey. When it is evaluated in comparison with other social histories of its period, its research methodology and interpretative focus on women are truly remarkable.

Anne Bobroff-Hajal's, *Working Women in Russia Under the Hunger Tsar: Political Activism and Daily Life*, is a fascinating, excellently researched study of a topic on which there is virtually no material available in the English language. Focusing on women industrial workers in Russia's Central Industrial Region, most of them employed in textile production, Bobroff studied their daily lives and family patterns, their gender socialization, their working and living conditions and their political activism during the Revolution: in political organizations, in food riots and in street fighting. The fact that these women and their families lived mostly in factory barracks will be of added interest to labor historians, who may wish to compare their lives and activities with other similarly situated groups in the U.S. and England. Drawing on a rich mixture of folkloric sources, local newspapers, oral histories, workers' memoirs and ethnographic material, Bobroff presents a convincing and intimate picture of working-class life before the Russian Revolution. Bobroff finds that the particularly strong mother-child bonding of Russian women workers, to which they were indoctrinated from childhood on, undermined their ability to form coherent political groups capable of maintaining their identity over a long period of time. Her thesis, excellently supported and well argued, may undermine some commonly held beliefs on this subject. It should prove of interest to all scholars working on gender socialization and to others working on labor culture, working-class activism, and class consciousness.

Rosemary Keller, *Patriotism and the Female Sex: Abigail Adams and the American Revolution*, is a sophisticated, well-documented interpretation of Abigail Adams's intellectual and political development, set firmly within the historical context. Compared with other Abigail Adams biographies, this work is outstanding in treating her seriously as an agent in history and as an independent intellectual. Abigail Adams emerges from this study as a woman going as far as it was possible to go within the limits of the gender conventions of her time and struggling valiantly, through influencing her husband, to extend these gender conventions. This is an accomplishment quite sufficient for one woman's life time. Professor Keller's sensitive biography makes a real contribution to colonial and women's history.

Elizabeth Ann Bartlett, *Liberty, Equality, Sorority: The Origins and Integrity of Feminist Thought: Frances Wright, Sarah Grimké and Margaret Fuller*, is another work of intellectual history. It attempts to define a common "feminism" emerging from the thought of these important nineteenth-century thinkers and concludes that feminism, in order to sustain itself, must balance the tensions between the concepts of liberty, equality, and sorority. The lucid, well-researched discussions of each woman's life and work should appeal to the general reader and make this book a valuable addition to courses in intellectual history and women's history and literature.

Mary Grant, *Private Woman, Public Person: An Account of the Life of Julia Ward Howe from 1819 to 1868*, is a sensitive, feminist study of Howe's life and thought up to the turning point in 1868, when she decided to dedicate her life to public activism in behalf of women. By carefully analyzing Howe's private letters and journals, the author uncovers a freer, more powerful and creative writer beneath the formal *persona* of the author of "The Battle Hymn of the Republic" than we have hitherto known. She also discusses in detail Howe's fascinating, never published, unfinished novel, "Eva and Raphael," which features a number of then taboo subjects, such as rape, madness and an androgynous character. This well-written biography reveals new aspects and dimensions of Julia Ward Howe's life and work.

Jane Jerome Camhi, *Women Against Women: American Anti-Suffragism, 1880-1920*, and Thomas J. Jablonsky, *The Home, Heaven, and Mother Party: Female Anti-Suffragists in America, 1868-1920*, are complementary studies that should be indispensable for any serious student or scholar of woman suffrage. They are, in fact, the only extant book-length studies of anti-suffragism. This important movement has until now been accessible to modern readers only through the somewhat biased lens of contemporary suffragists' observations. They consistently underestimated its scope and significance and did not engage with its basic paradox, that it was a movement by women against women.

Jane Camhi's comprehensive study of nationwide anti-woman's suffrage movements makes this paradox a central theme. Camhi analyses the "antis' " ideas and ideology and offers some thought-provoking theories about the competing and contradictory positions women took in regard to formal political power. Her insightful profile of a noted anti-suffragist, Ida Tarbell, is an additional contribution this fine book makes to the historical literature.

Thomas Jablonsky's study is focused more narrowly on the organizational history of the rise and fall of the movement. The book is based on extensive research in the organizational records of the anti-suffragists on a state and national level, the records of Congressional hearings, biographical works and the manuscripts of leaders. Jablonsky takes the "antis" seriously and disproves the suffragists' argument that they were merely pawns of male interest groups. He offers a sympathetic, but critical evaluation of their ideas. His detailed attention to organizational efforts in states other than the major battle-grounds—Massachusetts, New York and Illinois—make this book a valuable resource for scholars in history, political science and Women's History.

The four remaining books in the series all focus on aspects of women's organizational activities. Taken together, they reveal the amazing energy, creativity, and persistence of women's institution building on the community and local level. They sustain and highlight the thesis that women built the infrastructures of community life, while men held the positions of visible power. Based on research in four distinctly different regions, these studies should prove useful not only for the intrinsic worth of each, but for comparative purposes.

Darlene Roth, *Matronage: Patterns in Women's Organizations, Atlanta, Georgia, 1890-1940*, is a thoroughly researched, gracefully written study of the networks of women's organizations in that city. The author's focus on conservative women's organizations, such as the Daughters of the American Revolution, the Colonial Dames, and the African-American Chatauqua Circle, adds to the significance of the book. The author defines "matronage" as the functions and institutionalization of the networks of social association among women. By focusing on a Southern city in the Progressive era, Roth provides rich comparative material for the study of women's voluntarism. She challenges notions of the lack of organizational involvement by Southern women. She traces the development of women's activities from communal service orientation—the building of war memorials—to advocacy of the claims of women and children and, finally, to advocacy of women's rights. Her comparative approach, based on the study of the records of white and African-American women's organizations and leadership—she studied 508 white and 150 black women—is illuminating and offers new insights. The book should be of interest to readers in Urban and Community History, Southern History, and Women's History.

Robin Miller Jacoby, *The British and American Women's Trade Union Leagues, 1890-1925: A Case Study of Feminism and Class*, is a comparative study of working-class women in Britain and America in the Progressive period. Although parts of this work have appeared as articles in scholarly journals, the work has never before been accessible in its entirety. Jacoby traces the development of Women's Trade Union Leagues in Britain and America, exploring their different trajectories and settings. By focusing on the interaction of women's and labor movements, the author provides rich empirical material. Her analysis of the tensions and overlapping interests of feminism and class consciousness is important to feminist theory. Her discussion of protective labor legislation, as it was debated and acted upon in two different contexts, makes an important contribution to the existing literature. It also addressees issues still topical and hotly debated in the present day. The book will be of interest to labor historians, Women's History specialists, and the general public.

Janice Steinschneider, *An Improved Woman: The Wisconsin Federation of Women's Clubs, 1895-1920*, is a richly documented study based on a multitude of primary sources, which reveals the amazing range of women's activities as community builders and agents of change. Wisconsin clubwomen founded libraries, fostered changes in school curricula and worked to start kindergartens and playgrounds. They helped preserve historic and natural landmarks and organized to improve public health services. They built a sound political base—long before they had the right of suffrage—from which they trained women leaders for whom they then helped to secure public appointments. They worked to gain access for women to university education and employment and, in addition to many other good causes, they worked for world peace. Steinschneider's description and analysis of "women's public sphere" is highly sophisticated. Hers is one of the best studies on the subject and should prove indispensable to all concerned with understanding women's political activities, their construction of a public sphere for women, and their efforts and successes as builders of large coalitions.

Margit Misangyi Watts, *High Tea at Halekulani: Feminist Theory and American Clubwomen*, is a more narrowly focused study of clubwomen's work than are the other three, yet its significance ranges far above that of its subject matter. Watts tells the story of the Outdoor Circle, an upper-class white women's club in Hawaii, from its founding in 1911 on. Its main activities were to make Hawaii beautiful: to plant trees, clean up eyesores, preserve nature and rid the islands of billboards. To achieve these modest goals, the women had to become consummate politicians and lobbyists and learn how to run grassroots boycotts and publicity and educational campaigns, and how to form long-lasting coalitions. Above all, as Watts's fine theoretical analysis shows, they insisted that their female vision, their woman-centered view, become an accepted part of the public discourse. This case study is rich in theoretical implications. Together with the other three studies of women's club activities it offers not only a wealth of practical examples of women's work for social change, but it also shows that such work both resists patriarchal views and practices and redefines them in the interests of women.

Gerda Lerner
Madison, Wisconsin

Preface

"Matronage" began with an impression and evolved slowly, through a wide-ranging, experimental investigation, into a cultural concept. When I reviewed the papers of the Association of Southern Women for the Prevention of Lynching, where this study really started, I was struck by the fact that Jessie Daniel Ames, who founded the association, was able to reach over 40,000 southern women merely by tapping into the machinery of their organizations. Here was an extensive and intricate network of association and communication among women of the South, the workings of which were intriguing. It was impossible to investigate the personae of so large a network on any meaningful basis—the women were too numerous and the points of their influence too spread out—so I chose to look at the network at a more controllable level and picked the city of Atlanta as my focus. Atlanta was the headquarters of the Women's Anti-Lynching Association, and as the regional center for the Southeastern United States, it was anticipated it would offer many insights into women's organizational lives, southern style.

It was my original intention to conduct a demographic analysis of organizational women and to compile a collective biography of them, drawing the names from as many organizations as I could identify, for the twenty years between the two world wars, which corresponded with the period of early intense interracial activity among southern women. I was persuaded by Letitia Brown, then my dissertation director, to set the parameters of the study by the materials available and not to be arbitrary in assigning certain decades for analysis. The result was an intensive demographic analysis that stretched to fifty years in scope, and the addition of thirty more years of background material into the story of the women's organizations in Atlanta.

The methodologies used for the study also evolved gradually and were derived from the available research materials. I collected names of women in official positions in women's organizations from every conceivable source, but ultimately restricted the collection to names drawn from organizational records directly. Very quickly I amassed a list of nearly 2,000 names from over 200 organizations. It was clear at that point that there was no end to the numerical compilation, and that analysis of a collection of such magnitude was more than a single researcher could handle using a hand-sort card retrieval system.

I decided to pick from the numbers of organizations those groups that seemed to bear a high degree of similarity, that grew from the early female leadership in Atlanta, and that offered good cross-racial comparison. The groups that I finally used for the statistical and demographic studies are listed in Chapter IV. I traced all of the women (508 white women, 150 black women) through as many other record sources, organizational as well as biographical, as could be found quickly, in order to fill out the pictures of their individual biographies. Then, I traced the women through the Atlanta city directories at ten-year intervals, under both the name and street listings, to plot each woman on maps of the city. It was at this point that real differences among the organizations began to appear, as club memberships began to take on geographic characteristics within the metropolis. Other details of the search and of the analysis are discussed in the appropriate chapters.

In addition to the original research for names, facts, and social connections of the organization women, I read widely in southern history and literature, local Atlanta and Georgia history, women's history (then a new, emerging field), sociology, urban history and geography, black history, organizational histories and theories, and more. This, too, could have been an unlimited occupation, but the wide reading not only acquainted me with the basics I needed for this study, it helped refine the notion of "matronage" that was taking shape in my mind.

Throughout the period of research and writing I was assisted by many people who deserve credit and thanks. My thanks, then, to Lee Alexander, archivist at Atlanta University, who was the first to open Atlanta archival doors for me; to Ann Pederson and Pete Schinkel at the Georgia Department of Archives and History, for their professionalism and their personal interest in my projects; to Linda Matthews, helpful, sympathetic, patient, and encouraging at the Woodruff Library at Emory University; and to the staffs of the Atlanta Historical Society, the Atlanta Public Library, and the University of Georgia Special Collections Department, all of whom endured research requests while they were undergoing the dislocations of reconstruction of their facilities.

Personally, I wish to thank Bernard Mergen for picking up the pieces after Letitia Brown's untimely death. To Anne Firor Scott, my thanks for encouraging me to get into women's history in the first place, and to C. A. Bacote for opening my eyes to the riches of Atlanta's black history. To Dr. Arthur E. Burns a special note of thanks for assuming I should pursue a Ph.D. degree when I had never considered it a possibility, and special appreciation to my former colleagues and friends from the Graduate School at George Washington, especially Kathleen Pope and Hallie Lou Blum. My gratitude also goes to my friends and colleagues in The History Group, Inc., who have not only taught me a great deal about history but also stood by patiently and resolutely while I finished up my work. Among them Colleen Keegan deserves special credit for the photographic work that was done and redone for my original narrative. Finally, my thanks to Dana F. White, whose belief in me never wavered even when my belief in myself did, whose strength often had to sustain the two of us, and whose sense of humor got us both through many a dark hour when I would begin to repeat the litany of dissertation blues just one more time.

D.R.R.

Matronage

ONE

Matronage: A New Word for an Old Phenomenon

This is an examination of one of the cultural manifestations of the separation of the sexes in America. It is not my task here to trace the origins of the idea of "woman's place," or to argue its pros and cons, but to look at how that concept has worked itself out in a part of American culture.

The phenomenon I examine is women's organizations—specifically, the local branches of those national associations, societies, clubs, federations, leagues, and other groups that were founded in the late nineteenth and early twentieth centuries, have become highly institutionalized over time, and are still in existence today. Institutions such as the Daughters of the American Revolution, the United Daughters of the Confederacy, the General Federation of Women's Clubs, the National Association of Colored Women's Clubs, the National Council of Jewish Women, and the amalgamations of early suffrage organizations into the National American Woman Suffrage Association (extant today in the League of Woman Voters) and of local Christian service agencies into the National YWCA, as well as a variety of lesser known bodies all had their foundations within the intellectual atmosphere of the Victorian era, which espoused the doctrine of separate male and female spheres and the theory of "distinctive womanhood."

The theory was a compromise position between those who argued the innate inferiority of woman and those who propounded her superiority. Briefly stated, "distinctive womanhood" required only that woman fulfill and develop her "own nature and function in life," a nature and function believed to be entirely different from that of men—not necessarily intrinsically better or worse than man's, merely different.[1] This was an ingenious cultural construct, for implicit in the idea of "distinctiveness" was the appeal of having a special life mission designed for women only, which had meaning for the total community. Implicit also in the idea was the requisite for sexual segregation, which allowed women on their own terms to create the forms and means of carrying out their special mission. In addition, the idea carried with it the possibility of almost universal applicability; it could be used to buttress any and all female factions: those women who adhered to a *Küche, Kinder, Kirche* philosophy could be satisfied that their special mission lay strictly within the home, and those adherents of a "new" womanhood could use the argument to uphold their less restricting views about women's roles. Female reformers regularly used woman's "special" nature as a defense of their own activism, and, indeed, the cause of woman suffrage itself was supported from this same point of view.[2] Other women translated "distinctive womanhood" into a position whereby it was woman's proper role, in fact her duty, to bring recognized feminine virtues out into the open community, with or without the vote. As a common cultural assumption, differential sexual value held currency among reformers and nonreformers alike; its expositors have been as diverse as they have been numerous.

Probably the most extraordinary proponent of special womanhood in the nineteenth century was Catharine Beecher, whose life, work, writing, and philosophy provide a consummate example of the proper concerns of distinctive womanhood. It was Beecher's own mission, through her writings and her school, to create a corps of domestic evangelists—women of dignity and social standing, whose backgrounds were impeccable, whose personal circumstances were blessed, and whose domestic credentials and training (under Beecher) were exceptional. To these women, Beecher granted the moral rectitude of a modern-day crusade army out to redeem mankind, whose soldiers were to serve as paragons of virtue, breeding, education, and sacrifice in their communities.[3] In a word, Beecher trained morally aggressive Christian wives and mothers.

Beecher's missionary zeal carried over into the twentieth century, where it appeared in more secular forms. Two proponents of distinctive womanhood who applied the idea of woman's special mission quite differently were the prosuffrage social worker Jane Addams and the antisuffrage muckraker Ida M. Tarbell. Addams emphasized the application of domestic talents to the needs of local governments, extending the language of the kitchen into the municipality, with suggestive references to "city housekeeping" as a natural concern of women. For Addams the vote was a means to an end and a way for women to offer more—and more effective—public service.[4] Ida Tarbell, on the other hand, stressed the importance of the domestic role itself over any extension of it into the public arena. Hers was no vague social prescription, but a direct advocation of the functions of maternity within the culture. The "meaning of woman's natural business in the world," she explained, and the part it has played in

civilizing humanity—in forcing good morals and good manners, in giving a reason and so a desire for peaceful arts and industries, the place it has had in persuading men and women that only self-restraint, courage, good cheer, and reverence produce the highest types of manhood and womanhood—that is written on every page of history.[5]

The point to be made is obvious, and the political realities of it as old as the nation itself. The key to woman's special mission lay, quite naturally, in her dual roles as childbearer and childrearer. In the early days of the Republic, the importance of these roles were established on the principle that a "model" mother was also a "model" female citizen; as such, she was inevitably "dedicated to the service of civic virtue; she educated her sons for it; she condemned and corrected her husband's lapses from it."[6] Christian thinking ladened the role of the female with the moral redemption of mankind in atonement for the Fall from Grace; certainly, early-nineteenth-century revivalism and missionary spirits (such as Beecher's) kept this idea squarely before the eyes of American women. The bearers of the nation's infants were also, metaphorically, the bearers of its culture per se, "culture" being everything from the teaching of simple morality and social graces to the prerequisites of "high" artistic appreciation. Women were to be the arbiters in all such realms.

The prescriptions of separate male and female spheres allowed women to expand their "distinctive" womanhood on their own territory, as individuals and as groups. Such expansion was encouraged as long as it was domestic in origin and expression. As the nineteenth century wore on, voluntary associations became prominent vehicles for the expression of model female citizenship as well as a favored setting for its expansion. In the eyes of most, this was a predictable step in the nation's growth, as a president of the National Association of Colored Women's Clubs once suggested:

That organization is the first step in nation-making, and that a nation can rise in scale no higher than its womanhood are principles which have come to be looked upon by the sociologists and all students of the development of just humanity as self-evident truth; hence, it seems quite natural to speak of one in connection with the other, i.e., organization and women.[7]

Certain of the women's organizations founded during the late nineteenth and early twentieth centuries promoted the special nature of woman's mission on earth with more vigor than others did, but none denied the centrality of motherhood to the notion of what "womanhood" meant within the culture.

The attention paid to motherhood by women's organizations accompanied massive technological and social changes in America, which affected the roles of women in their homes—as did, in fact, industrialization, urbanization, and the privation of the home. It also correlated with new intellectual theories about the anatomically predictive destiny of women within their "proper" environments and their own communities. From the sexology of Sigmund Freud to the social application of Darwinism to the anthropology of Robert Briffault, the psychological and sociological responsibilities of mothers were being reinterpreted, refined, and reassessed, as was their communal value. What is of more specific interest here, however, are the women's own actions toward augmenting (some would say inflating) the duties, rights, roles, responsibilities, and honors befalling motherhood in the public eye, and how it was that women sought recognition for motherhood as appropriate social functioning.

The organizations that resulted from their efforts are worth individual attention on this very point, but the conglomeration, in Atlanta alone, of their doings in this vein is truly staggering and offers a vivid case study. What did the women do? First of all, they took care of their own: they created organizations for women and children in innumerable guises—orphanages, homes for destitute mothers with children, schools for children, but also schools for mothers. "Mothers' meetings" indeed were a common form of basic self-education for women, which became as well a convenient means for assimilating foreign women to American ways and poorer women to middle-class standards of domestic maintenance.

The women attempted to affect their children's upbringing outside the home by either supporting the creation of schools (including Sunday schools) or by creating bodies of women to influence those schools. Significantly, and not surprisingly, the first such influential body, itself founded by a Georgia woman, was known as the "Congress of Mothers" (now the PTA). On other external fronts, the women supported legislation, both locally and nationally, that not only protected their familial rights, but expanded their legal rights as mothers. For example, they fought for the right of a woman to have custody of her children at the time of divorce or widowhood, which transfer of parenthood was neither customary nor common in Georgia until the early nineteenth century. Or, to use a twentieth-century example, local members of the National Woman's Party avidly fought for the right of matrilineal citizenship for the children of mothers married to non-American males.

The women invented institutional forms to protect motherhood in controversial situations: the Florence Crittenden Mission, for example, was not only an effort to "save" unfortunate "fallen" girls, but it was also an effort to preserve the "natural" bond between mother and child, despite the social ostracism of the former and the so-called illegitimacy of the latter. In other ways the local women worked against the separation of mother and child by lobbying against the employment of young children and mothers of young children outside the home. They established kindergartens and nurseries for the children of women who had to work outside the home so the youngsters would get some semblance of maternal care. And for the proud but poor, who would not or could not leave their homes, there was the chance to make products from their own domestic skills, which would be sold at the Woman's Exchange at a genteel profit for the producers.

Atlanta women embraced domestic "science" and the arrival of "professionalized" home management with a vengeance—as individuals and as groups. They broadcast its virtues and preached its practice through their organizations—not only through the Home Economics League, but also through "home" demonstrations at the local woman's club, through "model homes" and "better baby" contests at fairs and bazaars, through classes and instruction they gave one another, through propaganda in their organizational media, and so on and on and on.

Acting often in loco parentis, the women concerned themselves with the social outlets of younger, unmarried women, as the YWCA did for women of the expanding, nonindustrial female work force. And in a similar way, the Debutantes Club and the Junior League tried to regulate the social outlets of unmarried and newly married young women, respectively.

At the beginning of the period under study, Atlanta women combined to commemorate their fathers, in such groups as the Daughters of the American Revolution and the Daughters of the Confederacy where they were very active, in what might be seen as a confirmation of patriarchal loyalties as well as a statement of their own birthright. By the end of the period, they were forming groups to commemorate their sons—as members of the Service Star

5

Legion—as an out-and-out statement of maternal sentiments. Ultimately, they simply created organizations for themselves; "mothers" and "grandmothers" clubs were common by the end of the period. And throughout, they passed on their own club memberships—not at all indiscriminately, but directly from mother to daughter. This has been the process of transmission.

Predicated on the ideals of good motherhood and the imperatives of sexual segregation, "distinctive womanhood" has been transmitted through single-sex organizations. A separatist tradition has developed, which has supported both "liberal" and "conservative" causes, both status-quo and change-oriented issues, and which manifests itself in a wholly separate entity within the domain of public affairs—an interconnecting network of social associations, a Female Establishment, one might call it, the functions, operations, and institutionalization of which I have identified as *matronage*.

The word *matronage* does not exist per se, but its meaning should be clear from a combination of definitions under the words *matron* and, to some extent, *patronage*. The *American Heritage Dictionary*, for example, lists the following under *matron*: 1) a married woman, especially a mother of mature age with established dignity and social position; 2) a woman who supervises a public institution, such as a school, hospital, or prison. Under *patronage* is listed the "support, encouragement or championship from a patron." *Matronage* would be, then, the status or function of a matron, i.e., of being a married woman, especially a mother of mature age; exercising the personal attributes of a matron within institutional settings; championing, encouraging, supporting as a matron, etc. The principal elements are the mature woman (who is a mother) and the institutions or groups through which she works to champion or support the people, ideas, and operations of her choice.

The patterns of activity found within matronage are identifiable through these principal ingredients and are marked by another distinguishing feature—the intentional nature of the involvement in these organizations. Discriminated against, subordinated, and excluded, the women in this study also consciously and willfully excluded themselves from male associations in the full belief that their sexual distinctiveness had political and social viability. The women "realized" their cultural differences through their organizations, establishing therewith both the means and the ends of their activities. Once founded, their organizations continued to function apart—serving wholly female constituencies, espousing feminine pursuits, fostering woman-to-woman relationships, nurturing individual women in otherwise often "hostile" environments, lending support, giving purpose to individual lives, commemorating the memories of deceased women, creating social differentiations not created through other social systems, and so on. Organizations for women have been founded for every conceivable purpose, but because of their separateness, their single constituency, and their social significance, women's organizations may be taken together as an identifiable cultural phenomenon.

This study, therefore, is an attempt to see women's organizations as cultural phenomena rather than as contending political bodies. It is also an attempt to analyze the various aspects of women's organizations at their lowest reducible level—the local chapters and leaders—to reveal their cultural functions and social characteristics. The term *matronage* is used here to describe the affairs of women in a particular place—Atlanta, Georgia. I found it to be a useful descriptive term for the cultural phenomena observed, but I do not use it with the intention of making sweeping declarative statements about women in general. It seemed to be appropriate for Atlanta, but just how appropriate *matronage* is to other times and places, even to other cultures, remains to be seen. Nevertheless, the examination of a long range of history of selected women's organizations in Atlanta, between 1890 and 1940, has supported some emerging approaches to the history of women in the United States, and challenged others.

There are basically two historical traditions that treat of women's organizations. The first consists of those general, local, and regional histories that mention women's organizations in passing as part of their story; the second consists of a more recent body of works in an expanding number of admittedly feminist histories. Both traditions concur in their adherence to liberal principles; essentially, both are concerned with two different aspects of female citizenship, which are "progressive" in character. They focus either on women's direct political involvement, social influence, or economic development, especially as related to feminism, the suffrage movement, or other movements concerned with getting women into the mainstream of modern life; or they discuss what might be termed local "community building," where the contributions of women to the local environment may range broadly, but are still categorized as acts that contribute to the "progress" of the community. Of the two, the feminist tradition is stronger and more thoroughly developed.

Women's organizations—as women themselves—have been discussed within the general context of social change, especially feminist social change. Thus, Carl Degler points to the great surge of women moving into the labor force as a particularly significant index of real social change. Eleanor Flexner and others have elaborated on the importance of the establishment of a variety of educational institutions for women to the successive achievements women made in the nineteenth and early twentieth centuries. Merle Curti described the woman's rights movement as a typical example of the relation of democratic philosophy to reform movements in the United States, and J. Stanley Lemons devoted an entire book to the successes and failures of female citizenship in the 1920s.[8] In the same way, the WCTU was once described as a veritable "school on a national scale for the education of women in social affairs and the need for social reform."[9] The example of the WCTU as a progressive agent is particularly relevant to a study of the South, where it is recognized generally to have been a major liberalizing force among the women. Belle Kearney called it the "generous liberator, the joyous iconoclast, the discoverer, the developer of Southern women," and Anne Firor Scott traced a pattern of reform activity in Southern (white) women that led them directly from their churches to the WCTU to the suffrage movement, and finally, into the interracial movement.[10] However, in this case, as in others, it is not the WCTU itself that is of interest to the historians but the causes it served, the momentum it created on the way toward its goals, or the reasons for founding it in the first place. The goals may change, the movement die, yet the organization still persists (which is true of the WCTU), but beyond its moments of progressive activity, the organization ceases to be of interest to the historian.

The assumption behind this kind of discussion is obvious: organizations are agents of social change, relate to political issues, fight for causes, achieve ends, make progress. Therefore, they are important historically only to the extent that they have influenced national politics or effected social change. A corollary to this position is that those organizations that have not influenced national politics or, worse, that have impeded positive social change, are not considered historically significant.

Such is the nature of most discussions that compare the General Federation of Women's Clubs, for example, with the woman suffrage organizations. William O'Neill's treatment is typical. Although O'Neill is willing to admit that women's clubs of the federation type were an effective "antidote to boredom" that offered comradeship and "extradomestic activity," he cannot see much value in them, and explains only that the General Federation "grew like weeds for no apparent reason." In addition, he finds that the federation's aims were consistent only with "traditional womanly concerns," not with radical or feminist ones; its actions, he feels, sacrificed purpose to organization; it was too massive to respond quickly to issues, and it knew it would alienate its great masses if it did become too radical. O'Neill's discussion is intended, in his own words, not as a "reproach" of the federation, but as an indication of the federation's liberalism (which is not too great in his opinion).[11] With that, the federation is dismissed: it is large, it exists for the time considered, but to no great purpose in O'Neill's mind.

The tendency to relate women's organizations solely to social change and liberal causes is increased by the scholarly recognition of "reform" in America as the special province of the female sex (although not its exclusively). Richard Hofstadter, the major historian of reform in the United States, sees exactly this division of labor and this version of sexual segregation: politics belonged exclusively to the men; reform, to the women. An active political role in the past was "practically a test of masculinity" according to Hofstadter, while reform fell within the realm of "ideals and purity," was thoroughly feminized, and "to be engaged in reform movements meant to be the constant associate of aggressive, reforming, moralizing women."[12]

The question is not whether reform is an appropriate context within which to discuss women's organizations; obviously, it is not. Nor is there cause to question the importance of female political identities, status, and influence as a central, perhaps the central, topic for discussion in women's history. Rather the question is this: is it not possible that the written history of women, since it has been addressed with so much emphasis to the reform activities of women for the period between the Civil War and the Second World War, has actually obscured part of the whole pattern of women's lives? The tendency to focus on suffrage especially as the elemental story of American women in the latter half of the nineteenth and the first few decades of the twentieth century has created a biased view of the full shape and substance of women's lives. William O'Neill again provides a good example of what is meant here.

Jane Addams served as the model for what O'Neill called "social feminism," a concept that has been adopted by many historians of American women, in fact, applied directly by them to describe the phenomena they chose to discuss. Social feminism, taken from the Addams model, tended to subordinate female emancipation to general social reform, unlike general feminism, which made female emancipation itself a political end. This concept has been applied by Lemons in *The Woman Citizen*, and by others. It has been applied and extended now nearly to the point of exhausting its usefulness. Lois Banner, continuing the model, has suggested that in addition to distinguishing between social feminism and feminism per se, other forms of feminism ought also to be

9

identified and described in the history of women: e.g., "radical feminism," "militant feminism," and "domestic feminism," to name some of her varieties.[13] The problem with this proposal, carried to its implied extreme, is that it is absurd: it makes feminism the measure of women's activities, as though that were the norm. The question has become of history not, "what happened?" but rather, "how feminist was it?" This single-minded approach has even led one scholar to conjecture, cryptically, that what might be needed are "more historical explorations of what was happening in the lives of American women *apart* from the struggle for the political right to vote in order to reach some final understanding of the suffrage movement itself."[14] Woman suffrage, political activity, and reform endeavors are all subject to misinterpretation if not seen in a broader context. Most of all, the grass-roots level of political activity and the processes of social interaction that go into making up a community need to be focused on.

This leads to the second historical tradition concerning women's organizations—their involvement in local community building. Here historians have been suggestive only. O'Neill admits that "clubwomen were probably most effective" on the local level, but he does not examine them there. Degler states that women's clubs "were actually enormously effective in the 1890s and later," and that "many a town or city owed its library, children's playground, or a charming park to the efforts of a local woman's club [as] frequently, there were no other civic organizations in town." He gives no specific examples, names no towns. Others, such as L. B. Wright, have perceived women's clubs to be "civilizers" on the frontier. Since most of America has been frontier country at one time or other, this is an important hypothesis, yet the true extent of women's clubs and of women themselves as "civilizers" in frontier living is more a popular theme than a serious historical one. A few black women's organizations have been dealt with as local community builders, but again, only as part of a larger picture.[15]

Generally speaking, here too the accent has been on organizations as progressive agents within local communities. They have good records of effective reform, good "city housekeeping" habits, and effective direct or indirect political input—from these, their historical importance is derived. In this way, women's organizations clearly fall within the character of voluntary associations described by Arthur M. Schlesinger: democratizing agents that serve as a "great cementing force for national integration."[16]

But what is the process through which they work? And what are the forces for (or against) national integration? What part do women's groups play in the total structuring of a community, which is itself a series of associations among people, taking place at a certain time and in a certain place? What is needed is not just a sense of women's groups as political agents, but a sense of the ramifications of a widespread, formally organized system of women's activities at the local level and its impact on the community and from the community outward. What more is needed is some adjustment of the national picture of women's affairs, as qualified from the local perspective. Their political, "democratizing" influence aside for the moment, women's organizations have manifold functions within a community, most of which are devoid of ultimate political significance. Historians are disappointed when organizations do not make powerful political statements or when they do not seem to involve themselves in political struggles, and as a result, historians often miss important social factors about organizations, which are operative at the level where the organization and the individual interact and at the level where the organization and its immediate ecology interact. Women's organizations, if and when they do not exercise political clout, still affect their communities: they confer social status and distinctions on their members; they exercise authority in many areas of adult female life; they define community structure through their "turf" identifications; they create life-style variations through their specific operations and locales; they create occupations and economic bases (albeit usually small ones); they perpetuate value systems through the institutionalization of their corporate bodies; and they stimulate psychological motivations through their extensive ego reward systems. Such functions as these have not been seriously examined by historians, or are only now beginning to be examined.

The aggregate effect of women's organizations actually serves to complicate the general outline of women's history: their influence is contradictory. Not all women's organizations are progressive bodies; even the most "liberal" of women's organizations is likely to have its conservative aspects, and the most conservative to have liberal causes at times. It piques the imagination, for example, to know that the suffrage movement in the South was marked by the indigenous racism of the region, as was the movement in the North by nativism in that region. The major liberal organization of feminist persuasion was socially repressive and progressive at the same time, while conservative groups, such as the Daughters of the American Revolution, from whom little progressive involvement is ever expected, supported at least one feminist issue, women's education, for years, e.g., when the University of Georgia was firmly set against admitting women to its ranks.[17]

11

Taken as a whole, women's organizations indicate that the matrix of adjustments made to female role expectations, as worked out through formally organized, single-sexed groups, is much more complex and much more varied than the single story of increased political involvement tells.

As stated earlier, there are aspects of women's organizations (indeed, of any voluntary organizations) that are best illustrated at the local level. This is particularly true when analyzing the structure of a community as it reflects the separation of the sexes.

To begin with, the most obvious—and most overlooked—aspect of sexual segregation is that it requires actual physical distance between the sexes. This kind of social distance seems to have been exaggerated in the nineteenth century, and it survives into the twentieth century, but in constantly challenged forms. While no history of the various effects and forms of sexual segregation in America seems ever to have been attempted, it is essential to understand its importance in the basic working of American social systems.

In the nineteenth century, social sexual distance was obviously meant to be preserved through the separate educational systems that were developed for boys and girls; not only were males and females required to learn different subjects, according to the different curricula made available, but they were to learn them in different places. Even institutions that operated coeducationally from the outset maintained physical separation through a number of sometimes ingenious, sometimes ridiculous regulations governing social intercourse. Separate dormitories for men and women, separate physical recreation facilities, even separate classrooms are still common enough today, but the tight regulations governing dating are certainly gone, as are situations such as one described by the historian of a local university in which young men and women were required to eat on opposite sides of the dining tables.[18]

Personal appearance is another area where sexual separation is evident. It is easy enough to observe that men and women dress differently, presuming thereby different modes of behavior according to what the dress allows. It is another matter to evaluate the separate consumer systems that have developed around the dress of each sex: separate retail outlets for the sale of clothing, discreetly separated clienteles, distinct vocabularies to describe quite similar garments, different manufacturing occupations, and different occupational technologies involved in the construction of each set of clothing, male and female. Even the modern-day department store—by its very name—is not a wholly integrated institution; it too preserves separate counters for boys' and girls', men's and women's wear.

The pattern is repeated everywhere, but not always so conspicuously. One example, which comes out of the nineteenth century and as an exercise in public education certainly deserves closer examination, is found in the series of world's fairs and expositions inaugurated in London in 1851 with the Crystal Palace. Their purpose was to celebrate "progress" by putting the industrializing nations on public display. The women's part varied from fair to fair, but generally speaking, their role was a contradiction to the industrial theme. Special women's exhibits tended to celebrate not "women's involvement in industrial society, but those achievements specifically identified and approvingly catalogued as 'woman's work.' "[19] Thus, needlework, china painting, and cookery were abundantly in evidence. The fact that at several of the expositions the women's exhibits were housed in their own separate buildings is clear evidence of the social distance between the sexes. This was the case with the Columbian Exposition at Chicago in 1893 and the Cotton States and International Exposition in Atlanta in 1895, both of which had enormous impact on organized women's activities locally, regionally, and nationally. John Cawelti, who has written of the 1876, 1893, and 1933 fairs, concludes that their treatment of women indicates a kind of social suspension—a "climactic moment between emancipation and assimilation" of women into the industrial economy. Assimilation, he notes, was marked by the disappearance of the separate women's building (there was no such building at the 1933 Chicago fair).[20] Assimilation was also marked by the disappearance of women from the management level of the fairs: at the early Chicago and Atlanta fairs, female managers had been prominent in the governance of the event—not so later—a displacement Cawelti failed to observe.

A particularly troublesome example of the physical separation of the sexes—which also comes out of the nineteenth century—lies in the land-use patterns of American cities, where the creation of planned, outlying residential areas set the pattern to be followed in twentieth-century suburbanization. The real distance between home and marketplace steadily increased. The suburban ideal, which was posited in this physical separation, was hailed as a great advance in environmental control; the suburb offered the healthiest atmosphere yet for the nurture and cohesion of family life, according to its builders. It was the consummate cultural concept brought to life—a suburban home, the perfect accommodation for the essential American social unit, the family. As one of its chief proponents firmly believed, "probably the advantages of civilization can be found illustrated and demonstrated under no other circumstances so completely as in some suburban neighborhoods."[21]

Yet the suburb brought cultural disadvantages as well. Even though it was intended to foster family life, it kept the father separated from the family for much of the time, and kept the mother with the family unit, itself separated from the affairs of the marketplace. The absence of the father from the family unit was "little short of absolute," and the rule of the mother paramount.[22] Separate urban and suburban spheres developed, which, as William Bridges has pointed out in an essay on family patterns in the nineteenth century, gave rise to opposing value sets. The acculturation process was now left in the hands of women, and "mothers were barraged with a many-sided campaign to save the world by means of the family," for then, both reformers and the populace as a whole agreed that the best means of human advancement was through the virtue, sacrifice, and excellence of the mothers of the culture. The sexes were not only separated physically, they were polarized spiritually, as "the male principle of material advancement" was to be reined and checked by the "female principle of moral advancement."[23] It was thus the woman's job to transmit the best of the culture to her children, and to see it passed on, generation to generation; her roles as conserver and transmitter of cultural values were buttressed by the social system around her, including the very living arrangements of American cities.

As it turned out, the family sphere was not the only place women could preach moral advancement and practice "mother-craft." As stated, another institution was created that offered all the necessary facilities for the practice of distinctive womanhood: opportunities to articulate high moral attitudes, occasions to preserve the family through concerted action on its behalf, exercises for special feminine sensibilities, environments appropriately unisexual yet engaging to the female imagination. The woman's club was not just the result of a rush to fill the vacuum of empty time, it also represented an assertive statement of woman's proper roles. Just as a man could be most comfortably a "man" at his club, so a woman could be most comfortably, most conspicuously, a "woman" in the company of her own sex. Through the club, women could encourage, inspire, scold, preserve, and conserve in force. Women could exert their feminine authority in concert, project their own image abroad, and act as a brake on unwanted, runaway (masculine) changes. "Conservation, then," an early historian of women's clubs asserted,

in its best and highest sense is the *raison d'etre* of the General Federation of Women's Clubs—conservation of life, of liberty and of happiness; conservation of child life, of womanhood, of civic and national integrity in matters of public and private import; conservation of the best and highest functions of womanhood which shall make her in very truth the conserver of all that is best in our advancing civilization, preserver of all that is good in the civilization of the past and the helpmeet in the daily battle of life.[24]

This is the expressed tradition of the woman's club, a tradition where woman is viewed as the servant of man, and sexual separation is idealized, subordination accepted. Like Catharine Beecher, who set up her school with a similar intention, the founders and fellows of the women's club movement tried to make an active platform out of their social "place." Feminine attitudes were fully internalized by the members of the organizations and pervaded the operations of the groups. Coming to rest far short of the feminist position, this middle vein glorified women nonetheless and operated out of a sense of moral rectitude and social sanction.

Every community in the United States saw some systematic, organized application of these feminine values within its borders, and the interplay of social, economic, political, and geographic circumstances would unfold a different story for every setting. Those organizations that were anchored securely to the values described above found particularly fertile soil for expansion in the South, especially in a city like Atlanta, which espoused conservative social values while embracing progressive economic ones. Women's social organizations have persisted tenaciously in the South among its female populations, and they offer the historian a fulsome view of their cultural significance. In addition, women's social organizations have developed distinct racial varieties within the segregated communities of the South, offering the historian a ready-made, indigenous comparison. Atlanta offers an excellent opportunity for a case study of the racial variables, the tenacity of organizations, and for the interplay of the processes of urbanization, suburbanization, and female organization, which developed simultaneously in this city. Atlanta has had a highly developed, intricate network of women's organizations, operative from its earliest history, and as a localized model, it provides a qualified comment on the generalized model of women's history discussed earlier. It also provides a southern model to compare to the national model of women's involvement in organizational life.

Since it is the South in which Atlanta is located and from which it derives its importance as a city, the city itself provides another dimension to the study of women's organizations. The sense of purpose, of distinctiveness, of loss, and of common nostalgia, which mark the southern region, spill over into the women's groups. The passionate acceptance of what it means to be a woman—*a southern woman*—permeates the activities of Atlanta organizational women and gives their organizations an emotional tenor that compounds what must have been the original emotions out of which the organizations stemmed. The organizations reflect not joy, but duty; not celebration, but solemnity; not license, but obligation; not freedom, but purpose; not entertainment, but service, even in the performance of simple rituals. The underlying beat of their organizational march is duty, duty, duty—of the woman to her home and family, to her community, her state and her country, to her race, and to her God. Atlanta organization women echo, clangorously, the sentiments expressed by Jennie June Croly, founder of the General Federation, who conceived of the women's club as a proper forum for the expression of womanliness, and who saw at the center of that womanliness a sense of duty. "The sense of duty is always strong in the woman," she wrote,

> if she disregards it she never ceases to suffer. Her convictions of it have made her the most willing and joyful of martyrs, the most persistent and relentless of bigots, the most blind and devoted of partisans, the most faithful and believing of friends, and the only type out of which nature could form a Mother.[25]

A woman, a matron, a mother, a champion of a cause, with a place from which to champion it—such are the foundations of matronage.

Two Steps Forward and One Step Back: Early Chronological Patterns of Women's Public Activities in Atlanta, 1860-1900

Atlanta is a thing of industrial creation, having little in common since its inception with its more rural surroundings. It has Old South ties, but barely any Old South origins, arriving on the Georgia scene in 1837, fully a century after the founding of the colony in Savannah under James Oglethorpe and just over two decades before the Civil War laid the Old South to rest forever. Atlanta was brought into existence by the railroads, and it has continued to thrive because of its intricate ties with the developing transportation and commercial systems of the nineteenth and twentieth centuries. By virtue of its looks, its foundations, its economy, and its aspirations, Atlanta is a thoroughly New South city.

Even before Atlanta's "First Citizen," Henry Woodfin Grady, nationalized the idea of the New South and made it so famous, Atlanta citizens were boasting of their city's newness, of its national allegiances, and of its importance as a harbinger of southern things to come. One of its first historians, E. Y. Clarke, for example, extolled it in 1877, proclaiming:

> The older cities [of Georgia], though boasting the enjoyment of relics and
> monuments of colonial times, have also clinging to them the barnacles of many

old fogyisms and effete castes; while the city herein described, with an experience of battle and flame none the less terrible by reasons of its youth [referring to General Sherman's destruction of Atlanta in the Civil War], is emphatically the creature of young America and progressive ideas.[1]

To itself and others, Atlanta has maintained an image of an eager, young city—boastful, proud (even vain), forward-looking, and hungry for conspicuous material success: its size has always been exceeded by its presumptuousness. In 1868, it wrestled the capital away from Macon and became the political as well as the economic center of Georgia. Not content with statewide importance alone, it began to aspire to regional influence. Throughout its history, Atlanta has conscientiously tried to "keep up" with the nation, to lead the South, and to absorb into itself all the things considered to be the most modern aspects of life—modern architecture, modern business practices, modern life-styles, and even modern ideas. In the late nineteenth century, Atlanta seemed to look especially to Chicago as a model. In envious recognition of that city's status as the transfer center of the middle U.S. and gateway to either coast, Atlanta dubbed itself the "Gate City of the South." Its suburbs imitated suburbs of other cities; in fact, its first planned suburb, Inman Park, resembles Riverside outside Chicago, though it is not a direct copy. Atlanta's greatest nineteenth-century endeavor, the 1895 Cotton States and International Exposition, *was* a conspicuous imitation of the Chicago Columbian Exposition two years earlier. And Atlanta's first skyscraper was designed by the Georgia-born but Chicago-based architect John Root.

Atlanta's boosterism is notorious, and apparently it has always been so. The Pioneer Citizens of Atlanta, writing of their hometown in 1902, quoted the good-humored confession of their president, that "it has been said that every citizen of Atlanta carries a horn with him and blows it on all occasions."[2] Of all its citizens, its greatest press agents have been, in fact, members of its own press: Joel Chandler Harris, Henry Grady, Ralph McGill, Frances Newman, Margaret Mitchell. From the first, they have performed their tasks with "unceasing and inevitable persistence," as one bitter Macon observer (later governor of the state) put it in 1888, touting the uniqueness of their city, which shares with the rest of its home state—according to one—only the color of its soil.[3] This boosterism, or the "Atlanta Spirit" as it is known at home, is a constant theme in the development of the city. It has fostered myriad self-promotions: international expositions in 1881 and 1895; drives to attract new businesses to the city (under the aegis of Chamber of Commerce "Forward

Atlanta" campaigns in the 1920s and 1950s); and today, conscious economic structuring that is geared toward the outsider (especially the conventioneer) coming to what is referred to now as "The Next Great International City" or "The City Without Limits" by the Chamber of Commerce.[4]

Atlanta's boosterism has had significant consequences for the history of its women, sometimes ironically, as in 1895, when the National American Woman Suffrage Association held its annual convention there at the invitation of the Georgia Association. The women were welcome, as the suffragists knew, not because Atlanta was in favor of suffrage, but because Atlanta "was always ready to help Atlanta."[5]

Atlanta's own history, in fact, is practically coincidental with the development of the women's movement in America, so there is a measure of chronological convenience in comparing the progress of the two. They started out about the same time: Atlanta was incorporated just a year before the Seneca Falls Convention of 1848 (the landmark date for the founding of the feminist movement), though the city was actually staked out a decade earlier in the 1830s, at which time there were the early rumblings of other kinds of feminist protest heard in some parts of the country. The city and the feminist movement—both phenomena integral to the processes of industrialization and urbanization—have grown up together, though they have hardly been constant bosom companions.

Atlanta was not terribly important to life in Georgia for the first decades of its existence; it was a railroad camp that had turned into a small frontier town. Life was rough, relatively speaking; certainly it was primitive compared to the sophistication found in older Georgia cities—Macon, Milledgeville, Athens, Augusta, and especially Savannah. One early female resident was quoted as saying that the only thing that broke the monotony of antebellum Atlanta was the "stage between Marietta and Decatur [that] passed every other day."[6]

If formal organizations are evidence of urbanization, then Atlanta was just barely "citified" by 1860, when the population slightly exceeded 9,500 people. For the general community there was an assortment of Odd Fellows and Masonic Orders, a YMCA, and a Hibernian Benevolent Society (among others), as well as a handful of churches. For the women, there is scant evidence, but the barest beginnings of formal cooperative activities can be discerned: In 1858 the Ladies Benevolent Society was established.[7] More important, the Atlanta Female Institute was founded in 1859.[8] A halfhearted attempt at founding a common school in Atlanta, its establishment is also a reflection of the city's booster spirit and of some community desire to keep young ladies at home while they studied. Seminary education for young white women had been widely available in Georgia, but in other cities: Macon, La Grange, and Milledgeville, to name a few.[9] But the Atlanta Female Institute, the first school to be established in the city, is evidence that this city too was taking part in what Carroll Smith-Rosenberg has described as the "real" revolution of the nineteenth century—the education of women.[10]

Other reform movements that have been described as part of the national antebellum history of American women were simply not visible in Atlanta and Georgia. There were no antislavery organizations, of course, and there is no record of activities in support of alleviating the restrictions on married women's property rights. A case has been made frequently for antislavery sentiments on the part of southern women, however. The outspoken criticism of one-time Georgia resident Fanny Kemble, the unique example of the South Carolina Grimké sisters, and the private thoughts of many southern women whose diaries formed much of the source material for Anne Firor Scott's *The Southern Lady*, have all been pointed to as illustrations of the lack of uniform opinion in the South, and even more, as proof of some sense of humanitarianism on the part of its women. In none of these cases, though, can the sentiments be considered full-fledged abolitionism, except in that of the Grimké sisters, who upheld the cultural solidarity of the South by leaving it; to follow their consciences they felt compelled *not* to live there. Fanny Kemble, of course, was not really southern to begin with. As for property rights, there were peculiarities in Georgia law that allowed women to establish independent estates before and in some cases even during marriage. If this was one form of a marital safely valve, divorce was another; and it is evident that all was not rosy in the antebellum marital world from the increasing divorce rate between 1810 and 1830. In those days, it required a special act of the legislature for a divorce to be granted, and in 1833, the legislators voted themselves out of the divorce business for the simple reason that it had become too great a burden on their time.[11] Later, the exigencies of the Civil War, the tradition of separate estates (not unknown also among free blacks),[12] and the influence of Reconstruction philosophies led Georgia to pass an act in 1866—immediately following the war—granting married women full property rights.[13]

For the city of Atlanta and its women, as for the South as a whole, the Civil War was clearly the turning point. Both southern myth and southern reality were altered by the struggle. Atlanta went into the war as a railroad junction of barely 10,000 people; it came out of the war with a population swollen to more than twice that size—a change that saw the black population increase by more than 400 percent.[14] Sherman's destruction of the city gave Atlanta both the impetus for its quick recovery and the symbol of its survival (a city "raised from the ashes" like the phoenix, which became the city emblem). More important for purposes here, the war meant the presence thereafter of a large black population in Atlanta (never less than 30 percent of the total at any time since 1865).[15] And just as Atlanta's revival from the war marks its true origin as an industrial leader of the New South, the experience of the war marks the emergence of new images and realities for its women. After the war, southern women found themselves in familiar surroundings, but the "old place" now had unrecognizable social formations.

The suffering and industry of southern women during the war have been excessively mythologized, with both "Yankee" and "Dixie" versions to the story. One picture of Atlanta is particularly luminous—the popularized account of the burning of the city according to its most famous author, Margaret Mitchell. Mitchell's account has become so famous worldwide, in fact, that it has virtually superseded the historical record. It has "overwhelmed and replaced" history to the point that "for many"—even now—"*Gone With the Wind is* Civil War Atlanta."[16] And, of course, Scarlett O'Hara is its true (and fascinating) heroine. On the other hand, it is still possible to read modern writers who are unconvinced that there was any heroism at all on the part of southern women during the war. Emily Hahn, for example, wrote:

> . . . no doubt how many folk tales we have heard about the gallant Southern ladies and their quick-wittedness and how they always saved the silver from the Yankees, they could not, on the average, have been much of a help in the conduct of the war.[17]

But one need not embrace the cherished Old South folk tales to understand and appreciate the harshness of the Civil War and its aftermath, nor to find credibility and valid argument in the increasing volume of scholarship on the subject of the war's effects on southern women. Works by Bell Wiley, Anne Firor Scott, and M. Elizabeth Massey have begun to present a much fuller, more complex picture of southern women, especially of the southern "belles."[18] Wiley has described the wide variety of female accomplishment and occupation during the war; Scott has shed light on the abrupt changes in life-styles that the war brought; and Massey has described with compelling sympathy the experience of women caught at the warfront. It is significant, to her view, that for most of the South the element of danger was added to the "normal" privations of war; there *was* a real possibility that southern women could be (and would be) robbed, raided, or even killed during the hostilities. It was so in Atlanta.

At the local level, the war produced the few heroines Atlanta admits to having: there are stories of Confederate spying among the women, stories of courage and incredible endurance; and even stories of "Yank-killing" by women in defense of self and property. Atlanta was not only a munitions depot, communications center, staging ground, and "impregnable" embattlement, it was also a large-scale hospital center, and treatment of the wounded and dying absorbed many Atlanta women in several different capacities (as it did everywhere). Women numbered among hospital nurses and administrators; they organized for soldier relief, held fairs and bazaars (along the lines of the northern sanitary fairs); they wrapped thousands of bandages, sewed clothing and uniforms for the soldiers and knitted sock after sock after sock. On another level, Atlanta also had its share of camp followers, prostitutes, boardinghouse keepers, and female vagrants. It had refugees by the hundreds, especially war widows and children, looking for something, anything, to sustain life in an overcrowded, undernourished city. It was a time of great turbulence and great tragedy, of deprivation and desperation, of occasional glamour and frequent gore, and it was a time when women were called upon to do almost everything in response to the uncertain demands of war. The hardships in Atlanta increased manifold when the city was under siege, and when the city was finally abandoned, the flow of refugees reversed for the first and only time in that decade—flowing out of the city instead of pouring into it. There are few surviving eyewitness accounts of this escape, as time and paper were much too scarce, but the forced departure from homes in and around Atlanta remained bitterly vivid in many later memories.[19]

Devastation, ruin, and the smell of death met those who returned to the city; the process of rebuilding began quickly, but under entirely new rules. Whatever else came out of the war, the South's women were no longer the same. As Scott and Wiley have suggested, they were no longer so dependent on the old patriarchal system to support them, for they had emerged from the war more heroic for their part in it than the men, who had "lost caste by suffering defeat in the war [they] had made and conducted."[20] Dislocation, widowhood, postwar dispossession, and hunger added new emergencies to the already grueling experiences of the siege. In the process of deprivation, the women earned the admiration of their region for their militant behavior, for their courage and resourcefulness, and for their defense of homes, families, and birthrights. However unwillingly at times, or stridently at other times, they had forged for themselves a new image, one made of "sturdier stuff than the popular concept of the delicate, overprotected, blanched, and perfumed Southern belle."[21] From now on, after 1865, it was as if the southern "belle" had a doppelgänger shadowing her—an altogether different woman, fiercely loyal, outspoken, ready to act, angry when aroused, strong, aggressive (not passive), patriotic, impassioned, clever, and courageous, one who would stop at nothing to continue to defend what she had already defended during the war—home, family, birthright. This new woman became a model, like the pioneer woman of the West, for successive generations to follow, and what a reputation she had to emulate: the woman of the sixties became not only the measure of what a woman could sacrifice, but also of what she could command.

While this new image served later generations as an exemplum of female behavior (and it did influence the later patterning of public activities), the real experience of living in an interdependent, maleless society during the war must have had a more immediate effect on female behavior. Collections of women, large and small, assembled for innumerable purposes, social or otherwise. Out of these self-supporting interactions had to come a belief in the potential of organized activities across family lines as a response to community needs. At the very least, the *habit* of formally organized group activity was established: war relief gave Atlanta women their first real opportunity to work together as a group. This group activity simply continued after the war. In peacetime it became an essential part of the postwar cleanup and the keystone in the foundation of female organizations.

Specifically, the Atlanta Ladies Memorial Society was founded in 1866, a direct descendant of war relief work. Today it is the oldest extant organization in the city. It proposed not only to commemorate the dead, but to manage the proper identification and burial of Confederate dead and the removal of Federal dead, when necessary, to more appropriate resting places.

This organization deserves to be remembered for its service to the Confederate dead, but its importance here lies in something else: it provided a direct link between the Civil War activities of Atlanta women and the network of women's organizations that developed over the next thirty years. The Memorial Society had only nineteen charter members, but out of that number, three are known to have served in (or were founders of) the Soldiers' Relief Association and the Hospital Association during the war. Undoubtedly, other charter members also assisted the relief effort. Two of the charter members busily organized large-scale philanthropies—"calico balls," for example—in the late 1860s and 1870s. One of them, Mrs. W. F. Westmoreland, even attempted, unsuccessfully, to get the city council to set up a public soup kitchen. The Ladies Relief Committee, founded in 1871 (with the same Mrs. Westmoreland as a member) distributed clothing to the poor and sponsored lectures, fairs, and once a circus, to raise money for charity. Two of the young members of the Ladies Memorial Association were later members of the distinguished Board of Lady Managers for the Cotton States and International Exposition, as was another young woman who had assisted Mrs. Westmoreland on the calico ball planning committee (namely, Mrs. Nellie Peters Black, later the most influential clubwoman of her day). Two of the original members became important officials in the DAR after it was founded in 1891; and the founding president of the association as well as four more of its presidents, who served before 1941, were also officers and leaders of other organizations in the city.[22] So it appears that long before Atlanta had its first "woman's club" per se, the practice of individual women serving their community through a network of interlocking organizations was established and can be traced directly to women's work during the Civil War.

Up to a point this was true for all women in the city, for black women too quickly became accustomed to working through organizations to help remedy the desperate circumstances of their community. However, their organizations were very different in kind and in structure, and at this point they were not single-sexed. What emerged from the black community was a very different picture from what has been described so far.

Blacks were the objects of hostile neglect in postwar Atlanta; if the city directory for 1867 is to be believed, there were no blacks at all in the city, but that is simply not true. Furthermore, and again according to the city directory, there were no black women in the city until 1877, when they were listed for the first time. Again, that cannot be true.[23] What it does show, however, is the "official" invisibility of black women that pervades language, custom, and historical convention, not only locally, but throughout the South and the United States in general. Tradition says "women" or "southern women" and means "white" women only. Or it refers to "blacks" and is really speaking of black men. These are difficult habits to break, especially when discussing a society that has assumed for so long that the white part of it was the whole and only part of it. The historian has almost insurmountable problems in trying to discuss "women" as a single group, cutting squarely across racial lines, without unintentional overstatements, misstatements, and offenses. The histories of black and white southern women—because of slavery and segregation—have been separate histories, experienced separately and written down in separate traditions. Yet the similarities between their public records are too numerous and the differences too striking (and too socially significant) not to take advantage of direct comparisons. Furthermore, the consciousness of race so permeates the public and private lives of southern women that any discussion of their modern-day, post-1865 lives must include consideration of both racial experiences.

With few exceptions southern black women have also been absent from recently published works in women's history,[24] and this is a serious shortcoming. The attitude seems to imply that southern blacks as a group have been so deprived that they could barely be expected to raise their heads above the twin oppressions of white supremacy and economic privation; and further, that they could really "succeed" only if they left the South entirely, which, of course, many of them did. The tendency for historians to follow black history north, so to speak, may point the finger at the grimness of white racism and black suffering in the South, but it obscures two essential ingredients of southern culture in the later nineteenth century that contribute powerfully to its complexity: first, the tenacious strengths of southern black communities in the cities, which were composed of those who stayed behind and of those who had once "gone up the spout" and returned; and second, the ironies of southern paternalism, which while keeping blacks in their place, allowed southern whites privately to help "their" blacks, and—more troublesomely—under hidden and peculiar circumstances even to love them. The presence of a fairly stable, large black population with roots extending back into the 1860s in cities like Atlanta and the nature of southern paternalism affect the story of women in the South on both sides of the color line—not equally, and not always similarly, but inevitably nonetheless.

It must be remembered that for quite a few decades after the Civil War the American black population remained largely a southern population. The first great wave of its migration out of the South occurred about 1910 and continued in several waves thereafter over the next forty years. The great shift in population out of the South was more a twentieth-century phenomenon than a nineteenth-century one, and the important demographic change for the black population in the late nineteenth century seems instead to have been its increased urbanization in southern cities.[25] The Atlanta community, as stated earlier, remained fairly constant between 1870 and 1900, about 40 percent of the total population.[26] Whoever left Atlanta was simply replaced by someone else coming from the countryside.

The story of black community building in Atlanta that took place after the Civil War is a story unto itself: important social foundations were created that had an effect on the later patterns of organization among the black women. Local black institutions, especially the churches, were either founded or strengthened in their missions to the community. The establishment of six black schools and colleges in the Atlanta area in the twenty years following the war has had a continuing effect in the community that cannot be overstated. Segregation itself meant separation from local whites, but the practices allowed a direct line of communication with northern whites, through the auspices of missionary societies, philanthropies, and other agencies allowing people to come south to "see" or to help the freedmen. What this meant ultimately for the women was that, if southern white women were looking to northern models for what "progressive" females were doing, so too in fact were the black women. To a large extent, both groups were receiving their information from the same sources.

As a result, parallel but separate black and white organizational networks developed among Atlanta women in the 1870s, 1880s, and especially in the 1890s. The systems were fairly well stabilized by 1900, at which time there were already in existence black and white church organizations for women, mission societies, literary groups, secret societies (such as sororities and auxiliaries to fraternal orders), alumnae associations, female-run orphanages and children's homes, WCTUs, women's clubs, and national federations of women's clubs with which the Atlanta clubs had affiliations. A decade later, by 1915, the networks included in addition black and white kindergarten associations, PTAs, exclusive hereditary societies, civic improvement associations, and state federations of women's clubs, which were begun under Atlanta leadership.

In general, it took the black women a little longer to "get there," but get there they did. A comparison of founding dates between black and white organizations not only shows a surprising degree of uniformity between the two systems but also a surprising state of contemporaneity with national organizational trends. This is important, as it is not generally granted that such widespread or early organizational activity has been present among southern women, especially among southern black women.[27]

The organizational networks among Atlanta women took firm root in the general climate of community redevelopment during the postwar period; in fact, the 1870s and 1880s exhibited a kind of organizational fervor in the city as a whole, as Atlanta was industrializing, rebuilding, and expanding rapidly. The year 1872, for example, saw not only the end of Reconstruction (and in the parlance of some, the beginning of "Reconstriction"), but also the establishment of a public school system (that excluded blacks at levels above elementary grades), the construction of the first street railway system, and the completion of part of the municipal waterworks. Commercial activity was significantly spurred on by the reorganization of the Chamber of Commerce in 1871, and cultural activities also increased: two music societies appeared in the 1870s along with a second library society, the first one having been founded in 1867. The 1880s saw the addition of exclusive social clubs to the Atlanta scene, professional sports, an athletic club, literary societies, a Chautauqua, and a brief exercise in legal prohibition. (Temperance organizations had been active in Georgia long before the Civil War.) Social welfare agencies of every description and self-help organizations—especially in the black community—began to appear in greater and greater numbers.[28] For the women, public activities centered on charitable, philanthropic, and religious aims primarily, and the churches were the institutional framework within which the most widespread organizational efforts took place.

Formally organized women's missionary societies—a more independent branch of women's activities within the churches than boards of deaconesses, prayer groups, and auxiliaries—began to appear throughout the South in the 1870s, as has been established by Anne Firor Scott. This coincided with the first appearance of single females sent from the South to serve abroad in the mission field (most of them in China). While women's organizations in churches in the South actually predate this decade, the evidence for them is sparse and scattered and it is the organizations founded during the 1870s that became the large national institutions that are still part of most American Protestant hierarchies.

The first white women's missionary society in Atlanta seems to have been the Women's Missionary and Benevolent Society of the Second Baptist Church, founded in 1873. Typically for that time, the society was organized with the active assistance and encouragement of two churchmen—the minister of the church and the secretary of the Baptist Foreign Mission Board, who had been urging southern women to "aid their heathen sisters" in 1872: his woman-to-woman appeal succeeded.[29] According to the records of the Second Baptist Church, this women's society was the third such group to be formed in Georgia. A few years later, there were apparently enough local associations to form a separate administrative committee for women's activities, and a central state committee was set up at the 1878 convention, held at the Second Baptist Church of Atlanta. Until then, it had been customary for men to head up women's work within the Baptist church, but this committee was headed by a woman—significantly, she was from the Second Baptist Church of Atlanta. Ten years after the formation of the Georgia committee, by which time other state committees had been formed throughout the South, a regional organization was established.[30]

The first local Methodist women's missionary organization on record appeared in 1878 at the First Methodist Church of Atlanta. In the same year, at the regular convention, meeting then in Atlanta, the women of the Methodist Episcopal Church, South, proposed having their own separate missionary society—churchwide, regional. The proposal came to fruition the following year. By 1880, the Women's Board of Foreign Missions was holding its own meetings in conjunction with the annual convention.[31] A few years later (1883) home mission work was begun with the establishment of the Trinity Home Mission Society in Atlanta, founded by Laura Askew Haygood, later a missionary to China. She established her first mission agency "for the promotion of helpful Christian work among the poor of the city,"[32] creating thereby a new form of Christian service that spread throughout the church and lasted for generations under its own administrative auspices; it was years before the home mission and foreign mission activities were absorbed into one board.

There were two stages upon which organized religious life appeared among black women—the local churches and the local colleges. Because the local colleges were mostly mission schools, they were the direct recipients of administrative efforts to form missionary societies on the campuses. The schools included, of course, Atlanta University (founded by the American Missionary Association in 1867), Morehouse College (founded in Augusta in 1867 as a Baptist seminary and relocated to Atlanta in 1879), Clark College (founded by the Methodist Episcopal Church in 1868), Spelman College (Baptist, 1881), and Morris Brown (African Methodist Episcopal, 1881). According to the historian of Atlanta University, student life there was already proscribed in the 1870s by certain kinds of missionary activities, since the Christian Endeavor (a female society) and the YMCA met jointly on Sunday evenings and devoted their time to missionary concerns.[33] Written records for this early period are simply not available for the local churches, but one thing is abundantly clear: the ties between the local churches and the local colleges were close and deep, so what happened at the educational institutions and what happened at the religious institutions were inextricably related. An 1894 history of black Atlanta gives information on active women's mission societies at several churches in Atlanta, unfortunately without indicating how long the societies had been in existence. *The Black Side*, written by Rev. E. R. Carter, a Baptist minister, is unique in documenting the institutional activities of blacks in the period following the Civil War. It is the best, and sometimes the only, record of the processes of community building that were taking place. Rev. Carter reported extensively on active women's mission societies at Wheat Street Baptist Church and at Friendship Baptist.[34] Friendship, where Rev. Carter was pastor, had a congregation predating the Civil War and was one of the few Atlanta institutions prepared to help the freedmen coming into Atlanta after Emancipation. Friendship was also an example of the close church-school ties that have existed: it was involved in the foundation of Spelman College and it hosted Atlanta University commencements for many of that school's early years.[35] Spelman College, in turn, affected the mission activities of the women of the local churches. It is known that the two missionary founders of Spelman, Harriet Giles and Sophia Packard, founded a mission band composed of women from a number of local churches in the first year of the school, for the purpose of securing local support for their school.[36] Shortly afterward, there were organized mission bands in black churches across the entire state, and one of their activities was, quite naturally, to raise money for Spelman College.[37]

The *1898 Atlanta University Publication* reveals that organizations within other Atlanta churches were also already in existence, probably for some time. For example, the First Congregational Church—which had very strong bonds with Atlanta University—boasted five organizations, including one literary society, two benevolent societies, one mission society, and one society to "aid the church." Unfortunately, no indication is given of the male to female ratio of participation in these groups.[38]

A particularly useful example of black-white parallel tracking in women's organizations, coming out of this same period, is the WCTU. The first local organization (white) in Georgia was formed in Atlanta in 1880, by a WCTU "missionary" from Ohio. The first state convention, held in 1882, was attended by delegates from Atlanta as well as Savannah, Augusta, and Rome, Georgia, and by Frances Willard herself. Willard made three trips to Atlanta between 1883 and 1890; on one of these she visited Atlanta University and "other colleges" in the area where temperance work was going on. Without doubt, Willard was the first really important, nationally known, northern female to visit Atlanta after the Civil War, and she made much of the southern courtesy extended to her during her stay.[39] In 1887, the West Atlanta WCTU (black) was formed in Friendship Baptist Church, and with it the black community had an independent women's temperance group, though it is not known if this was the first. Rev. Carter paid a great deal of attention to the West Atlanta WCTU in his history, implying that it was an important organization in the community and also suggesting that by 1893 it was following a program of activity that was in effect among black women throughout the state.[40] (The fact that this WCTU also began its life in his own church may have something to do with his assessment of its importance.) The relationship of the West End WCTU to the National Union is not clear: it could have been a member of the national organization; it was never a part of the statewide organization. It is important, however, to point out that one of the departments in effect nationally and on the state level was a division for work among blacks. The national department was headed by a black woman, poet-reformer Frances Ellen Watkins Harper. Locally, some white members of the Georgia WCTU apparently also did work "among colored people," at least according to the association historian who reported on the warm reception given white WCTUers by Spelman girls and of the many Bands of Hope formed at the school among temperance pledge signers.[41] Spelman was a veritable hotbed of temperance activity, according to articles appearing in the *Spelman Messenger* between 1885 and 1900.[42] Not only were the school's founders firmly dedicated to the cause, but the school also had frequent contact with local and national temperance leaders. For instance, Spelman students were permitted to attend a public lecture given by Frances Willard in 1889, and in 1892, the students were addressed on their own campus by Frances E. W. Harper. When they graduated, Spelman girls went on to further the temperance cause, by setting up units of the WCTU in other parts of the city and state, by holding mothers' meetings, by founding social purity groups, and the like, wherever they happened to settle.[43]

In addition to temperance societies, literary societies—the precursors of Greek letter sororities—were also known at the girls' schools. The first recorded sorority in the United States was founded as a literary club at Wesleyan College at Macon, Georgia, in 1851. The Adelphean Society, as it was originally known, survived the Civil War "untouched," changed its name to Alpha Delta Pi in 1904 to conform with the trend toward Greek letter identifications, went "national" in 1906 at a time when many other sororities were being founded in the U.S., and joined the intercollegiate, intersorority organization, Pan Hellenic, in 1909. Today, Alpha Delta Pi has no chapter at Wesleyan, which has banned Greek letter societies, but it does maintain chapter houses in numerous schools across the country and has its national headquarters building in Atlanta. A similar and doubtlessly competitive organization, Philomenthean (later Phi Mu), was also founded at Wesleyan and at about the same time as Adelphean.[44] These two organizations are important for several reasons: first, they are the earliest evidence of the close tie between school and club, between education and sisterhood, which appears to be an essential ingredient in the formation of women's organizations; second, many Atlanta women who were prominent in organized activities were graduates of Wesleyan and were probably members of one sorority or the other;[45] third, these two groups are antecedents (possibly even prototypes) of the later self-education clubs, which began to be found in Atlanta in the 1880s, such as the 19th Century History Class (founded in 1886), the Every Saturday Class (1894), and the Wednesday Morning Study Class (1906).[46]

The 1880s also saw the appearance of literary clubs among the women students at Spelman College and Atlanta University. In 1884, the Phillis Wheatley Literary Club was formed at A.U. when the girls were excluded from the all-male Phi Kappa debating club entertainments. In the 1920s, Phillis Wheatley and all similar literary groups were superseded by Greek letter organizations, although fraternities and sororities as such never received official sanction from the university.[47] As in the example above, these school groups were antecedents of later social and educational groups formed in the early 1900s, such as the Inquirers (founded 1909), the Chautauqua Circle (1913), the Mo-So-Lit Club (date unknown), and the Utopian Society (1916).

There were still other beginnings during this period besides activities for religious, literary, missionary, and temperance purposes. Independent female-run benevolent societies were established in the black, white, and Jewish communities by 1890. The great preponderance of these were set up to meet the needs of orphaned and indigent children. The Baptist Orphans Home (white) was established in 1871, the Home of the Friendless (white) in 1874, the Home of the Women's Christian Association (white) in 1885, the Carrie Steele Logan Home for Orphans (black) in 1888, the Hebrew Orphans Home in 1889, the Atlanta Children's Home (white) in 1890, and the Leonard Street Orphanage (black) also in 1890.[48] As stated earlier, formally organized benevolent and charitable activities among Atlanta women did not originate in the years indicated by these associations, but had precedents in work done before, during, and immediately after the Civil War. The differences between the earlier groups and these later ones is institutional, and that is a critical, qualitative difference. Each of these later societies was identified with a place as well as a name; each had its own facility—a building or set of rooms—that it owned or rented and from which it dispensed its services. Each had a board of lady managers (or board of directors)—only occasionally an all-male advisory board—and each had at least one resident, supervisory staff person on the premises. These groups did not just hold meetings and dole out charity; they maintained institutions, and as a result, had a community visibility that would probably startle some modern generations. Some of these early charities have survived: The Baptist Children's Home and the Carrie Steele Orphanage still exist as private institutions (though Carrie Steele gets some appropriations from United Way). The Jewish Children's Home was absorbed into a larger welfare network of Jewish community services. The Home for the Friendless began to receive city subsidies as early as 1900,[49] and its replacement by a municipally run service should not be surprising.

By 1890, though Atlanta had no Woman's Club, it had clearly developed systems of women's organizations working for self- and community development. Its WCTU had followed on the heels of the formation of the National Union by a short six years. Its women's church organizations had been at the forefront of church activities in the South for nearly twenty years, especially in denominations that were split from northern counterparts. In one important case, the Trinity Home Mission movement, the pioneering work had actually started here. Atlanta had literary societies, and it had a whole series of benevolent agencies established and run by women, who were following directly in the path of mainstream America, concerned in the late 1800s with self-education and community altruism. By 1895, Atlanta had chapters of at least three hereditary, patriotic organizations (the United Daughters of the Confederacy, the Daughters of the American Revolution, and the National Society of the Colonial Dames of America); it had suffrage associations, at least one Free Kindergarten Association, two hospital auxiliaries (The King's Daughters Hospital Association and the Grady Hospital Woman's Board); and alumnae associations at the girls' schools (including Spelman College, Agnes Scott College—founded in Decatur in 1889—and Girls' High, the public high school for girls); and it had representation on the governor-appointed Board of Lady Visitors for the State Normal School in Milledgeville, established in 1889. By the end of 1895, it had three Woman's Clubs formed almost simultaneously, and in the following year, the three clubs were affiliated with their respective national federations. The 1890s was a decade of tremendous organizational expansion, and the greatest boost to the women's club movement came with exposure to the World Columbian Exposition in Chicago in 1893 and—more important here—with involvement in the Atlanta Cotton States and International Exposition of 1895.

The Atlanta Cotton States and International Exposition, held between September 18 and December 31, was described by its chronicler, Walter G. Cooper, as "Atlanta's greatest public enterprise," a phrase that probably still holds true. In the history of this city it stands out as one of Atlanta's most glamorous events and as one of those historical moments that reveal a great deal—quite self-consciously—about the city. There was no small degree of regional competition involved—against Chicago and the great Columbian Exposition—but the official reasons for giving the fair in the "Chicago of the South" were to stimulate trade and to promote local recovery from the Depression of the early 1890s, two quite legitimate purposes. Unfortunately, the Cotton States Exposition did not make money and had to be bailed out at the last minute by one of its backers; it did, nonetheless, entertain more than 800,000 visitors and offered some 6,000 exhibits for their enjoyment. If the fair was an economic failure, it was a splendid one, and in other ways it was not a failure at all. The exposition netted worldwide publicity for Atlanta and firmly established the city as the transfer center of the Southeast. It is generally believed too that the fair was a boon to the community despite its financial fragility; and, if it is remembered for nothing else, it is remembered as the occasion for Booker T. Washington's famous speech, giving verbal affirmation to the policy of racial segregation.[50]

The importance of the exposition to the history of Atlanta women has really never been explored, nor has its relation—in more general terms—to the kind of female public participation that it represents. My discussion is suggestive only, and it is limited to only two aspects of the importance of the exposition in this regard: first, it is the best evidence for this period of the long interrelationship of women's organizations and the tradition of fairs, exhibits, and expositions held during the nineteenth century; second, because of the close parallel between sexual and racial segregation, which is present at the Atlanta Exposition in a more obvious way than at the Chicago Expo, the 1895 fair offers an even clearer example of the nature of social segregation, a fundamental element of this study.

That the world's fairs and expositions of the late nineteenth century stimulated the development of women's clubs is not a new observation,[51] but the connection between those fairs and the participation by women in all types of expositions, fairs, and exhibitions, at all levels of community life, has never been admitted as a part of that stimulus to organize.[52] The tendency seems to have been to assume that women were passive visitors to the events of the early part of the century and active participants only at the later ones, since Chicago, Atlanta, and Philadelphia (1876), for example, were known to have had viable women's committees as a part of their managerial structures. Yet, even the lowly bake-off or baby contest would require some amount of woman-to-woman communication, possibly even some group cooperation; certainly, these required the *active* participation of the women of the community. Women's part in local, county, and state fairs is simply too universal a phenomenon to ignore, yet historians have overlooked this as another probable root—alongside quilting bees and sewing circles—of the fully developed, formally organized groups that appeared in the 1890s.[53]

In Atlanta, for example, as early as 1850, a special place was marked off at the southeastern fair for the women's displays, and the women themselves were urged to cooperate, as "their assistance, in many departments of the Fair, [was thought to be] absolutely necessary to a proper management."[54] This became a tradition. Obviously, by the time the Civil War came along, the women of Atlanta were well versed enough in giving bazaars and fairs on their own to use them as a means of raising money for the Confederate armies. This was also the case in Philadelphia and New York, where sanitary fairs of massive scale were held that had women's committees as part of the management.[55] The tradition of ladies' fairs continued, and by 1876, women's pavilions and female judges as part of major expositions were commonplace. As the nineteenth century wore on, the question was not *if* women were to participate in any public exhibitions, even industrial ones, but rather how to define the special contributions to the festivals the women should make, and how to manage those contributions. The trend was to more specialized behavior and to more separated structures, and by the 1890s, the answer to both questions was to have a Board of Lady Managers that would make its own decisions and administer its own choices.

The Boards of Lady Managers at Chicago and Atlanta are important historical bodies in themselves; that is, who they were, what they represented, and what they actually did during the fairs, as well as what they went on to do organizationally. The Atlanta Board is dealt with at some length later, since its membership went on to set the pace and style for leadership in the developing women's clubs. But one of its members is pivotal and should be mentioned here: Rebecca Latimer Felton served on the board of the Chicago fair, and before her duties there were finished, she was appointed to serve on the board of the Atlanta exposition. The pattern of her involvement, of bouncing from one fair to another, is typical of the continuum of service and the accumulation of experience that the women established between fairs. Felton had attended fairs before Chicago: it is known that she went to Philadelphia in 1876 (even though her husband had opposed the centennial celebration in the U.S. Congress).[56] Her biographer guesses that she also attended the Cotton States exhibition in Atlanta in 1881. At any rate, after Chicago, she was an official observer, a judge, or a committeewoman at all of the fairs that occurred in the next decade.[57]

Felton was an agent in creating an informal system through which the management of women's affairs passed, fairly smoothly, from one exposition to the next. But there were other connections that illustrate the importance of the fairs for the growing organizationalism among women. The fairs were a meeting ground of the first order, and a number of organizations were actually founded at the fairs, such as the National Council of Jewish Women and the National League of Nursing Education at Chicago.[58] Others met in national convention, or had special commemorative "days" during the fairs. Atlanta was a mini-Chicago in this respect.

The Atlanta Section of the National Council of Jewish Women was founded during the Cotton States Exposition,[59] while the Baptist, Unitarian, and Methodist women all had meetings.[60] The first statewide Georgia convention of the DAR was held in conjunction with the exposition, and the DAR invited the Colonial Dames to meet in session with them.[61] The several branches of the United Daughters of the Confederacy got together the day after Confederate Day to organize themselves into a state division.[62] Several days were set aside to honor individual professional women, to listen to lectures by them, and to give their organizations a chance to meet.[63] The General Federation of Woman's Clubs, itself only a few years old, held "Federation Day" at the Exposition, affording "clubwomen of the North, East, West, and South an opportunity to see the great progress which has been made by the Southern states during the quarter century just passed."[64] This and the Congress of Colored Women undoubtedly served to quicken the formal organization of both a white and a black Atlanta Woman's Club.[65]

Naturally, the fairs were also showplaces. They not only tried to exhibit the "progress" of women as a class and to celebrate the achievements of individuals, but also to attempt to reveal something of the nature of

"Womanhood" in its totality—from the "lofty genius of Rosa Bonheur to the daintiest confection of real old southern housewifery," as it was expressed by Mrs. Joseph Thompson, president of the Atlanta Board.[66] The fairs were an advertisement for women's club activities: the Atlanta Woman's Press Club, as an example, had a display room in the Woman's Building in 1895.[67] The WCTU was also there.[68] The Free Kindergarten Association ran a kindergarten as an exhibit.[69] The DAR was highly visible, arranging gala social affairs, special events, and Revolutionary War exhibits (including the Liberty Bell).[70] And the Atlanta chapter of the United Daughters of the Confederacy formed itself quickly in July of 1895 (just two months before the fair opened) in order to put together an exhibit of Confederate relics.[71] (One wonders if its founders did not think too much attention was being paid to the Revolutionary War.)

As in Chicago, the Woman's Building itself was a tribute to organized womanpower. It was designed by a woman; the money for its construction was raised by women, and its entire management was under their control, along with the management of the hospital, the day care center, and all other women's exhibits at the exposition. The Woman's Building was a popular spot at the fair, and in the words of one observer, who was none too impressed with the exposition as a whole but singled out the Woman's Building as something to comment on: ". . . the ladies exhibited a commendable degree of enthusiasm, energy, and enterprise, and contributed no little to the success of the Exposition."[72] The Woman's Building was a costly undertaking, and one of the ways the women raised the $35,000 it took for its construction was—as the generation-old tradition held—by holding "entertainments, fairs, bazaars" and the like.[73]

The mutual dependence of fairs and women's organizations benefited the organizations in ways besides creating precedents for fund-raising. The Atlanta Chapter of the DAR acquired one of the exposition buildings for its use as a chapter house. The building was not built to last, but it did serve until 1909, when plans for a new house were undertaken—for a replica of the exposition building, which had been itself a replica of a building in Massachusetts.[74] After more than a decade of postexposition delay and deterioration, the city finally turned the old fairgrounds into a municipal park, razing whatever remained of the original buildings and landscaping. Piedmont Park, as it is now known, quickly became a favorite civic memorial ground, and today contains many monuments erected by Atlanta's women's clubs over the years. Almost as if to signify the importance of the site to the early days of the Atlanta DAR, both DAR chapter houses are located across the street from the park.

In another direction, the management of women's activities at the annual fair held in Atlanta by the Southeastern Fair Association, a descendant of the 1850 fair mentioned above, was ultimately—and officially—turned over to the Georgia Federation of Women's Clubs.[75] The federation was founded in 1896 under the auspices of the Atlanta Woman's Club and the Elberton, Georgia, Sorosis, and it attributes its origins to the inspiration of the exposition.[76] The influence of the women's clubs on fair activities continued at least into the second decade of the twentieth century, when it peaked just before World War I in a series of local agricultural fairs and rallies, co-sponsored by the Georgia Bureau of Agriculture and the Georgia Federation, under the direction of Nellie Peters Black, president of the federation. Mrs. Black was also a member of the Southeastern Fair Association's Women's Committee, and years earlier she had been (it hardly needs saying) a member of the Board of Lady Managers of the 1895 Cotton States Exposition.[77]

As suggested, the relationship between the fairs and the organizations form a tight circle.

There were no black women on the Board of Lady Managers; there were no exhibits by black women in the Women's Building; and there were no black children in the model school or nursery. But within the display rooms of the Negro Building, black women were everywhere. There were probably not many exhibits from women's organizations, though some schools and social welfare agencies were presented—Spelman College, for example, was one of numerous educational exhibits, as was the Carrie Steele Orphanage[78]—but exhibiting by women's clubs per se is questionable. No mention is made anywhere of exhibits from either of the two national associations of black women that had been established by that time: neither the National Federation of Afro-American Women (Josephine St. Pierre Ruffin's group from Boston) nor the National League of Colored Women (organized in Washington, D.C., by Mary Church Terrell) was there, apparently. An Epworth League from South Carolina sent a quilt for display, but other such items are not plentiful in the official program. Female visibility consisted primarily of a preponderance of fancywork exhibits; there were more of these, according to one observer (herself a woman) than demonstrations of industrial, agricultural, and business achievement.[79] If the entries listed from Atlanta alone are any indication of the "preponderance," she was probably right. The list shows about two dozen entries of foodstuffs, including canned, preserved, and baked goods, and more than twice that many entries for various kinds of needlework (not including hats!).[80] And Atlanta was only one Georgia city among several, and Georgia was only one of fourteen states exhibiting.

There is no indication of the exact organizational structure that managed the women's exhibits, if it was handled entirely by the men or if some of it was provided, formally or informally, by the wives of the members of the district and state committees comprising the black management at the exposition. There *was* an auxiliary committee for the Congress of Colored Women held during the exposition, and membership on that committee is significant. It represented twenty-four states plus the District of Columbia, and included a number of women who had already been, were then, and would certainly continue to be important to women's organizational life: Frances E. W. Harper (already mentioned in connection with the WCTU), Mrs. Booker T. Washington (first president of the National Association of Colored Women, formed in 1896 out of the two organizations mentioned above), Lucy Laney, Lucy E. Moten, Victoria Earle Matthews, Fannie Barrier Williams, and Mrs. J. W. E. Bowen (of Atlanta), to name a few of the most notable.[81] Thus, the relationship between the stimulus to organize occasioned by the fairs and the later management of women's organizations, which was seen among the white women, also existed among the black women, but present research does not prove (or disprove) that the same kind of continuity of female personnel went from one fair to another. This pattern of continuous involvement from fair to fair certainly did exist for the black community as a whole and also individually for some of its men,[82] so it is not unreasonable to assume that it was also true for the women. It is important to note that just two years after Atlanta, in 1897, the Tennessee Centennial included a Negro Woman's Board as part of its management.[83] It would be interesting to know who was on that board.

The creation of the Negro Building in Atlanta gave blacks their own exhibition hall for the first time in the history of national expositions, and it set a precedent. In fact, it was followed immediately by a larger, more expensive Negro Building at the Tennessee Centennial. The Atlanta building was designed, constructed, and managed by blacks, but it did not wholly escape the kind of controversy within the black community that had been so condemnatory of the Chicago Exposition. Judged suspiciously by some, by others as a gracious and friendly gesture by the white community, and by still others as a triumph of black achievement, the building was actually required by the same law that granted a small subsidy to the fair from the U.S. Congress—making it official, whether liked or disliked. Even though there was not universal support for a segregated building, it had to be admitted that the number and size of exhibits in Atlanta outdid the black exhibits in the Hall of Government in Chicago.[84] The Negro Building made racial segregation *look* almost viable.

So did Booker T. Washington. His speech on opening day was heralded by local, national, and international presses as an unprecedented signal for promised racial harmony. President Grover Cleveland declared that it—by itself—made the entire occasion of the fair worthwhile.[85] The speech hurled Washington into national prominence as the leader of his race in the United States, and his wife, correspondingly, inherited some of the same national prominence. Out of recognition of her club work at Tuskegee, but probably more out of recognition of her husband's importance, she was elected in 1896 to the first presidency of the National Association of Colored Women, an organization she continued to influence for several decades, long after her husband had died.

At the moment of her election to NACW, Mrs. Washington was the *only* southern woman to head a national federation of secular women's clubs of any kind in the country. All other federations were dominated by easterners and northerners, including the suffrage, temperance, educational, and general federations. Even most religious groups were also so controlled, with the obvious exception of the Southern Baptists and Methodists.[86]

Mrs. Washington's unique position points up one of several differences between the black and white female participation in the Atlanta Exposition. In most other respects the fair was a provincial event: international exhibits were few, and the managing personnel with rare exceptions were local Atlantans. Black participation, however, as the auxiliary committee for the Women's Congress clearly indicates, depended on regional, even national representation. Furthermore, only the black presence at the fair got much prolonged national attention, that is, for the novelty of the blacks having their own exhibition hall, but more especially, for Booker T. Washington's landmark address, later called the Atlanta Compromise.

There is great irony in Washington's speech: Atlanta fostered the occasion for—even saw its name given to—the speech that helped catapult him into national leadership, but as a result of the Atlanta Compromise, national attention was diverted away from Atlanta and onto Tuskegee and what that school—its emphasis on industrial education, its politics of accommodation, and its essentially rural economics—represented. Even more ironically, shortly after the exposition, Atlanta became the base of operations of the young W. E. B. DuBois, who joined the faculty of Atlanta University in 1897[87] and whose integrationist policies came into increasing conflict with the separationist tone of the "race leader" from Tuskegee. The competing strategies of Washington and DuBois vied for public attention, but the measure of the national black ideal from 1895 until the eve of World War I—certainly in the eyes of monied, white America—lay with Booker T. Washington and Tuskegee and not with W. E. B. DuBois and Atlanta University. Atlanta was quickly overshadowed as the power center of black America; apparently, the black side of Atlanta, although projected into the image of the New South city, was not a conservative enough example of race development for either the city itself or the rest of the nation to be comfortable with. The policy of accommodation voiced by Washington in 1895 was all too timely; it was followed in 1896 by *Plessy vs. Ferguson*, the Supreme Court decision making segregation the law of the land, and Washington's rise to fame from that platform in Atlanta, in the words of his biographer, "coincided with a setback of his race."[88]

The consequences for the women were similar. The momentum for organizing, so strongly manifest in the Women's Congress, was not dominated by Atlanta after the fair, but moved with Margaret Murray Washington to Tuskegee and from there to a national (and largely nonsouthern) arena. Simply by participating in the exposition a few Atlanta black women became part of a small, upper-echelon group of leaders, who provided the direction for women's organizations at the state and national levels for years to come. But local Atlanta organizational efforts, like most such efforts in the South—in the amount of national attention they could draw—were overshadowed, again, by the prominence of the Tuskegee model.

No such dominant personalities as the Washingtons emerged for the white population, and the effects of the fair were more pronouncedly localized. The impetus to organize stayed with the Atlantans, and white women went on to set examples and take the initiative in much of the organizational life of the state. The scope of their activity stretched out citywide, statewide, and regionwide into the New South, but it did not have the same national connotations as the black connections did. Two different cultural ecologies had been created, within which the women's organizations had to define themselves: one white, with strong local roots and appeals to regional identifications, and one black, with strong local roots and appeals to national identifications.

Another part of the cultural differences in the women's participation is inherent, again, in the example of the two buildings. It may seem obvious, but it is essential to point out that the Negro Building was racially segregated but sexually integrated, while the Woman's Building was both racially and sexually segregated. The nature of social segregation affecting each female population group was different, and the difference was integral to how the women of each group would approach questions of sexual solidarity through their organizations. The black women would always have to take into account questions of racial solidarity, while the white women would always suffer (or enjoy) dual isolation. The viability of social segregation was at the heart of each emergent organizational system, but the character of the segregation affecting each has differed over the course of time, so much so that the struggles for (and against) social segregation—from the southern female perspective—look very complex indeed.

The Exposition of 1895 might be seen as sitting at the apex of an age in which both sexual and racial segregation were embraced as fundamental principles of social government. Correspondingly, groups that were affected by these principles—male and female blacks, and female whites—would be encouraged to form their own organizations, in which they could "prosper" and "achieve status," and these organizations in turn—if they themselves endured—would project the principles of separation into future generations. One scholar of black America has already analyzed the situation in terms of race, and his penetrating statement is worth quoting at length:

> White discriminatory and exclusionist policies were the direct cause of the establishment of segregated institutions such as the Negro churches and fraternities. . . . Such institutions, once established, have a way of stimulating and perpetuating Negro ethnocentrism and of fostering attitudes favorable to group separatism. . . . And the increased separation that these institutions encourage reinforces the mutual ignorance, suspicion, and hostility that exist between the Negro and white groups. Ordinarily, it is true, segregated institutions are justified as a temporary form of withdrawal that will vanish once prejudice and discrimination disappear. Yet the continuing uncertainties, discriminations, and psychological attitudes built up over the years perpetuate group consciousness and the justification of segregated institutions.[89]

Racial "uncertainties, discriminations, and psychological attitudes" have not disappeared, nor have segregated institutions, and ideologies of separation, as outlined in the above, applied not only racially, but sexually as well.

The particular binds of sexual segregation are evident from a few comments about the Woman's Building by a northern visitor to the exposition. First the writer bemoaned the need for separate women's exhibits, which along with the works of "the Freedmen, the Indians, the blind, the feeble-minded, and other defectives" it was unfortunately considered unfair to judge by the "usual" standards. Then the writer felt compelled to explain that the separation by sex was actually a "voluntary" effort by the women and more a reflection of their own estimate of their position than of the men's estimate. The author's final comments, though intended as a criticism, are better read as a statement of the problem. "Someday," the writer concluded,

> there will be a world's fair without a woman's building or at least the woman's building will be devoted to *distinctively* feminine pursuits and interests [*Küche, Kinder, Kirche?*], and the women whose tastes or accomplishments lie in directions ordinarily followed by men will either take their chances in the main building or keep out of it altogether.[90]

So much for the realities of female emancipation where the choices are limited: be separate and therefore redundant or peculiar, or assimilate and disappear from view.

Even though it was not so evident in the Negro Building, the principle of sexual segregation was also operating in the black community, for the idea of "distinctive womanhood" transcended race. Two localized examples indicate that some evolving attitudes toward the roles of black women in society were not substantially different from attitudes about white female roles. W. E. B. DuBois, in an address before the Spelman College women in 1902, outlined three specific areas of duty he saw as incumbent upon the women of his race: 1) motherhood—"the hard work of bringing forth and rearing children" and "the burden of peopling the future earth"; 2) homemaking—"the spiritual force which, guided by deft hands and molded by trained minds, builds the foundations of human life and living"; and 3) the organization of human relations—that is, leadership in "society in the narrower sense of that term."[91] Mrs. Booker T. Washington, in a later statement to the same audience (1915), echoed these sentiments and was even more explicit about their meaning:

> Over and over again scholars have told us that no people can rise above their source—the mothers of the land—and there at the fountainhead must the work begin. The home and the family is the starting point. Since the spirit of the age demands that the mother should have a wide knowledge of all matters pertaining to the moral, spiritual, and intellectual training of her children, we women must meet the demands *by making organizations avenues of help* to the better way.[92]

The phenomenon of capturing the various responsibilities of motherhood within a coherent social construct, of extending them into the community, and of making them the heart of organizational behavior (as described by Mrs. Washington) was the essence of what I call "matronage." It might even be described as a system that began as a way to use maternalism as a defense of organization and organizations as a defense of maternalism. It became, at the very least, a self-reinforcing system that, because of the idealism surrounding motherhood, compounded the social consequences of segregation for the female sex. If motherhood were to be seen—as it was—as the first duty of women, as the rock upon which civilization rested—and upon which also depended "the perpetuation of the race, the transmission of the culture, [and] the ultimate triumph of right"[93]—then motherhood was a central role to be played in the development of the consciousness of each racial group. An appeal to the importance of motherhood could be effectively employed in the defense of both the "preservation" of the white race and the "survival" of the black race, though there is—to put it mildly—a qualitative difference between the two causes. Nonetheless, the role of "mother" as the preserver-transmitter of culture and of race led to questions of what race, what culture, and what heritage would be transferred. Thus it was that motherhood represented simultaneously not only the ultimate distinction between the sexes (a universal idea) but also the means for the ultimate distinction between the races.

The ironic burden of matronage as an organizational system, then, is simply this: by asserting the distinctive responsibilities of maternalism in the community as a whole, the implied coordinate values of sexual and racial differentiation were also asserted. It is paradoxical, but motherhood, often seen as the common female experience, the basis for sexual solidarity, and the one thing that would bring women together, could also be seen, historically, as the very thing that would keep them apart.

It is this mix of race/sex identities and the prevalence of separatist thinking during the so-called Progressive Era that makes the multitude of organizations founded in that period so interesting, for they were often combinations of positive reform values and negative or reactionary sexual and racial values. The Atlanta Exposition gives a clear view of the back-stepping processes of social discrimination that were at work at that time; in fact, Atlanta offers a clearer view of these than Chicago, because, in terms of race, it is more explicit. The exposition, Rebecca Felton said of it years later, "gave a definite impetus to associations of women that never has slackened, and from that year on women wielded an ever-increasing influence in Georgia."[94] The exposition extended and strengthened networks of women's organizations, giving birth to some and directly inspiring many more. It remains to be examined what transpired in the organizations born under this star, so to speak, in the 1890s and early 1900s, as they became well-established, durable institutions in the community. How has matronage functioned? What have been the long-term effects and the legacy to the next generations of these organizations? What have been the nature and importance of their memberships? What relationship do they bear to society and culture in the city of Atlanta itself? After they got started, in the simplest sense possible, what happened?

THREE

Matronage as a System: Institutional Patterns of Women's Organizations, 1890-1940

Atlanta grew between 1890 and 1940, and it grew rapidly. Typical of other American cities undergoing industrialization during this time, Atlanta grew especially fast right after the turn of the century. The city developed from a small base of just over 65,000 people in 1890 into a large base of over 302,000 people in 1940, with the greatest increase occurring between 1900 and 1920, when the population more than doubled (from almost 90,000 to over 200,000 people). In terms of relative size, Atlanta was exceeded only by Memphis and New Orleans in the South, but by national standards—in comparison with New York, or Philadelphia, or Chicago, for example—Atlanta was still not large.[1] The city had three sources for metropolitan growth: it took in rural migrants from the rest of the state and elsewhere; it received a trickle of foreign-born immigrants; and it annexed property. Over the fifty years of this study, a great number of suburban settlements were absorbed into the municipality, with the result that the city expanded geographically as well as demographically.

Certain features of Atlanta's population persisted throughout this time period and must be taken into account in establishing the special character of the community. First, Atlanta was typical of the southern urban population model: that is, it had a large black population and a small foreign-born population, just the reverse of what was common to the rest of urban America. While it is true that the national black population was redistributing itself during this time, and blacks were leaving the rural South for cities in the North, the West, and the South, the percentages of the population affected thereby varied greatly from region to region. The percentage of blacks as a portion of the total population of southern cities remained high, while it remained low in other parts of the country.[2] In Atlanta, between 1890 and 1940 the black population never constituted less than 31.3 percent of the total, while in the other parts of the nation it never constituted more than 8.4 percent of the whole urban population. By the same token, the foreign-born population in Atlanta reached an all-time high in 1910, with a figure of 2.8 percent of the total, while the rest of the nation's cities showed 22.6 percent of the total for the same year.[3]

Between 1890 and 1940, Atlanta was essentially a biracial society in a nation that was accommodating itself to ethically mixed and multiracial compositions in its urban populations. In addition, Atlanta was overwhelmingly native-born—both black and white—in a nation where mixed parentages and foreign births were as numerous as native births. Closer to home, Atlanta was a city with a large black population in a state where the total black population was declining: while Atlanta remained substantially black, Georgia was becoming increasingly white. Furthermore, Atlanta's black population was not only large and growing, it showed impressive stability, as Richard Hopkins's exhaustive study has demonstrated.[4]

While the racial composition of Atlanta's population must be considered its most obvious feature, the sexual composition of the population is equally pertinent. First, there were continuously more women in the city than men, as had been true since the end of the Civil War. The war had created "a generation of women without men," throughout the South,[5] an imbalance that persisted thereafter in the cities. The sexual balance among Atlanta whites evened out in 1890, when rapid urbanization brought more men into the city, but then it began to drop again, irregularly, until it reached a new low in 1940. Among blacks, the male-female ratio was one of the lowest in the nation, and reached a high point in 1920, with only eighty-six men to every 100 women.[6] During this time Atlanta also had a very high rate of widowhood; it was high enough among the whites, but it was exceedingly high among the blacks, explaining to some extent the low male-female ratio among them.[7]

The characteristics of the participation of women in Atlanta's labor force are a source of some additional exceptional features of the city's population. During this period, an excessively high number of women—almost exclusively black women—appeared in domestic service. Though the percentage dropped slightly between 1890 and 1940, it was still in 1940 nearly twice the national average for that year. Except for the entrance of women into clerical fields, which occurred in especially large numbers between 1910 and 1920, there were no very perceptible changes in the distribution of female workers throughout the labor force for these fifty years. The female labor force grew, but the percentage of women in all fields and occupations in Atlanta, again with the exception of clerical service, remained about the same; and, with the exception of domestic service, the percentage of women participating in all fields of labor remained considerably lower than the national averages.[8] Other analyses of the labor force show another important difference: the preponderance of white female workers were single (i.e., never married), and the preponderance of black female workers were either widowed or divorced, or still married.[9]

Three observations ought to be made in connection with these demographic data: first, the patterns of female participation in the labor force did not vary significantly between 1890 and 1940, but showed instead great resistance to change. Any "progress" or improvement, or change of any sort, beyond the introduction of women to clerical fields was negligible compared to the rest of the nation. Once the 1920 distribution level was reached, the female population, in employment terms, remained fairly static. Second, the women of Atlanta—the white women, that is—had ready access to domestic assistance; in fact, they probably had more service, more easily available, than anywhere else in the country. While women elsewhere turned from "maids" to "appliances,"[10] Atlanta was slow to change in quite the same way, and domestic servitude continued to be the most frequent point of contact between white women and black women in an otherwise heavily segregated society. Third, all of the exceptional qualities of Atlanta's female population—its feminization, its high rate of widowhood, and the unusual profile of its labor force—are racially based factors. These characteristics were inordinately more pronounced in the black population than in the white. Thus, in every respect, the racial dimensions of the Atlanta populace were not only its most obvious feature, they constituted its most inescapable feature, one that had particular meanings for the women of the community and that showed up in their organizations. As the city grew, so grew the organizations. But first, the city.

Given the bilateral structure of Atlanta's population, the quickened pace of urbanization around the turn of the century spelled trouble for the city. Race relations were bound to be exaggerated in a place that had no buffers between the race groups, and the inability of the whites in power to conceive of a public welfare that extended to both the races usually meant that public welfare was simply not considered at all. In the early years of the twentieth century, conditions in Atlanta in almost every respect were alarming. According to one estimate, at least a third of the population was not served by sewers, and more than half of the residential streets were not paved. Epidemics of diphtheria and typhoid were common, and the number of tuberculosis cases was reaching an all-time high. There was a high death rate, a high crime rate, and a high rate of juvenile delinquency and vagrancy. In 1905, more children were arrested for disturbing the peace in Atlanta than anywhere else in the United States.[11] In every situation the burden fell heaviest upon the black population, and as to the state of race relations, the 1906 race riot speaks for itself—brutal, senseless violence perpetrated by the whites of the city against the blacks.[12]

The small Jewish population was itself an occasional scapegoat for the frustrations both blacks and whites felt. Antisemitism was not only common, it too was violent, as the lynching of Leo Frank in 1915 made plainly visible.[13] Furthermore, since Russian Jews comprised the largest single segment of the foreign-born population in Atlanta, the Jews as a group suffered the dual stigma of being not only un-Christian but un-American as well.

To aggravate Atlanta's other problems, the city operated under a cumbersome municipal government and an antagonistic state one. At least twice Atlanta voters were asked to consider reform: once, in 1911, for a commission type of government, and later, in 1927, for a city manager type, to replace the topheavy arrangement they had, which included a mayor, a council, and a board of aldermen. Both efforts failed, though some small reforms were instituted.[14] Before being submitted to the public, all city charter changes had first to pass through the state legislature, which was dominated by rural interests; nonurban representatives outnumbered those from counties with large cities in them by wide margins. Additionally, the "rule of the rustics"—it was once aptly termed—rested in a statewide electoral system that kept political power concentrated in the least populated areas of the state, while wreaking havoc in the most heavily populated areas. Neither governors nor United States congressmen from Georgia during this time ever truly represented Georgia's urban populations. The long-term effect on Georgia cities, especially Atlanta, was negative, and the outlines of that political story between 1890 and 1940 are vividly intelligible, bracketed as they are by two of Georgia's most famous and powerful figures: Thomas E. Watson on the one side, who rose to prominence in the early decades of the period, and Eugene Talmadge on the other, who began to dominate Georgia politics in the 1930s. Neither man, to put it mildly, supported urban interests.[15]

The 1920s were an especially critical period in Atlanta's development, for it was then that the city began to deal more adequately with its internal problems and at the same time to strengthen its position as a regional metropolis. Under the sponsorship of the Atlanta Chamber of Commerce and with the blessing of numerous other civic groups, Atlanta launched a "Forward Atlanta" promotional campaign in 1925, designed primarily to increase Atlanta's attractiveness as a commercial center, but aimed also at general municipal improvement. The campaign was successful: over 700 enterprises chose to locate in Atlanta over other southern cities. Atlanta's regional importance was sealed in 1929 with the city's purchase of Candler Field, an airport then in its infancy, which over the years has transformed Atlanta into the major air transfer center of the Southeast. Banking also expanded in the 1920s, and the construction industries mushroomed as the downtown built upward and the suburbs built outward. New buildings were erected, streets were paved, highways were laid, and a system of viaducts was installed downtown to accommodate the rapidly increasing automobile traffic. A bond issue for schools, sewers, and waterworks was ordained early in the decade, and schools, sewers, and waterworks were added to the growing list of accomplishments for the public good.[16] Among the new schools was a public high school for blacks—the first one in the city and a sign that Atlanta was beginning to take its black community more seriously.[17] Indeed, work for interracial cooperation began in earnest during this time, which work was most strikingly marked by the assertive stands of the Commission on Interracial Cooperation (CIC) headquartered in Atlanta.[18] But, though the 1920s were a period of improved efforts to solve race problems and reduce racial tensions, it was also a decade of heightened racial consciousness generally, with the unhappy result that racism did not abate. Even the CIC was committed to "racial integrity," and Atlanta—ever a barometer of such things—was not only the home of the CIC, but also the imperial headquarters of the recently revived Ku Klux Klan, which flourished zealously in the early 1920s.[19]

The boom of the 20s did not last. While white and black Atlantans were enjoying a comparative prosperity, most of the rest of Georgia was suffering from an agricultural depression. Throughout the decade, local attention was riveted to the worsening rural situation, replete with declining farm prices, migrating workers, and overdependencies on cotton and other cash crops. Ultimately, the bad economy swept up all of Georgia, as it did the entire nation, and Atlanta shared fully in the deprivations of the Great Depression. As with the rest of the nation, the city did not revive until World War II.[20]

This study ends a year before United States entry into World War II; 1940 is a convenient cut-off date; it is also a logical one in terms of the city and the women's organizations. After the "take-off" decade of the 1940s, Atlanta became more metropolitan, more cosmopolitan, and more prominent nationally than ever before.[21] More important, the very essence of southern culture changed, as one by one—swiftly and dramatically—the stanchions of racial oppression were knocked down: first, the white primary, then the county-unit system, and finally, segregation itself.[22] In addition, the Second World War is generally accepted as a milestone in the lives of American women, which changed their economic reality, if not their social and political conditions.[23] Following suit, women's organizations were different after the war too. First of all, *no new* national women's organizations were founded after the end of the war, with the single exception of those directly concerned with the issues of the recent women's liberation movement. *All* major, familiar national women's groups were founded before World War II, though many saw additional branches, chapters, and imitations formed afterward. This indicates a clear break in women's public activities as well as their role expectations. At the local level, the story of women's organizations is even simpler: after the war, Atlanta groups were occupied much more with questions of integration and survival than with questions of expansion and origin. It is, for example, not the origin of the League of Women Voters, but the integration of the League of Women Voters (or the YWCA, or the General Federation) that piques historical curiosity for the postwar era.

It is impossible to enumerate every activity of every woman's organization from 1890 to 1940, or even to list every woman's group that was then active in Atlanta. There were literally hundreds of them. Rather, it is my purpose to give some indication of major trends in the women's activities and major patterns of their associationalism. The description of Atlanta history above, brief as it is, gives clues to the patterns. Basically, there are four important lines of development that reflect the changing urban environment in which the clubs were situated: 1) the growth, extension, and institutionalization of the organizations themselves, which parallel the city's growth; 2) the professionalization of the early charities and the disestablishment of public welfare as a private (female) concern, which represents the typical situation in a city trying to improve its capabilities to meet welfare needs; 3) the creation of separate, often competing, organizational networks, accompanied by increasing group specialization, which reiterates the disjunctions between Atlanta women along race, class, status, and issue lines; and 4) the "ruralization" of the organizations, a complex phenomenon that occurred because rural problems in Georgia seemed to everyone to outweigh and outnumber the urban problems. The attention of the organizations was distracted from urban locales to rural ones, and even at home the city clubs tended to turn from public projects to more private concerns.

It is certain that Atlanta organizations grew in size between 1890 and 1940, but group size is a problem. It is difficult to measure organizational growth with any accuracy, when the organizations themselves have kept poor records (as is the case with most voluntary associations). Membership records are particularly unreliable, as they usually contain gaps, inconsistencies in reporting methods, omissions, and inflations. However, a look at membership rolls over a long period of time for a number of organizations in the city reveals this general pattern: individual organizations founded in the 1890s and early 1900s tended to increase in size, though unevenly, through the late 1920s, and then to decline. The decline became quite sharp in the 1930s.

The (white) Atlanta Woman's Club is a representative example. Founded in 1895 with only twenty-five members, it grew to include some 297 people just over a decade later. By the mid-1920s, the membership had swelled to 784 women, not counting associate and "deceased" members also listed on the roster. By 1932-33, however, that number had shrunk to just over 500 members, including 397 "active" members, 95 "life" members, and a few honorary and affiliated persons. By 1935, the membership, as reported to the State Federation that year, included only 219 people. Obviously, the Depression caused much of the decline, as club dues became a luxury item beyond the means of many women in the 30s, but there were also internal problems. In 1928-29, a contested election became so heated an issue that it was taken to Fulton County Superior Court for settlement; naturally, the matter caused some bitterness, and resignations ensued. By 1930-31, the club was having severe financial difficulties—so severe that personal loans were taken out in the club's behalf by several of its members. The 1941 report shows that the club survived, but with its membership fallen off, its credit gone, and with more wartime problems to come.[24]

The development of the Atlanta Woman's Club was part of the much larger growth of general women's clubs nationally, which growth occurred in three ways: individual clubs grew in size and added to the total membership strength of the national organization; new clubs were founded and added to the parent body, increasing the total number of affiliations; and a hierarchy of authorities was established between the single club unit and the national unit, which added to the bureaucratic weight of the organization. The pattern was similar, but not identical, within the numerous national federations of women's organizations, of which the General Federation of Women's Clubs (GFWC) is probably the most familiar example.

The smallest unit in the General Federation is the club itself, which is part of a district federation (usually corresponding to the local congressional district), which is a part of a state federation, which in turn composes part of the national body. This structure took some years to develop. When the General Federation was first established, in 1890, state units and individual club units had the same national membership status. Gradually, the individual clubs were subordinated to the states, and then to districts within the states. This affected the status of numerous city federations—of which Atlanta was one—that began to appear across the country at the same time the state federations did.[25] In the process of structural rationalizations, the city federations were also subordinated to the districts, and for the duration of this study, they never held a level of affiliation above that of an individual club within the General Federation. The significance of this will be clearer below in a discussion of the membership of the Atlanta Federation, but the inherent duplication and the confusion of hierarchies is obvious from this single fact: though the Atlanta Woman's Club was a member of the Atlanta Federation of Women's Clubs, both the club and the federation had the same status in the district, the state, and the national units of the General Federation.

Georgia's part in the development of the General Federation was considerable. Georgia was the first southern state to organize at the state level and affiliate with GFWC. This was in 1896, in which year there were approximately twenty other state federations. The founder and first president of the Atlanta Woman's Club, Rebecca Douglas Lowe (Mrs. William B.), was also the founder and first president of the Georgia Federation, and in 1898 she was elected to the national presidency. Mrs. Lowe served two terms, being reelected in 1900. During her tenure as president, the membership question was settled, by the reorganization that subordinated the individual clubs to the state federations. In the process, the "color question" was also solved: now no club could belong to the national federation without the recommendation of the state board of admissions. This was "states' rights" of a kind, but it was tacitly understood that no state board would recommend an organization that after investigation showed a mixed membership or a black membership.[26]

Different national organizations had different patterns and rates of growth. The hereditary, patriotic organizations, for example, which grew up side by side with the General Federation, responded to different membership stimuli. Quite obviously, periods of great national feeling would swell their ranks, and periods of national quiet would not. The National Society of Colonial Dames of America (NSCDA) in Georgia is such an organization.

In this case membership is internally managed not only in terms of "quality" but also in terms of "quantity," as the Colonial Dames exercised tight control over the number of chapters in Georgia (which they call "Town Committees") as well as the number of members admitted to each. The group organized in 1893 with a handful of people and received their charter in 1894 with twenty-eight members. In 1896 a resolution was adopted, "whereby, when the membership should have reached one hundred, there should be twenty admissions yearly, and a waiting list formed."[27] In 1898 the membership reached 100, and for two years thereafter, only twenty members were admitted each year. The rule must have been relaxed in 1902, when twenty-seven members were brought in, but, then, between 1903 and 1918, the quota exceeded the number of persons actually admitted; only once in those fifteen years was it met—the average was instead eleven admittees per year. World War I precipitated a boom in registration: fifty-one new members were admitted in a single year (1919), and registrations remained high through the early twenties, when an average of thirty-one new names were added to the roster annually. Between 1927 and 1938, the number dropped to an average of twenty-two names per year, and after 1937, the exclusiveness of the organization was reconfirmed by a lowering of the entrance rate to only fourteen names a year. The quota was not increased again until around 1950, when it was raised to "one non-resident member, one member-at-large and two members from each Town Committee" (of which there were then eleven), for a total of twenty-four enlistees per year.[28]

The Dames not only controlled their membership tightly, they also concentrated the statewide authority of the organization by keeping most of it in Savannah, Georgia's original colonial city. Not only were the headquarters located there, but the majority of the officers—the president, one vice president, two secretaries, and the treasurer—were also required to be from Savannah.[29] The importance of Atlanta as the major Georgian metropolitan center was thus diluted in this organization; all town committees regardless of size had the same relationship to the state society. All state societies existed in a loose confederation with the national society, but because of the structural relationships within the state, Atlanta was at once more constricted and more exclusive than much of the rest of the state society.

The United Daughters of the Confederacy (UDC) provide further contrast in the picture of organizational development. The most southern of the patriotic, hereditary organizations—less restrictive in its membership than the Colonial Dames and less national in its orientations than the DAR—the UDC may be the most representative example of southern women's involvement in this type of association. The growth pattern of the UDC resembles that of the Colonial Dames only in that it also experienced a spurt of growth in the early 1920s. The UDC peaked in the 1920s, but there had been almost no leveling off of its growth prior to that time as there had been with the Dames; furthermore, a great part of UDC growth, unlike that of the Dames, was accomplished through chapter development throughout the state, not just through increases in individual membership. According to the best historical source on patriotic societies, there were already 11,000 UDC members in the South by 1898, and Georgia was one of the Daughters' strongholds.[30] Because of the regional importance of the UDC, I studied its growth rate for the entire state as well as for the city, all the way up to 1960.

Until 1921, the Atlanta Chapter (#18) was the only UDC chapter in the city. It was founded in 1895 as the 18th chapter in the federation, one year after the national federation was set up.[31] By 1903 it had an enrollment of 200 members. The membership doubled by 1915, when it numbered 448 women, at which point it began to decline a bit. The number picked up again with World War I, and by 1920, the membership totaled 502 women, and then, quickly, 610 women just two years later. At its highest point—in 1923—the membership included 659 women, after which it began to decline and continued to decline through World War II. In 1942, the chapter reported a low of 220 members in annual convention. A small spurt of renewed interest in the UDC in the 1950s was barely perceptible in this chapter, and in 1960, #18 reported only 248 members.[32]

The growth of the organization, in terms of total membership throughout the state, closely parallels that of the Atlanta club specifically. The greatest growth occurred in the first two decades of UDC existence in Georgia, between 1895 and 1915. At the end of the second decade, the UDC was 6,345 women strong in Georgia. That the organization continued to flourish in the state well into the 1920s is obvious from the fact that 8,120 women were still on its rolls in 1928. A sharp decrease occurred in the 1930s and continued in the 1940s with, for example, a membership of only 5,431 women reported in 1933 and a membership of 3,775 in 1942. By 1960, only 3,190 women were counted as members of the United Daughters of the Confederacy in the state. On the evidence of numbers solely, the development of the chapters throughout the state appears to follow that of the general membership, again with the greatest increase occurring between 1895 and 1915, when the number of chapters in the state grew by leaps and bounds—from four in 1895 to 116 in 1915. After that the rate of growth was much slower, with only a half-dozen or so new chapters established each year, until after the mid-1930s, when the number of chapters itself began falling off, and a pre-1905 level and new low was reached at seventy-seven chapters in 1960.

There is, however, a qualitative difference between chapter development and membership growth that is not apparent from the numbers. In the very early years of UDC development, between 1895 and 1900, virtually all of the major cities in Georgia established UDC chapters, including Albany, Americus, Athens, Augusta, Columbus, Macon, Milledgeville, Rome, and Savannah as well as Atlanta, in addition to numerous smaller cities, such as Dalton, Waynesboro, and Marietta. The growth in chapters that occurred between 1900 and 1915 was largely due to the establishment of chapters in the small towns and cities in the rest of the state, but after 1915 another pattern began to emerge. Between 1915 and 1925, fourteen new chapters were established in Georgia, two of which were in the greater Atlanta area, within a radius of thirty miles from the center of town. Between 1925 and 1933, eleven chapters were added, six of which were in the greater Atlanta area, and in the years between 1933 and 1942, there were four chapters established, three of them in the greater Atlanta area. The fourth was located halfway between Atlanta and Athens. Finally, in the 1950s there were seven chapters established—two in greater Atlanta, one each in suburban Augusta and Macon, and others outside Albany, Savannah, and Bainbridge.[33] The momentum of the organization—where new life was being put into it—is reflected in this geographical spread of chapters. It went from Atlanta and the other major cities in the 1890s, was dispersed throughout the state to the mid-1920s, revived in the Atlanta suburban areas, and then dispersed again, chiefly to additional metropolitan and suburban areas. The importance of the suburban spread of chapters will suggest itself in the discussion later concerning the nature of membership in the UDC (Chapter IV).

There is not the same consistency of information, chapter by chapter, available for the Daughters of the American Revolution (DAR) in Georgia, but two characteristics of growth seem to follow those of the UDC: the DAR saw its greatest increase in numbers in its first two to three decades of existence, and chapters also proliferated in Atlanta, but not to the extent of the UDC. The first DAR chapter in Atlanta was founded in 1891; it was one of the earliest chapters in the nation and was called simply the Atlanta Chapter. A second chapter was founded in 1900 under the title the Joseph Habersham Chapter. Today, there are half a dozen DAR chapters in the Atlanta metropolitan area, and both the Atlanta and Joseph Habersham chapters survive.[34]

The growth of individual organizations gives some idea of the survivability of female organizations in Atlanta after 1890, and organizational permanence is an important concept; institutionalization is an important pattern of that same growth. Institutionalization itself is a complex process; however, two of its aspects are essential qualities of matronage: the establishment of organizational permanence through the longevity of the "ruling class" within the organizations (Chapter IV) and the establishment of organizational permanence through the assumption of property ownership and the identification of women's groups with actual physical sites in the city (Chapter V). Both long-term service in an organization and organizational ability in a "home" address are attributes of the matronage system that developed. Take, for example, the Colonial Dames, who referred to their own maturation in 1927 this way:

> . . . we had up to that time been solely a voluntary organization, without one penny's worth of real property and with no legal ties. We did one piece of work after another, quietly and well, and turned over the accomplishment to others' maintenance. But having voted a headquarters for the Society, we acquired valuable real estate; a historic mansion and a large endowment fund; we formed a corporation to hold the property; we equipped a museum with the highest standard for comparison; we set up housekeeping; we maintained a social status in Washington; we invited the world and his wife to visit us; we are women of property.[35]

The Dames of the 1890s were simply a group of polite women who met in various founders' homes to establish their society; their successors had substance as well as politesse. They were "women of property."

While a number of women's groups were establishing their permanence in the community through the acquisition of property, other women's groups were losing ground—literally—through a reversal of the same process. This was especially the case with the small charity organizations that had been established in the late nineteenth century. Quite clearly, these small operations were insufficient, on their own, to meet the worsening urban conditions in Atlanta. Larger, more efficient, more effective organizations were needed, and more of them. It is a typical story in Atlanta—one that is already familiar—of the gradual assumption of the responsibilities for public welfare by public agencies, accompanied by the professionalization of welfare work and the demise of charity as a special province of women. The outlines of this story as a national phenomenon are known from a variety of excellent sources, as are its general effects on the changing roles of women in the country.[36] The effect the transformation of charity administration had on women's organizations is particularly acute at the local level. Not only were some organizations eliminated from female control, but other effects were felt as well.

The first feature of the shift in philanthropic control can be perceived in the growing reliance of private charities on public subsidies and regulations. The Home for the Friendless and the Carrie Steele Logan Home, for example, were both receiving monies from the city in 1900, when each was about ten years old.[37] The Home for Incurables began receiving money from the city from its inception in 1901.[38] When the city built the Battle Hill Sanitarium, about 1910, Atlanta's capacities to deal with tuberculosis were increased immeasurably, but the sanitarium nearly put the Home for Incurables out of business by absorbing all of its TB patients.[39] The association that ran the home itself was superseded by the Atlanta Anti-Tuberculosis Association, which was not only coed and professional, as opposed to female and amateur (which the Home for Incurables had been), but it was also—at some points of its operation—interracial. The Confederate Veterans Home is another case in point. It was begun in 1889 with the collection of private subscriptions for its construction, but it was not actually opened until 1901, under the reluctant management of the State of Georgia. The United Daughters of the Confederacy had been one of the major proponents of the Veterans Home, but their functions under the state were ancillary and consisted primarily of providing special entertainments, comforts, and refreshments for the men who lived there.[40]

The proliferation of small charity organizations in the early 1900s made some control over them and some direction of their purposes desirable, and a communitywide committee for the "Associated Charities" was formed in 1905 with the object of "coordinating" and "motivating" proper social work rather than of doing the work itself. This committee was a direct predecessor of the Community Chest, which was formulated—as such—in 1924, and which has sometimes been a double bind for service organizations, as three brief excerpts from the YWCA's history might serve to show:

> In May 1922, the Y.W.C.A. became affiliated with the Community Chest and was no longer dependent upon its own campaigns for finances. [The Chest is seen relieving the Y of burdens and hurdles to the performance of its tasks.]

> In July 1926, the Y.W.C.A. discontinued its employment service and it was established as a separate agency of the Community Chest. [Part of the Y's function is being replaced by the other body.]

> In March 1935 a day school for unemployed girls was established because of pressure from the Community Chest and the community. [The YWCA is no longer entirely independent in the choice of which services it will offer.][41]

One of the best examples of the complex of processes in operation during the transition from charity to social work can be seen in the Neighborhood Union in Atlanta.

The Neighborhood Union is undoubtedly one of the richest chapters in Atlanta social history. Founded in 1908 by black women on the West Side of Atlanta, its purpose was simply stated: to become better acquainted with one another and to improve the neighborhood. To improve the neighborhood the women undertook an eager, comprehensive program of activities—from petitioning the city for sewers, street lights, and pavements, to establishing playgrounds for neighborhood children, to creating health clinics, to surveying housing conditions, to investigating school problems, and so on. The union was designed to serve a single neighborhood to begin with, then expanded its operations in 1911 to include five Atlanta neighborhoods, and ultimately all Atlanta neighborhoods, as its plan of organization was adopted by the Anti-Tuberculosis Association in a house-by-house search for tuberculosis cases. As the union grew, it acquired property; its first neighborhood house was located very near the Leonard Street orphanage, and its second location was on Fair Street, just a few blocks east of Morehouse College.

The primary force behind the union was Mrs. John Hope, wife of the president of Morehouse College and of Atlanta University. Mrs. Hope was an indefatigable community worker, dedicated, along with her husband, to racial betterment. Both were committed to the application of scientific principles to the improvement of racial and urban conditions. Her commitments were obvious through her organizational work—the union, the YWCA, the NAACP, the Commission on Interracial Cooperation—and her contact with racial and welfare leaders throughout the country. His were obvious through his own organizational ties as well as through his exceptional leadership of Morehouse and Atlanta University. At the latter institution, for example, he rehired W. E. B. DuBois, negotiated with the affiliation of the Atlanta School of Social Work with the university, and supported the development of University Homes, the black half of the first public housing project in the United States, as a potential laboratory for the social work school.

Mrs. Hope's ambitions for the Neighborhood Union met much apathy and resistance along the way—some anticipated, some not. For one thing, the aims and activities of the union were shared by competing—and stronger—agencies, including the white-male-dominated Community Chest, which severely limited the union's program of service, and the black-male-dominated Urban League, which claimed to bring with it to Atlanta a new, "scientific" approach to urban problems and precipitated a debilitating controversy between itself and the union as to which had actually originated social service work among blacks in Atlanta. Probably nothing, though, is as symbolic or eloquent of the forces at work to change the nature of social service than the destruction of the union's house on Fair Street in order to make way for the federally funded University Homes housing project.[42]

"Progress" in social work caused not only the *de*institutionalization of some women's organizations, it also caused a change in their expectations toward public projects in general. They no longer anticipated managing affairs, but they did expect to continue to serve—the difference being, perhaps, between the early job of sitting on the board of the Home for the Friendless and the later job of serving the same institution as a Junior League volunteer. Gradually, the women's organizations took on less of the burden themselves and expected more involvement from all levels of government. The Atlanta Woman's Club, for example, set up a curbside market in Atlanta in 1919, as part of a Georgia Federation drive to encourage diversified farming in the state and to provide outlets for produce farming in the cities. When the club opened its market, the women had no intention of creating their own institution; quite the opposite—while running their curbside stand, they also lobbied the City Council to build a special municipal market. They succeeded in 1925, and the city of Atlanta is still in the meat and produce business. The

Atlanta Woman's Club, meanwhile, continued to have some responsibilities for the market—as far as the organization was concerned—but these were not a direct part of the market management. The women operated a rummage stall inside the market and kept watch over the building, petitioning—when so inclined—for improvements in the place (a post office substation, a fire hose, a couch in the ladies room, etc.). After the market was built there was not only no official relationship between the market management and the local club, there was no further relationship between the local market committee of the club and the rest of the program of the Georgia Federation. The Atlanta Municipal Market was a completely localized project.[43]

Certainly women as individuals profited from the professionalization of welfare work by being able to find employment in a new career, but women's organizations per se did not. There is no doubt about it: their local effectiveness was much diminished in the process. Not only were they eliminated from official, recognized responsibilities in social work, they could not compete independently for institutional viability. As a result, women's organizations lost both public visibility and public participation; they became not only separate as organizations, but isolated as well.

The isolation of women's organizations from affairs of the general community, which seems gradually to have increased during the decades under study, was accompanied by another kind of isolation—that of individual women's organizations from one another. From 1900 on, whole new constituencies of women, as well as new issues for their concern, began to be served by wholly new sets of organizations. These groups formed themselves all but simultaneously at the local and the national level, so that even as new groups formed they were part of a nationally affiliated system. In some cases, national federation was a matter of strengthening the superior body, such as with the YWCA. In some cases it was a matter of joining somewhat independent and disparate units into a communications confederation, such as with the Association of Junior Leagues. In other cases, such as the Girl Scouts, the national organization and the original local groups were synonymous, and geographic expediency required that the national headquarters be located somewhere else (i.e., New York instead of Savannah). A different case still is the League of Women Voters, which built a new organization on the remnants of an old network of organizations.

The special needs of groups of women were met with special associations; new groups of women not formerly organized sought new associations, and the general trend of development—noticed by everyone—was *from* the general woman's club *to* a more specialized club, one with limited appeal or with very specific goals and less obvious socializing purposes.[44] Still, every organization served not only its stated purposes, but also the social needs of its constituent members. Mothers of public school children had sets of problems not related to private schools; they also had a new bond with one another through the schools and the local PTA. Professional women were now numerous enough to assert their occupational desires through their organizations, which they could also use to identify with one another as special groups of people—subcultures within subcultures. The sheer number of young women entering the labor market, especially in white-collar positions, required some adjustments in communities not geared to handle the job placement, housing, and dislocation problems of single women, let alone their needs for sorosis and social intercourse with the opposite sex. The YWCA was one of the first organizations to respond to the needs of this group of women, and out of the YWCA grew the Business and Professional Women's Clubs in 1920, itself a federation, with over a thousand clubs and tens of thousands of members in a few short years.[45]

The process was at work in Atlanta. There was no concern, no issue, no political cause that did not capture the imagination of at least some Atlanta women, no social grouping that was not represented by a band of local adherents, however tiny the organization.[46] The organizational picture among Atlanta women began to reiterate the divisions within the social fabric itself in a more complex way, with different population groups and different portions of those groups being served by separate organizations. As the organizations persisted over time, they tended to develop their own "characters," distinguishable from one another on the basis of loyalties, social status, member attributes, age, educational level, interests, and so on.[47] On the basis of appeal and member compatibility, every woman could now have "her" club, and the clubs in turn buttressed differences in taste and life-style. Because of the proliferation of clubs, the increasing number of national affiliations, and the new networks of association, organizations—though they did draw women together into groups—tended to segregate and insulate women's groups from one another. This was especially true after 1920: the suffrage question was settled, and the huge suffrage machinery collapsed. No issue remained to unite the women or even to command their undivided attention, and at that moment the most catholic of national bodies was the General Federation of Women's Clubs. However, the General Federation ceased, rather quickly, to be the only—or even a major—meeting ground for clubwomen, because it could not (or would not) accommodate increasing specialization among women. The recession of the federation's influence is mirrored in the annals of the Georgia Federation, which offer, at the state level, a very clear view of what happened.

Originally, "everyone" belonged to the Georgia Federation; there were few restrictions on club membership beyond the federation's obvious racial and political aversions, and for a long time, the directory of the Georgia Federation read like a catalog of white women's organizations in the entire state. The proliferation of clubs and the growth of the federation itself dictated an expansion of its bureaucracy, so a system of district offices, to correspond to state congressional districts, was instituted about 1912. Prior to that time, the numerous city and county federations—such as the Atlanta City Federation—had been respected as amalgamations of the member clubs from their respective geographic areas of the state. After 1912, all city and county federations were subordinated to the district administrations—in Atlanta's case, to the Fifth District.[48]

Membership in the Georgia Federation was not mandatory for membership in the Atlanta Federation, and vice versa. But membership in the Georgia Federation was now obligatory for representation in Fifth District affairs. This was not important in itself except to those individuals and clubs that wished to pursue careers and/or rewards within the General Federation system. For a time, there continued to be many crossover and duplicate as well as exclusive memberships in the city and the state federations, as organizations joined either one or both, depending on their circumstances. It made sense for organizations organized at the local but not the state level—such as the YWCA—to join the Atlanta federation but not the state federation; likewise, state-level organizations—such as the Georgia Division of the American Association of University Women or the Georgia Association of Women Lawyers—tended to join the state federation but not the city one. It made little difference except for the convenience of communication, until late in the 1920s. Beginning about 1928, the Georgia Federation began to distinguish among memberships.

There were now four categories of membership: Group One was reserved for regular club memberships, where participation in federation business was based on a club head count for both dues assessments and votes. Group Two was specifically set aside for city and county federations. Group Three now contained all those "affiliated organizations or clubs having a specialized purpose, and which may belong to other state and national organizations," and Group Four specified charitable organizations. Groups Two, Three, and Four had the same privileges of representation—one vote per club (or federation) in state business—but the dues structure was different. City and county federations that affiliated with the state prior to 1928 (which was virtually all of them) paid higher dues per federation than other members did as single organizations, plus they had an additional assessment for all member clubs in their federation in excess of twenty clubs. In 1935, the Atlanta City Federation was the single organization in the Georgia Federation that met the requirements of both the category and the surtax, as other city and county federations were either small or already extinct. Thus, the Atlanta Federation paid more money for less participation in the state organization than its individual members did, a circumstance that lacked some appeal, not to mention rationality.

Another problem arose because the city federation differed substantially from the Fifth District Federation and represented an open channel through which nonfederation clubs could participate in the conduct of federation affairs. The city federation appealed to many women: more sororities, alumnae organizations, literary societies, educational groups, not to mention BPW clubs, labor auxiliaries, welfare agencies were members of the city federation that were of the state.. Both the YWCA and the Girl Scouts were members, alongside the WCTU and the Junior League and, early on, one UDC chapter. In 1935, there were sixty-nine member organizations listed for the Fifth District of the Georgia Federation, of which only twenty-six were Group One members. One Fifth District member, the Atlanta Federation, meanwhile, had something between ninety-eight and 108 member organizations and made no distinctions in the type of membership they held. Obviously, the tail—given a chance—could wag the dog, and the Georgia Federation, in imitation of the Georgia legislature, did not wish the city to dominate the state. City federations and associate members were unmanageable and unwelcome within the structure of the state federation, and ultimately both associate memberships and city federations evaporated, as did the interest of many women.[49]

There were some Jewish organizations and some Catholic organizations within the body of the Georgia Federation, but there were no black organizations, and no blacks, except indirectly—invisibly—through white-controlled organizations such as the YWCA and the Anti-TB Association, which had a Negro Branch and a Negro Department, respectively. The separate, parallel tracking of women's organizations along racial lines was a continuing feature of organizational life throughout this period. Increasing public segregation and a rigidifying caste system meant that women's groups would have to develop separately, racially. Furthermore, the caste system precluded the possibility of the systems developing identically. Inevitably, there would be differences. The chronological pace of organizational foundations, the range of their programs, their autonomy, their size, their community responsiveness, the bases for their memberships—all responded to different stimuli in the black community, and the entire network that resulted resembles the white network only partially. There were, of course, many duplicate organizations in the two networks—BPWs, PTAs, kindergarten associations, and nursing associations, along with the older organizations—the women's clubs, state federations, alumnae associations, and charities. There were, however, profound differences.

At the upper echelon of black society, for example, there were no patriotic, hereditary organizations—no Colonial Dames, no DAR—though there were organizations for which correct family background was a requisite for membership. By the same token, there was nothing quite like the elite Chautauqua Circle among literary societies in the white community. There was nothing stemming from the Civil War in the black community that vaguely resembled the United Daughters of the Confederacy; it is lunatic to think there might have been, but there was also nothing organized around the Union cause either. On another level, no white organization in Atlanta ever approached the total neighborhood involvement of the Neighborhood Union. In fact, it was years after the union got started before white neighborhood groups began to appear with any substance to them.

Importantly, there was no organized support—in fact, very little interest even—in the suffrage question among black clubwomen. The socially superior Chautauquas politely entertained the question "Should Women Have the Right to Vote?" at their first recorded regular meeting in 1913, but could not have been very interested in it, as they failed to record the outcome of their debate in the minutes. In 1919, when the woman suffrage question was all but settled, the question reappeared in Chautauqua discussions, but this time with a compelling racial emphasis: "Resolved: That the Responsibility for the Political Condition of the Negro Rests Upon the Women of the Race." The question was apparently hotly contested, the debate noted in the minutes, and the affirmative barely won.[50]

It seems logical to think that the young women being trained at Spelman College or Atlanta University might be interested in woman suffrage, but such was apparently not the case. The *Spelman Messenger* reported no suffrage organizations on the campus, indeed, no suffrage activities at all, except a solitary debate between Spelman women and Morehouse men (which the women lost). The *Messenger* itself never advocated suffrage or argued the pros and cons on its pages.[51] Some individuals in the black community were suffrage sympathizers (Mrs. Hope, for instance), but "race leaders" were not in general agreement. W. E. B. DuBois openly championed suffrage, but Mrs. Booker T. Washington was less enthusiastic: "Personally," she once wrote, "woman suffrage has never kept me awake at night."[52] She was not opposed to it, but as a southern black woman she was undoubtedly persuaded that the white woman suffrage movement was simply no concern of hers—a political reality for most black women in the nation because most of them lived in the conservative South.[53]

The distance between black and white women, specifically the difference in the cultural expressions of their eliteness through their organizations, can be seen in a comparison of some of the traits of the local DAR and the Chautauqua Circle, which comparison is neither specious nor ridiculous, but serves to point up some pertinent variations.[54]

The DAR is that familiar organization about which more is assumed than is actually known and that has had an insurmountable national image problem since the Marion Anderson incident.[55] At the local level, a Daughter may be less formidable, though no less genealogically obsessed—a "pleasant, somewhat parochial gray-haired woman [who may do] well behind the tea urn, but never could sustain any protracted interest in public affairs such as her critics ascribed to her," in the characterization of one writer.[56] In Atlanta, the chapters have done much good, for which they have never received proper credit, but their reputation still attaches itself to unprogressive involvements (Stop-ERA, for example). However, with ninety-nine chapters and 7,400 members in Georgia, the Daughters cannot be overlooked.[57]

In addition to size, a major difference between the DAR and the Chautauqua might be said to be that between an organization that concentrates on genealogy and one that emphasizes heredity. The Chautauqua Circle is functionally hereditary but not constitutionally so, such as is the DAR. At its founding in 1913, the circle consisted of fifteen of the most socially prominent black women in Atlanta, including at least one pair of sisters and one mother-daughter combination in its small membership. Membership has since passed to daughters and granddaughters; one membership may be extending into its fourth female generation. While membership has never been limited solely to family members, the hereditary right to membership has been given preference when the question has arisen.

The circle certainly has not been patriotic in the same sense as the DAR, nor has it ever been "Africanist" to the degree, say, that the Colonial Dames are "Anglophile." One hesitates to describe the Chautauquas' singing of the Negro National Anthem at their meetings, which they adopted during World War I, as anything but a statement of race identity and pride, which became—like the Lord's Prayer—a religious habit. The Chautauquas started as a self-improvement organization, which meant in the early days that the women did their own teaching, their own research, their own studying and writing, their own speaking and reporting before the group. The Chautauquas concentrated on English, current events, parliamentary procedure, great books and plays, and notable black achievements and personalities. Like most female study groups, they ultimately reverted to a less demanding, more passive form of education.[58]

The DAR actually started out in the same tradition, with members giving their own historical papers at meetings. Thus, early meetings of both the DAR and the Chautauqua would have had much in common: a program item, a business session, some entertainment, prayers, and refreshments. In addition, the Chautauquas devoted some meetings to parties—to celebrate the anniversary of their founding and public holidays. The DAR also celebrated its anniversary and all patriotic holidays. The circle celebrated the birthdays of its members and also mourned their deaths. The DAR mourned the deaths but ignored the birthdays. Guests at DAR meetings would likely include representatives from the UDC or the Atlanta Woman's Club, and occasionally, the Colonial Dames would come over for a joint session. The Chautauquas shared their meetings with visiting dignitaries and guests from the other elite literary societies—the Inquirers, the Mo-So-Lit Club, the Utopian Society, among others.

Like the DAR, the Chautauquas were concerned with juvenile upbringing and especially with juvenile education. They discussed it a great deal, and like the DAR, they offered scholarships to local high school students. The circle's program, however, never reached the proportions of DAR educational projects. Unlike the DAR, the Chautauquas were affiliated with their city federation of women's clubs, but they were never part of a national network of organizations (as an organization, though as individuals they were), having only the most tenuous relationship with the original Chautauqua. The circle was small and exclusive, limiting membership by number as well as by social acceptability; the DAR was equally exclusive, but not small. Like the DAR, the circle was not a service organization, but an educational one, and most of its "service" was in the form of contributions to worthy causes and welfare organizations. Although educationally committed to black culture as well as Western culture, the Chautauquas never involved themselves in the creation and preservation of local history, as the DAR did. Unlike the DAR, the circle was obliged to meet in the homes of its members; it could not afford a chapter house, though it envisioned one for itself, which, by its description—had it been built—would have resembled quite a bit both of the two white-columned DAR houses in Atlanta.[59]

Clearly, the "best" of society, which both of these groups represented, operated within different spheres inside their separate communities—with divergent attitudes, social habits, interests, and effectiveness. Their social encounters were substantively different, and their club life-styles were dissimilar. Moreover, white and black women, isolated from each other, were ignorant of each other in those very associational situations they held dear in their own experience; at all levels of club life, there were no points of contact between the races. Beyond the inconsistent paternalism of the YWCA and a few welfare agencies, contact simply did not take place, and in most cases, was not wanted. There was no "mixing" of any consequence, really, until after World War I, when the formation of the Commission on Interracial Cooperation gave southern women their first opportunity to assume a responsible public position in racial affairs.

By that time, the need for some racial cooperation was already apparent to women in some quarters—in the churches, in the YWCA, in some schools, and in virtually all black organizations. A series of cautious meetings in 1920 between white and black women produced a tentative beginning to a new set of working relationships between women's groups. The initial reactions showed how wide the gap was between the races, how ignorant they were of each other, how much work they would have to do to overcome their basic mutual distrust. One of the white women reported her embarrassed surprise at what she found among the black women:

> I saw these colored women graduates of great institutions of learning. . . . I saw women of education, culture, and refinement. I had lived in the South all my life, but didn't know such as these lived in the land."[60]

The black women were also tense and distrustful, and at the same time were surprised by what they did *not* find among the white women, as one of them later admitted:

67

I want you to know that the Negro women had great suspicion, when we were called to that conference, that you could not get Negro servants, and that you were calling us together so that you could get help.[61]

From such an inauspicious beginning, a start was made on a very difficult job. Interracial work in the South gradually developed its own network of organizations, as people who could be trusted in race relations got to know one another and regularly showed up for the meetings where interracial matters were discussed.[62] But the interracial network never supplanted the separate white and black systems of organization during this time, as the Association of Southern Women for the Prevention of Lynching perfectly illustrates. The ASWPL, as it was referred to, was an educational campaign against lynching, begun in 1930 by Jessie Daniel Ames of the CIC, which ultimately encompassed tens of thousands of white women in the South by reaching out through their organizations—those networks of women's federations, churches, and YWCAs, which had been going strong for years and into which the programs of the ASWPL could readily fit.[63] The ASWPL, however, never incorporated black women into its membership, so its existence was enlightened without being integrated, a point that is made poignant by the fact that the ASWPL actually subsumed most of the authority, momentum, and action of the Women's Division of the CIC, whose committees *were* interracially composed.[64]

Interracial work did strengthen some female ties across race lines and weaken some within race lines. Many white women became estranged from organizations that they came to believe were either apathetic toward racial justice or hostile to it. And the black women often argued with one another—sometimes bitterly and wastefully—over the degree of aggressiveness or circumspection that should be shown over each issue. Women committed to the idea of racial cooperation moved from group to group in search of the idea's rationalization through some sort of group action, and in the process they laid down important groundwork for later integration in the South.[65]

Cooperation among women's groups, whose rationales were increasingly at odds, was difficult to obtain; consensus, almost impossible. When pushed to it, the women would revert to the "safe" things, the things they still felt special responsibilities for—home, children, education. When the early Women's Division of the CIC, for example, was casting about for a project of major proportions that would meet their group priorities as well as the needs of their region, they committed themselves to a ten-year program for the improvement of rural schools. BETTER RURAL SCHOOLS, NEGRO AND WHITE—exactly so inscribed—was their motto, and their intention was to work through their own organizations, using tried and true techniques such as model classrooms and mothers' meetings to accomplish their goal. Unfortunately, the full monetary support needed for the project never materialized, and the efforts of the CIC women were diverted to other objectives, namely, the campaign against lynching.[66] But the expression of CIC interest in rural schooling was added weight to what was becoming a national movement, as rural problems began more and more to occupy the attention of women's groups and other bodies.[67] Such an interest had been a "natural" in the South for some time.

The phenomenon of "ruralization" of the women's clubs included many distinct manifestations, of which an interest in rural education was one of the most important and widespread. The deterioration of conditions in the rural South and the high rate of illiteracy there led, for one, the National Association of Colored Women to create a special department for "Conditions in Rural Life" in addition to their departments of forestry, mothers' meetings, and night schools, which had country as well as city components.[68] Meanwhile, major northern philanthropies with long records of gifts to black education also turned their attention to the rural areas, including the Rosenwald Fund, the Slater Fund, and the Jeanes Foundation—all of which ran rural programs (sometimes at the expense of urban ones).[69] Rural education among whites—for women and children—saw one of the most forceful exercises of female philanthropic muscle in the country, from which a number of direct legacies stem today—a system of mountain schools stretching the full length of the Appalachians; home economics curricula in universities, agricultural colleges, and county extension centers; regional and county libraries; visiting nursing services, and the like.

Looking back in 1938 on what it considered a long history of "urban-rural cooperation," the Georgia Federation took stock of its major activities in the field. The women had done work in rural Georgia under such diverse titles as "Natural Resources and Forestry," "Memorials and Trees," "Library Extension," "Illiteracy," "Education in Rural Districts," and "Country Life" under their Department of Applied Education; "Good Roads and Highways" under their Department of American Citizenship; and "Home Economics Teaching" and "Home Demonstrations" under their Department of the American Home. Among their accomplishments they could list obtaining an increase in state appropriations to provide extension teaching for rural women in 1910; getting home economics included in the legislative appropriations for education in 1911; setting up scholarships for rural girls; raising money for salaries for home demonstration agents; entertaining rural girls in the homes of Atlanta clubwomen; building traveling exhibits; participating in agricultural rallies cosponsored by the federation and the state Department of Agriculture in 1915 and 1916; furnishing the women's dormitory at the state college of agriculture; setting up a student aid foundation for rural girls to prepare them at college level for home economics and vocational teaching; setting up curb markets for Georgia-grown foodstuffs in 1919; holding Georgia products dinners and festivals from 1919 on; supporting traveling libraries in rural counties from 1900 on; and last, but certainly not least, building their own rural school at Tallulah Falls, Georgia, in 1909. In the 1920s and 1930s the women continued many of their rural interests, concerning themselves with conservation, highways, planting trees, with "buy cotton" campaigns, with Georgia products dinners and bazaars, and with Tallulah Falls—always Tallulah Falls. The school actually enjoyed support from many women's organizations outside the Georgia Federation—an indication of the widespread interest in this school and others like it.[70]

The clubwomen's efforts to improve rural life were often marked by considerable feelings of superiority over the farm women. Sometimes the tone of their dealings was merely patronizing, as when the president of one Atlanta club explained in an interview that

> farm women have been able to lighten their drudgery by incorporating ideas into their work, ideas which club women in the cities through their advantages have discovered and are broadcasting through the newspapers.[71]

Other times the feeling was demonstratively hostile, as when one suffrage leader dismissed the entire rural population as "ignorant and hopeless."[72] None other than Tom Watson criticized the joint program of rallies produced by the Georgia Federation and the Department of Agriculture as "citified"; he found the efforts of "these benevolent Atlanta ladies" misplaced and their endeavors to "tell our wives how to keep house" laughable.[73] Mrs. Nellie Peters Black, who had instigated the rallies, was unaware of the contradictions in her own views on the subject. In the same speech explaining the rallies, she regretted the fact that farm women had not gained their "rightful" place alongside city women in the expanded sphere of modern womanhood while at the same time she argued that if only farm life were more attractive (hence the rallies), not so many women would be tempted to move to the cities.[74]

Ruralization was a contradictory development; in part, it was as much a negative response to the city as it was a positive response to rural problems. At least, it was so in Georgia, where urban-rural tensions were a state malady. This is apparent from the other qualities of organizational development already discussed. As the women were displaced from their urban philanthropies—or, as they removed themselves—they turned to other parts of the state, less well developed, to practice their "womancraft," and they created rural charities. Likewise, the growth of their organizations turned mountainward. The organizations grew out from the cities to the small towns and counties; in the process club growth in the smaller places outdistanced growth in the cities—especially Atlanta, and the state federations of the oldest, major women's clubs all reveal an anti-Atlanta bias in their corporate structures. There was no way Atlanta could dominate state women's affairs in any of the major associations as long as it could be outvoted by women from Calhoun, Cartersville, Valdosta, and Rome. Furthermore, Atlanta's "natural" political dominance in the state, by virtue of its commercial, governmental, and financial advantages, was lost on a female population that did not share a very large part of the power over those advantages and that was growing more heterogenous, suburbanized, and segmented with time. No single social grouping could contain the women or appeal to them all. As the older clubs matured and institutionalized, newer clubs were added to the scene, and the whole matrix of women's organizations in the city became larger and more diverse. It also became more disconnected and more insular. More clubs meant that more women could create "careers" for themselves through the organizations; more clubs meant more choices and a wider variety of club experience as a substitute for other kinds of experience. Just what that experience was like is disclosed in a closer look at the women themselves who constituted the backbone of the matronage system.

FOUR

Species "Clubwoman": Patterns of Organizational Involvement, 1890-1940

In 1941, as part of the Golden Jubilee celebration of the General Federation of Women's Clubs, the Georgia Federation picked one deceased woman to represent it among the roll of outstanding members of the national federation. That woman was Nellie Peters Black, a superior example of what the clubwoman could be, who is offered here as the quintessence of matronage—the matron herself. Contained within Mrs. Black's biography and career in organizations are all of the elements that might be described under the collective female identification, "Atlanta Clubwoman, 1890-1940."

Nellie Peters Black, nee Mary Ellen Peters, was born in 1851 into a large Atlanta family, daughter of Richard Peters (1810-1889)—railroad builder, cotton manufacturer, pioneer developer, and wealthy landowner—and Mary Jane Thompson, eldest daughter of one of Atlanta's first citizens, Dr. Joseph Thompson. Nellie was the oldest surviving child of eight, including two sisters and five brothers (three of whom died young). Nellie was educated in private schools, including Miss Eastman's in Pennsylvania, her father's native state. In 1877, she married—somewhat "late" according to custom—George Robinson Black, a widower with four children, who was a lawyer, state legislator, and himself a wealthy landowner. To his children, the couple added three more, two daughters and a son, but in 1886 George died, leaving Nellie a widow with seven children to raise and a farm to run. He also left her financially self-sufficient. Nellie never remarried, but she did raise the seven children and manage the family farm; in addition, as a well-to-do widow, she embarked on an extraordinary career of public activity the breadth and depth of which are truly impressive.[1] Following are some of the highlights of that career:

1. founder and member of the board, King's Daughters Hospital (1892), the first free hospital in Atlanta
2. local president (1893) and first state president (1905), Woman's Auxiliary of the Episcopal Church, Diocese of Georgia; Bible teacher from her youth until her death in 1919
3. founder of the Holy Innocents Mission (1905)
4. member of the Board of Lady Managers, Cotton States and International Exposition, chairman for hospital and day nursery department (1895)
5. woman commissioner from the state of Georgia to the Tennessee Centennial (1897)
6. charter member and member for life, Atlanta Woman's Club
7. president, Atlanta Federation of Woman's Clubs (1903)
8. president, three terms, Georgia Federation of Women's Clubs (1916-1919); committee member and committee chairman, many committees (1912-1919); elected delegate to national convention three times from Georgia Federation; director for life, Georgia Federation
9. member, kindergarten committee, Georgia Federation of Women's Clubs
10. founder and officer, Anti-Tuberculosis Association of Atlanta, and member for life (1909-1919)
11. charter member and vice president, Atlanta Pioneer Club
12. vice president, Home for the Friendless
13. president, women's department, Southern Conference on Education and Industries (1916)
14. delegate to Southern Sociological Congress (1912)
15. honorary appointments from Governor Dorsey of Georgia and President Woodrow Wilson (1917, 1918)
16. life member of other organizations; Every Saturday History Class, Georgia Society of the Colonial Dames of America, United Daughters of the Confederacy, Daughters of the American Revolution[2]

In her many civic roles, Mrs. Black repeatedly advocated reform of various kinds: the admission of women to the University of Georgia and to the Georgia bar; the promotion of diversified farming in what was still a cash-crop, cotton state; the institution of compulsory education and the eradication of illiteracy; the amendment of child labor laws; and—her most precious crusade—the establishment of a free kindergarten system throughout the state. Mrs. Black's reforms grew gradually and inevitably from her early church work and philanthropic activities, and she arrived in the Georgia Federation full-blown, so to speak, as a woman already known for her devotion to education and children. Added to what must have been obvious leadership abilities, Mrs. Black had other attractive features for a Georgia clubwoman: she was a "farmer"—or was so considered by the state federation—which was a decided asset in situations where she had to appeal to women from agricultural as well as urban sections. Furthermore, Mrs. Black had grown up during the Civil War, the memory of which remained personal and vivid and could be called upon to serve as a point of reference for her own sacrifice and courage. "From the ashes of her city," one admirer once recalled it, "she caught the fire that kindled her spirit through life."[3] Mrs. Black then made the ultimate sacrifice: she died in office, while serving her third term as president of the Georgia Federation of Women's Clubs.

Obviously, Nellie Peters Black had all the appropriate personal qualities and the correct interests for a successful club career: she came from a prominent family, had high social standing, was educated, and had rural as well as urban roots. She enjoyed the independence of a wealthy widowhood along with the admiration of her peers for her plucky persistence. Her causes were womanly ones, and her favorite cause, early childhood education, a most admirable one. She involved herself deeply in a variety of organizations, while maintaining affiliations in the socially necessary ones—the DAR, the UDC, and the Colonial Dames, without whose certification she might not have acted with full public, female endorsement. She was a supreme model for the women who followed directly in her footsteps, the reformers of the twenties, described similarly by Anne Firor Scott as also having a "common impressive social standing and family background, intelligence, courage, and a degree of inner security that permitted them to survive criticism."[4]

With Mrs. Black as the historical example, then, the questions began to arise: How typical was she? How important were memberships in the UDC, the DAR, and the Colonial Dames to the performance of public duties for southern women? What, if any, changes occurred over time in the retention of memberships in those organizations. For whom did they remain important? What were the weak and strong relationships between these organizations and other groups? If Mrs. Black represented—as she did—the first generation of organization women in Atlanta, that is, those who blossomed forth in the 1890s, then what would the second and third generations look like? Would the same mix of organizational ties and dependence on social standing occur among black women and Jewish women, and if so, how?

In order to begin to find some answers to these questions, a sample of women was selected against which Mrs. Black's model career of organized activities could be compared qualitatively and quantitatively. The sample had to be self-defined and as consonant with Mrs. Black herself as possible, else the variables in organizational involvement would be uncontrolled from the beginning and the conclusions therefrom, meaningless. Thus, names were taken from the rolls of the upper status groups—social clubs and hereditary organizations from which social credentials could emanate—and then traced through other organizations to check for crossover memberships and sundry leadership positions held. It was hoped that a collective picture of the organizational woman would emerge from this, which would provide the basis for two kinds of comparisons: 1) the similarities and differences in the general pattern of associationalism between white and black women, and 2) the changes in associationalism between the first generation of white clubwomen and the last generation of clubwomen studied.

The first sample included the following categories of white women from the organizations indicated below, for a total of 508 names:

1. all of the officers and board members of the Atlanta Chapter, DAR, between 1891 and 1921; the regents of the Atlanta Chapter between 1922 and 1941; and the regents of the Joseph Habersham Chapter between 1900 and 1941
2. the officers and board members of all the local chapters of the United Daughters of the Confederacy for the years 1895, 1905, 1915, 1925, 1933, and 1942
3. the members from Atlanta of the Georgia Society of the Colonial Dames of America from the cumulative rosters of 1927 and 1938 (which included the names of the earliest members)

The following categories of black women were included, for a total of 150 names.

1. the full membership of the Chautauqua Circle between 1913 and 1941
2. the full membership of the Inquirers, between 1920 and 1940
3. the original membership of the Junior Matrons, another elite social group, founded in 1923
4. the names of the participants in the Negro exhibits at the Cotton States and International Exposition along with the names of prominent local women mentioned by E. R. Carter in his history, *The Black Side*, published in 1894

The statistical reliability of the black women's sample proved to be not strong enough for direct comparisons with the whites, as the biographical data were too inconsistent. Consequently, the names of the elite social club members were discarded. Likewise, an original selection of Jewish names, the presidents of the Atlanta Section of the National Council of Jewish Women between 1895 and 1940, proved to be too small a sample to be very useful for statistical comparisons.

The names were checked through a variety of local source materials: Atlanta histories, city directories, who's whos and other biographical compilations, organizational records, school and church records where readily available, and newspapers. The 1890s names were checked against the listings of the special Atlanta census of 1896. An important part of the effort was to check the names of these women from the "conservative" social groups against the rosters of the progressive organizations—those on the "liberal" edge of the spectrum of women's public activities. For the white women, the suffrage associations and the League of Women Voters served to fill this definition, and for the blacks, the NAACP nationally and the Neighborhood Union locally. The city directories turned out to be a useful source for a broad range of data: full names, addresses, address changes, approximate time of marriage and widowhood, occupation of husband, and so on. The data collected on individual women were not perfectly consistent, but they were sufficient enough to indicate certain patterns of women's activities and certain changes in those patterns. What follows is a summary of those trends.

To begin with, Mrs. Black's career—as a model of club activity—offered many points for comparison. It was a direct challenge across racial lines, for one thing, to find a comparable career in the Atlanta black community. There were any number of black Atlanta women who rose to national attention within the network of one organization or another: e.g., Mrs. Hope's work was known outside Atlanta; Alice Dugged Carey had a national reputation within the Federation of Colored Women's Clubs, as did Mrs. J. W. E. Bowen, wife of the president of Gammon Theological Seminary, but of all of them, the career that most resembled Mrs. Black's was that of Selena Sloan Butler.

Selena Sloan was born about 1870, grew up in Atlanta, and married Henry Rutherford Butler, a physician, in 1893, after a brief career as a teacher in Florida. The couple had one child, Henry Jr., who also became a doctor. Mr. Butler was a graduate of Lincoln University and of Meharry Medical College, and Mrs. Butler was an 1888 graduate of Spelman College. Both were very active civic leaders in Atlanta, and among Mrs. Butler's many associations were these:

1. first president of the Georgia Federation of Colored Women's Clubs, and honorary president of the federation
2. active member for twenty-five years and one-time president of the Chautauqua Circle
3. founder and first president of the Colored PTA in Georgia

4. founder, first president, national committee chairwoman, and adviser, the National Congress of Colored Parents and Teachers
5. active member of the Eastern Star, the Neighborhood Union, and the First Congregational Church in Atlanta
6. cofounder and early officer of the Spelman College Alumnae Association; member of Sigma Gamma Rho Sorority
7. organizer and early officer of the Phyllis Wheatley Branch of the Atlanta YWCA
8. member of the Georgia Division, Commission on Interracial Cooperation
9. appointed to the National Commission on Childhood Health and Protection by President Hoover
10. continued active organizational life upon removal from Atlanta to London, then Arizona, and finally, California[5]

There are many similarities between the organizational careers of Mrs. Black and Mrs. Butler, and some significant differences. Both were church women; both enjoyed relatively high social status within their respective communities. Mrs. Butler was by no means as wealthy as Mrs. Black, but her husband was a property owner in Atlanta of some worth.[6] Both women were educated; in fact, Mrs. Butler was probably the better educated of the two. Both were progressive in some of their causes, serving female advancement and racial advancement, respectively. Both gained national prominence and reputations through their commitment to the education of children. Both were active members of at least ten organizations each, the bulk of which they served in official positions, some of which they had themselves founded, and their organizational careers spanned three decades of service: Mrs. Black's roughly between 1890 and 1920 and Mrs. Butler's between 1910 and 1940 approximately. Both were wives and mothers, though Mrs. Butler was not a widow for the duration of her organizational career, while Mrs. Black was. Both had occupations outside their organizational lives—one a teacher, the other a farmer—but Mrs. Black had never been actually employed for self-support or financial gain, while Mrs. Butler most assuredly was as a single teacher at the State Normal School in Florida. Both women had outstanding careers in voluntary activities and were recognized as leaders in their communities.

The two women together offered a paradigm of organizational service against which the activeness of the other women in this study could then be measured. Here were two nearly identical careers in terms of the length and quality of their leadership. Both women held many official positions in many different organizations over a long period of time. With this serving as the optimum in organizational involvement, the question then was, how would the other women measure up? In a similar manner, the two women illustrated certain potential points of divergence between the black club experience and the white, where the question might be, how did factors such as widowhood, employment experience, and education affect organizational patterns?

For the first question, a simply statistical analysis was done of the participatory patterns of the 508 white women, of whose records four questions were asked: 1) Over how long a period of time (expressed in decades) did the records show they were individually involved in organizational activities? 2) How many years did they actually spend in leadership positions, as officers, founders, board members, and committee chairmen for their organizations—as much as could be reconstructed from the records? 3) How many organizations did they retain memberships in? 4) How many different organizations did they serve in leadership positions?[7]

Approximately 24 percent of the sample (125 of 508) could not be considered leaders. Either they appeared as members of organizations without official positions (true of many of the Colonial Dames members), or the nature of their involvement was unspecific to the point that it could not be dated or certified, and therefore not counted. Others included in this category were those who for one reason or another could not be traced. The remaining 75 percent (383 women) were split about half and half: 48 percent of them (184 women) showed activity over two, three, four, even five decades, and more than a third of the whole group (131 women) were active over a period of two decades.[8] This seemed to indicate that involvement in organizations for a long period of time was common, and that a ten-year period of active involvement (i.e., holding offices) was already a clear indication of commitment and leadership of a type that constituted a long-term, adult pursuit—in a word, a career.

Having a career in women's organizations should be interpreted not only to mean holding a continuous stream of offices, one after another, but also that the interests of the women, their loyalties, and activities were traceable over a long period of time and were, in fact, much governed by the organizations they belonged to. Actually, the course of service itself was usually intermittent. The records for the Atlanta Chapter DAR officeholders between 1891 and 1921 show long, faithful memberships and broken service records. For example, Mrs. Archer Avary is typical: she served as an officer for three years, rested from office for three years, then served four more years in various capacities. Cora Brown served three years, was off one year, served two more years, was off one more year, served again for two years, was off for six years, then came back into office for another two years. The more contiguous the service, the more important the individual to the leadership core of the organization, of course. Nellie Bowen was almost constantly in office between 1906 and 1921, but still she had three breaks in her service: two of one year's duration and one two years long. The most dominant DAR figure, Mrs. Joseph H. Morgan, had a similar pattern of constant officeholding between 1893 and 1921, but in twenty-eight years of service, she had one break of three years duration and four additional ones of a year each. It was not uncommon on these rolls to find very long breaks between periods of service: several women (e.g., Mrs. W. A. Newell and Mrs. J. M. High) held office in the DAR in the 1890s and then not again until the late 1910s. In this case the women were frequently active in other quarters, while resting from DAR duties. This was certainly true of Mrs. High, who held state and national offices in other patriotic societies in the interim.[9]

Organizational careerism could be described as continuous active involvement in organizations, but that involvement took different forms. The record of continuous service could be established through multiple officeholding in multiple organizations (such as with Mrs. Black and Mrs. Butler), or through multiple (usually consecutive) officeholding in a single organization (Nellie Bowen, perhaps), or in the long-term possession of one office in one organization. Some women, such as Dolly Blount Lamar and Mildred Lewis Rutherford, established their reputations primarily on the basis of one office alone: Lamar and Rutherford were historians-for-life of the Colonial Dames and UDC, respectively. Though they occasionally held other posts, both seem to have been considered irreplaceable as historians. This fixation of some offices—usually lesser ones—on single individuals was a common phenomenon and part of the gradual institutionalization of the organizations. It was even found in such a small group as the Chautauqua Circle. The presidency of the circle circulated among the members with democratic regularity; it was a one-year term, but most women were reelected for a second term before being replaced. But the roles of secretary and treasurer were held continuously by the same two women from 1937 on: it was apparently one thing among the fifteen women to hand around the president's gavel and quite another to pass on the minute books or the treasury, once it had been determined they were already in good hands. Otherwise, officeholding in the Chautauqua resembled the long, broken affiliations in the DAR, for which Mrs. Butler again serves as a good example: she was president for two years, held no offices for three years, served one year on the program committee, was inactive for four years, served again on the program committee, was off again for two years, then served for a third time on the program committee, then for three consecutive years as circle reporter. Meanwhile, of course, she filled in the gaps with responsible positions with other organizations.[10]

Once these variations of officeholding were established, tabulations were made to ascertain what the actual spread of officeholding was among the 508 white women. First, it was apparent that though the term of office itself was likely to be short (one to two years only), the entire tenure in official positions was likely to be longer—stretched out over many years in intermittent pieces, spread over several positions, sometimes over several organizations.

There were two strong trends: those many women who did a little bit in their organizations, and those—few in number—who did much. If more were known in every instance about the women in the sample, more substantial involvement on the part of more of the women might be evident. Nonetheless, between the 25 percent who maintained memberships but did not appear to seek office and the highly visible public leaders (i.e., the Mrs. Blacks of the organizational world) were the bulk of the women, who fulfilled at least some official functions within their groups.

Something that reinforces the sense that this pattern represents a low estimate of actual involvement is the fact that the women in this sample were themselves often reluctant to admit publicly the extent of their service. Time and again, the assessment of their own involvement would be devalued or only moderately valued, one example of which will illustrate: in an interview with newspaper columnist Mildred Seydell, Mrs. Elijah Lewis Connally (nee Mary Virginia Brown, and daughter of Georgia governor Joseph E. Brown) said of herself,

> I am the general manager of my husband's house, and a large family has kept me busy, but I join every worthy club which asks me. . . . I cannot always go to meeting but I send my dues and my name is on the books.[11]

One would judge from this that Mrs. Connally was not a very active clubwoman, but the records do not support that. She paid dues and had her name "on the books" of at least fifteen different organizations, not counting her church groups. She served very early in her missionary society (one of the first in the city) as auditor and as president; in 1912 she held office simultaneously in the UDC and the DAR in Atlanta; she was a longtime vice president of the Uncle Remus Memorial Association, and was secretary to the Georgia Baptist Orphans Home for twenty-four years!

Multiple memberships were the norm; some 70 percent of the women were shown to have memberships in more than one organization (265 of the 383 women). This figure, too, is probably understated, as the tallies do not always take church affiliations into consideration, and the whole spectrum of involvement could not be reconstructed for every one of the 508 women.

In terms of serving as an officer, here there is even less of a tendency for the women to spread themselves over many organizations; the overwhelming majority of the women represented made their organizational careers within one or two groups. The organizational careers of the women in this sample seem to be based on concentrated activity in a few organizations, not spread out over many, as the careers of Mrs. Black or Mrs. Butler would seem to imply. While there were plenty of women who collected memberships in organizations like so many Girl Scout badges, the number who undertook leadership in as many organizations was much smaller.

The fact that club careers evolved around so limited a number of organizations was significant and had importance beyond the mere numbers it represented in this study: i.e., 84 percent of the active women (320 of 383) made their reputations on the basis of leadership in not more than three organizations. This close equation between individual officers and individual organizations indicated a clear identification of certain women with certain clubs in the city; this then is the way the women were known to one another and, by extension, to the public at large—as representatives of the interests of specific groups. It was the norm for women to be known for one concentrated endeavor, no matter what the whole spectrum of their involvement might have been. This was as true of those women who had the broadest organizational experience and the largest reputations (or public visibility) as of those women who served their organizations with less public fanfare. Mrs. Black, for all of her leadership in the Georgia Federation, was most known for her work in the Atlanta Free Kindergarten Society, which organization she founded and served as president for twenty years. It was, in fact, her entry point for the federated women's clubs. In the same way, Mrs. Butler established her reputation through her work with the Colored PTA despite her many positions in other organizations. The community memory of other important Atlanta women fits the same pattern. Mrs. A. McDermott Wilson, though the founder and chief officer of a host of organizations, is most remembered for the preservation of the Wren's Nest, through the creation of the Uncle Remus Memorial Society, an organization she served as president for life. Mrs. Hope was noted for the Neighborhood Union most of all, though she was also active in her literary circle (the Inquirers), the Anti-TB Association, and the NAACP. Another excellent example is Mrs. William Lawson Peel, who quite simply *was* the Joseph Habersham Chapter of the DAR until her death. And it was in this same vein of identification that Emily Hendree Park, another "prominent and useful leader in all good public work," was memorialized:

> So broad were her sympathies and interest that she did not confine her activities to any one organization, and her great ability, energy, and capacity for leadership made her prominent in every organization to which she belonged; but her best efforts were given to the work of the Daughters of the American Revolution.[12]

The identification of organizations with certain personalities in the community had meaning for the organization and for the community. For one thing, it tended to personalize the organizations. It became, for example, the practice of women's organizations to record their own histories in terms of the accomplishments of the women who served as presidents (or regents, or directors, or whatever), so that the record of the club each year was synonymous with the record of its chief officer. This practice in turn reinforced the personal identification of the women with their organizations and kept many leadership evaluations and organizational activities at the level of personalities. As for the larger community, the implication is obvious: the identification of certain women with certain organizations, or certain functions within organizations, was the process of social differentiation at work; the organizations were serving as clear indices of the distinctions being made among the women.

There is no question that these women were personally, seriously, heavily committed to their organizations. For many, their organizational work was a form of occupation that shaped the hours of their days and gave purpose to their lives. Their clubs, even the most social ones, were not simply a way of filling leisure time, but often a way of eliminating leisure altogether. Their offices took on the aspects of a regular job, with all the incumbent responsibilities, accountabilities, restrictions, challenges, and duties of any job—complete, sometimes, with an expense account. There was always psychic income, though usually not monetary income. The retiring general director of the Georgia Federation put it this way: after "23 years of active service in federation work . . . I retire as a multi-millionaire in the richness and fullness you have brought into my life."[13] Every outgoing official reported not only her own (and the club's) accomplishments while she was in office, but in the process wrote the job description for the incoming official, and each year the demands and expectations of official performances grew. One wonders, for example, how the next president would top this—in 1915, the outgoing head of the state federation reported her year's activities as the following: writing 1,514 personal letters, 500 circular letters, and 437 postcards; sending out ninety-eight yearbooks, forty-one telegrams, and ten special delivery letters; submitting forty-three articles for publication in newspapers and magazines, visiting six individual clubs and seven district federation conventions (out of a possible twelve), visiting Tallulah Falls School twice, holding five executive board meetings, and attending the national biennial convention. In all, she spent $381.43 and was reimbursed for $262.50 of her expenditures; the balance was, most assuredly, her cheerful donation to the continuation of federation work.[14]

Most of the white women, indeed, did not have any actual job experience outside their organizations. Among the ranks of the most active clubwomen, there were a handful of unmarried teachers and a society columnist or two from the local newspapers, but these were the exception. Of the 508 white women, only fifty-nine showed any connection with an occupation, a vocation, a business, or employment of any kind. Twenty-two of these were teachers—five widowed and seventeen unmarried at the time of their educational service. Thirteen additional women inherited some position in their husbands' firms—"jobs" that were more titular than actual and that perpetuated the business under family control after the husband's death. Six women were associated with newspapers, two were salaried heads of women's organizations, and six others (from late in the sample) were white-collar workers. Of the entire fifty-nine, fifty-two were either widows or unmarried at the time of their "employment." Only one could truly be said to have practiced a profession—a banker, active in women's organizations in the 1930s, who worked in the same bank as her husband.

As a rule, a club career substituted for a career in another field; it was intended for mature married women, not single women and not young mothers. One's career in clubs succeeded one's career in childbearing and childrearing, as Mrs. William Greene Raoul perfectly exemplifies. After twenty years of steady childbearing, in which time eleven children were born, she "threw herself zestfully into a sphere wider than that of one family,"[15] a sphere that in her case included the Free Kindergarten Society, the suffrage movement, the Every Saturday Club, the DAR, the UDC, and the Atlanta Federation of Women's Clubs. As with Mrs. Raoul, it was only then, when the outcome of motherhood was relatively assured—when it was known whether the infants would survive birth and whether the youngsters were going to conform to the better part of societal expectations of them—that it was permissible for a woman to pursue some of her own interests. Volunteer activities were woman's special province, and although the sphere for them seemed to grow wider and wider, the enforced succession seemed also to hold: the older the woman, the more freedom she was granted to involve herself in public activities. One sees this general attitude continued throughout the period under study, and it was no surprise to see Ruth Bryan Owen, child psychologist and daughter of William Jennings Bryan, encourage Atlanta women in 1930, by saying: "While the young woman's place is properly in the home, there is no reason why a grandmother should not go into politics."[16]

This particular mix of characteristics—maturity, motherhood, marriage, possibly widowhood, and the absence of other career identification or occupations—gives a good general description of the organization woman, but it must be carefully qualified. For one thing, the question of employment experience is one of the points where the black women diverge somewhat from the white.

Among the black women, employment experience was much more extensive than among the white women, even among so small a group as the members of the Chautauqua Circle. Among the thirty-four women who appeared on the rolls of the Chautauqua during the years studied, half of them (seventeen women) showed some kind of employment experience or were employed in some capacity while they were members of the circle. Every single one of the women was, or had been, a teacher; some were principals of local schools. One woman had been a teacher and moved on to become director of the Carrie Steele Logan Home. A few of them were music teachers and practiced their craft as members of the circle, having their children and pupils frequently as guests at circle meetings to perform for the enjoyment of the ladies. None of these women was employed as a domestic, as the greater percentage of black women were in Atlanta, but they had been (or continued to be) employed in some fashion. Even at their relatively high status in the community, they had some experience outside the household that was definitely found to be lacking in the experience of the white women. A 1921 observation made about Gainesville, Georgia, black women would seem to apply also to Atlanta:

> While the entry of [white] women into fields of occupation outside the home represents a new departure since the antebellum days, the withdrawal of the Negro woman from occupations outside the home to become housewives represents a movement just as novel and destined to produce just as great changes upon the social and economic life of the town.[17]

The fact was that the Chautauquas regarded themselves as housewives, which was reflected in the minutes of their meetings, for example, in the sentiment that the "Circle was organized with the thought that household cares and burdens would be forgotten for one afternoon a month."[18]

Another aspect of the clubwoman description—widowhood—was not so prominent a factor among the black women as the white women. A few of the women were widows; Mrs. Butler, for instance, was widowed in 1931, but she had been active before then and remained active afterward. It was not until nearly twenty-five years after the Chautauqua Circle was started that widowhood began to be an operative factor on the circle, and that primarily socially. In 1937, the minutes record that some of the women were now bringing "dates" to the annual evening with the husbands, since their own husbands were dead; in 1940, the annual event itself was temporarily abandoned, presumably because so many of the women were so affected.[19] This is a very different situation from the white women, who did not necessarily share their club activities with their husbands and for whom widowhood sometimes seemed a prerequisite for organizational involvement in the first place, as typified by Mrs. Black.

Another aspect of the organizational configuration that is different among the black women is so by virtue of being more pronounced than among the white women—i.e., the close ties to education. The black women were not only educated, as were the whites, they were educated at certain schools and retained, through their organizations and in other ways, close ties with those schools. Present among the members of the Inquirers, for example, were the wives of the presidents of Gammon Theological Seminary (Mrs. J. W. E. Bowen), of Morehouse College (Mrs. John Hope), and of Clark College (Mrs. Matthew S. Davage)—three of the local black schools in Atlanta now part of the Atlanta University Center. Another pattern of connection was found among the Junior Matrons, where eleven of the twenty-six names appearing on the rolls there were graduates of Atlanta University, seven of whom were among the original fifteen charter members of the organization. The Chautauqua Circle—studied in more depth—showed an even stronger pattern of connections. More than a third of them (thirteen women) were graduates of either the college or the normal school of Atlanta University; three more were graduates of Spelman College. The education of many of the other Chautauquas was not discovered, but there were other ties with local Atlanta colleges present among the membership: six of the women were married to faculty members, deans, or presidents of local schools (including the president of Morris Brown College and the president of Atlanta University); two were themselves teachers at Morehouse and Spelman; six more were married to men who had graduated from either Morehouse or Atlanta University. Six women could not be certified as having any connection with one or another of the local schools, but among them were connections with other schools and other educational ties—one, for example, left Atlanta to become a teacher at Bennett College. Three others were married to ministers, one of whom was the wife of the minister at First Congregational Church, which was not only the most prestigious black congregation in the city, but also the church with the most intricate and closest ties with Atlanta University.[20]

The importance of education—of education at Spelman, Morehouse, and especially at Atlanta University—is thus spelled out in the creation of a local black elite, personified by the Chautauquas. The Chautauquas represented a class with both education and longevity in the local area. At least fourteen of them were born in Atlanta or somewhere else in Georgia, so they were natives. Their persistence of interest in the local area is obvious in the tenure of their relationship with the circle itself: of those who were graduates of Spelman or Atlanta University, the average of club membership was fifteen years; some of these had been members for twenty-five and thirty years. For women who were nongraduates or who did not have local educational affiliations, the average of membership was only nine years. Beyond admitting their married daughters first, the Chautauquas were not very specific in their requirements for membership in the circle, but their preferences were predictable, and on at least one occasion they gave themselves away in the minutes. In 1932, a membership decision had to be made, and the following was recorded:

> . . . another lady was nominated and seconded [for membership], but when it was shown that she [,] although a charming and agreeable person [,] was only a newcomer and that there were others who had lived among us just as eligible [,] her name was readily withdrawn.[21]

As with women of their position everywhere, their own sense of belonging and of the rightness of their place was very strong.

This tie between education and black women's organizations was no local phenomenon; national reputations were based on just such a combination. The most prominent black female leaders were usually prominent in all varieties of club life, and they were also, usually, educators. The list would include, among others: Mary McLeod Bethune, Lucy Laney, Mary Church Terrell, Charlotte Hawkins Brown, Hallie Quinn Brown, Mary Burnett Talbert (a nurse turned lecturer), and Emma Frances Grayson Merritt. Education for black women was the route to achievement as it was also the basis for all forms of recognition, social as much as professional. For white women, the factor of education was not so tightly tied to specific schools (though certain such patterns might emerge, if enough incidental biographical information were known in each case). The closest thing in the Atlanta white community to the kind of education-tied model of the Chautauqua Circle might be the Emory Woman's Club, but membership in this organization was restricted to the wives of faculty members and to female faculty members and was therefore not rooted in any "natural" selection based on educational background. As seen earlier, especially in the case of the expositions, the nature of sexual segregation for black and white women—out of which these single-sexed organizations grew—differed. There were more schools for women among the whites than among the blacks, but the most important black educational institutions were open to women, while the most important white institutions (the University of Georgia and Georgia Institute of Technology) were not.[22] Nonetheless, education, as a function of the creation and the perpetuation of women's organizations on both sides of town, should not be underestimated.

Even with these suggested modifications, the general characteristics of the clubwoman stated previously seemed to persist. Yet the club world is anything but static, and many changes occurred between 1890 and 1940, to the extent that the clubwoman going into 1890, in a manner of speaking, was not the same clubwoman coming out in 1940. In order to determine the nature of the changes, the 508 white women were again turned to, and a group of them from the early era compared in detail with a group of them from the later era. That is, all women who were active between 1890 and 1910 in this sample (effectively, between 1895 and 1910) were set against the women active between 1930 and 1940, and the characteristics of their personal biographies (age, marital status, social standing, birthplace, etc.) were compared as well as the characteristics of their organizational involvement (especially the number and kind of their multiple organizational memberships). The early group consisted of 143 women; the later group of 196 women.

Briefly stated, the early group could be described as a collection of tightly knit, relatively young, educated women of society, while the later group of women were less tightly knit, older, still educated, but whose social standing was considerably lower. In addition, the early group was very generalized in its activities, the later group more specialized; the early group contained many prominent female leaders, the later group very few. The importance of these observations is contained within the sample itself: these are women who served in official positions or held memberships in the *same* organizations, in 1890 and 1940.

Some idea of the caliber of women involved in the early days of organizational life can be seen in the Board of Lady Managers for the Cotton States and International Exposition. There were seventy-seven women involved, including the ladies on the board, the members of the newspaper committee, and the members of the socially elite reception committee. Of this number, thirty-five women showed up in other organizational circles; they did not just show up, they were, by and large, the leaders of Atlanta women's affairs for their time. (Probably more than thirty-five of the women were active, but some of the names were of single women, whose married names were not known and who therefore could not be traced.) Among the forty women actually on the board itself were many family relations: there were at least five sets of mothers and daughters, three sets of sisters, five sets of in-laws and cousins, and at least two pairs of aunts and nieces. Again, there may have been more such combinations, but without full genealogies on all of the women, these could not be known. The women were relatively young: the average age of the board members was slightly less than forty years old. Mrs. Thompson, the chairman of the board, was a stately fifty. The oldest member, Rebecca Felton, was sixty-one, and the youngest, Nettie Sergeant, was twenty-five. The newspaper committee was much younger, with an average age of twenty-six years. Its oldest member, a society columnist, was forty-three, and its youngest two members were each twenty years old.[23]

So many of the 1895 board members were part of the 1890s sample that, obviously, the two groups shared some characteristics. For one, at least a third of the women in the 1890s group were known to be related—as mothers and daughters, cousins, sisters, and so on—to other organization women in the sample of 508. The average age of the 1890s group was about forty-five years old in 1900, putting them directly in line with the age of the Exposition

Board. The women were married—90 percent of them; and they had children—2.26 children each, on the average. They were overwhelmingly the daughters of the South and of Georgia, as 70 percent of them were born in Georgia. By comparison, the later women were less often related to other organization women; they were older, and even more married as a group. In the 1930s sample, only one woman in five showed any kin relationships within the total sample, as opposed to the one-in-three ratio above. The later group was fifty-five years of age in 1935, on the average—fully ten years older than the earlier group. More of them were married—96 percent, an increase over the 1890s group; but they had fewer children—an average of just two each. They were still overwhelmingly the daughters of the South and of Georgia, as 72 percent of them were born in Georgia.

In one aspect these women fit neatly into the demographic picture for Georgia, for as late as 1942, 60 percent of all Georgians were born in Georgia. The fact that these women show a slightly higher percentage than that can undoubtedly be attributed to the nature of the organizations studied, which require a somewhat localized social background. A second feature of the profile of these women, however, stands out in sharp contrast to other realities of their state and region, where fertility rates in the late nineteenth and early twentieth centuries were extremely high, with 40 percent of families numbering ten or more children in Georgia alone.[24] The indication of a lower birth rate here is important and raises many questions about a complex of social phenomena that must have been occurring—questions about the practice of birth control among these women, about the relationship of their education to the obviously reduced family size, about the influence of their own limited motherhoods on the extension (and defense) of maternalism and the home through their organizations. Certainly, in this respect these southern urbanites had more in common at the time with some of their northern counterparts than with their southern neighbors.

One of the most important characteristics of the organization women was carefully considered—their social standing in the community. The close ties between membership in women's clubs and social status in American communities is so familiar it hardly needs comment, but changes in that social standing do need explanation. In this case, the 1890s group of women were significantly more socially "acceptable" than were their successors of the 1930s. An assessment of the 1890s women put their listings in the Atlanta *Blue Books* at 57 percent of the total (eighty-one of 143 women), while the listings among the 1930s women dropped to 40 percent of the total (seventy-nine of 196). Most of this drop can be explained by what happened to the UDC.

As discussed earlier, the United Daughters of the Confederacy went through several periods of growth. During one of the expansion periods, a number of new chapters were established in and around Atlanta, which were open to a broader social base than had been the case before. The oldest chapter (#18) started out with members in high social standing, but their standing slipped with time: among the #18 officers in the 1890s group, 58 percent were registered socially, but in the 1930s, only 33 percent of them were (forty-four of seventy-six women in the first group, and twelve of thirty-six women in the second). The chapters that were established later apparently never had high social standing in Atlanta. In the 1930s group, there were sixty-two women representing officers in these chapters, of whom only two were listed in the *Blue Book*. This drop indicates an elemental change in the organization itself and suggests thereby a qualitative adjustment in the organization's perspectives, which became—with time—more strident and racist. However, it also demonstrates what may be a more general principle of organizational development, and that is the trend downward in social standing between the first group of participants and the later participants. The same phenomenon occurred, for example, among Atlanta teachers between 1881 and 1922, and some adjustment downward was noticeable among the student bodies, too, of the girls' schools in Atlanta.[25] Furthermore, this drop in social status reiterates the parallel decrease in the importance of "society" among women or in the community as a whole.

At the same time that the social status of these women was regarded, so too were their involvements in more "progressive" activities. How many of them were to be found among the ranks of the suffragists or later members of the League of Women Voters? Not very many. Only thirteen of the 1890s group (about 9 percent) were found among the active suffragists; of the 1930s group, 6 percent (twelve names) appeared in early listings of the League of Women Voters (from 1920 and 1925) and twenty-six names from a later listing (1948) for a total of 13 percent. Since, for the most part, the names in the 1930s group appeared on league rolls very late, it was plain to see that they joined the league when it was well established and less controversial. As a further test of progressive "activism," the names of these women were also checked against those in the Association of Southern Women for the Prevention of Lynching; three names were found. Considering the very strong bonds among the three organizations represented by these women and such other organizations as the Atlanta Woman's Club—bonds that are discussed below—the ties among these and women's rights or other progressive activities were weak indeed.

Other characteristics in the profiles of the early women and the later women also showed differences. Their educational backgrounds differed, but only slightly. Among the early women, private girls' finishing schools and tutors were prevalent, along with many local schools: Girls High and Washington Seminary in Atlanta, Lucy Cobb Institute, Madison Female College, Shorter College, and Wesleyan, all in Georgia. A few out-of-state colleges were represented by out-of-state women, Mississippi State Women's College, Rollins and Mary Baldwin Colleges, for example. The educational backgrounds of the later group were similar in that the same names of colleges and girls' schools showed up, but occasional other, higher-level, institutional names also occurred: Emory (law school), University of Georgia extension, Harvard Summer School, for example.

Employment experience among these women was not impressive in either group. The 1890s women showed that 13 percent had some experience with a business or other employment situation; most of them were teachers. A few inherited husbands' businesses. The 1930s group showed an even lower percentage of employment, 11 percent, but the range of situations was slightly broader. Still, the largest number of them were teachers, but there were also a banker, a genealogist, several clerks, a telephone operator, and a librarian. The slight downward trend in employment may not be statistically significant enough to suggest an actual downturn, but the fact that the number of employed remained so low in the face of a growing female labor force in Atlanta is important.

The first group of women was better known and more highly visible in the historical records of Atlanta than was the second group of women. This in itself is significant, and it speaks of a basic difference between the two groups. More personal information could be collected on the 1890s sample than on the 1930s, indicating the difference in the relative status of the two groups in the historical memory of the Atlanta community. The earlier women were better known and are still remembered; the later ones have been forgotten or were never known.

Cleavages between women and women's groups are more apparent in the later group than in the earlier group. For one thing, there is the clear distinction between women who worked and women who did not, more especially, between organization women who worked (who in the 1930s would probably have belonged to other organizations such as the Business and Professional Women's Clubs) and these organization women who did not work. The continued state of unemployment among these women also speaks of the life-style their organizational activities could create for them.

The cleavages among Atlanta women's groups were visible also in the "mix" of organizations that was found in each group—or what the multiple memberships consisted of. Two things were compared: simple memberships, and the names of organizations in which any of these women held positions as officers simultaneously (within the same decade) as they held positions in the DAR and the UDC, or maintained membership in the Colonial Dames. Briefly, the early group was spread out over a much wider net of organizations, held more leadership positions, was more prominent in the Atlanta Woman's Club and the federated women's clubs, and appeared in general to be far less specialized in its organizational interests than the later group. The 1890s group appeared as officials in all of the following organizations in addition to local, state, and sometimes, national offices in the DAR and the UDC: the 1895 Exposition Board, the Georgia Baptist Hospital Auxiliary, the Children of the Confederacy, the Atlanta Woman's Club, the Atlanta Federation of Women's Clubs, the Georgia Federation, the Atlanta Ladies Memorial Society, the YWCA, the Home for the Friendless, the Atlanta Woman's Press Club, the Grady Hospital Woman's Auxiliary, the Woman's Pioneer Society, the Georgia Library Association, the Atlanta Writers Club, the Florence Crittenden Mission, and the Uncle Remus Memorial Association. In addition, memberships were found in these organizations: the Order of Old-Fashioned Women (precursor to the Atlanta Junior League), the 19th Century History Class, the Daughters of the American Colonists, the Fine Arts Club, the Music Study Club, the Atlanta Art Association, and the Daughters of the Founders and Patriots of America. It should be noted that there are only a few additional patriotic/hereditary associations besides the DAR and the UDC in this group. At least five of the 1890s generation held the presidency of the Atlanta Woman's Club; several presided over the Atlanta Federation; and several moved up to the presidency of the Georgia Federation. (All memberships and positions accounted for here were held between 1890 and 1910.)

The difference with the later group is obvious in the names of the organizations served as officers. Only nine such affiliations occurred in the sample: the Atlanta Federation (only one woman in this generation held the

FIGURE 1

Statistical Profile, Organization Women, 1890s and 1930s

| | 1890 | | 1930 | |
	#	%	#	%
Number in sample	143	100	196	100
Officers in the DAR	124	87	49	25
Officers in the UDC	60	42	106	54
Members, Colonial Dames	44	31	91	46
Members, Atl. Woman's Club	57	40	42	21
Listed in *Blue Book*	81	57	79	40
Family ties within sample	47	33	43	21
Married	129	90	176	96
No. of children known	69	n.a.*	57	n.a.*
Birthdate known	20	n.a.	14	n.a.
Birthplace known	50	n.a.	22	n.a.
Church affil. known	29	n.a.	17	n.a.
Education known	22	n.a.	12	n.a.
Employed	19	13	21	11
Teachers	8	5	8	4
Widowed	52	36	52	26
Active as widows	29	20	24	12
Suffrage, LWV supporter:				
1920s	13	9	12	6
1940s			26	12

* Note: Not applicable, number does not pertain to the total samples of 143 and 196 women, but to some portion thereof. The numbers are included only to indicate the availability of information on each generation of clubwomen.

presidency); the PTA, the Baptist Church Women, the Northside Study Club, the Spanish War Veterans Auxiliary, the Pioneer Women's Society, the Rabun Gap-Nacoochee Guild, the Reviewers Study Club, and the Atlanta Service Star Legion, in which three of the 1930s women were prominent leaders. In addition, memberships were found in the Atlanta Woman's Club, the Atlanta Historical Society, the Red Cross, the Woman's Auxiliary of the Scottish Rite Hospital, the Atlanta Art Association, the League of Women Voters, the English Speaking Union, the Georgia Bicentennial Commission, and six additional patriotic/hereditary societies, including the Descendants of the Huguenots, the Daughters of the Confederacy (a separate organization from the UDC), the Daughters of the Barons of Runnymede, the Colonial Dames of the 17th Century, the Daughters of the American Colonists, and the Daughters of the Founders and Patriots of America. No one in the 1930s sample held the presidency of the Atlanta Woman's Club, and no one was prominent in the Georgia Federation. There was much more concentration of organizational efforts into the local historical, memorial, patriotic, and hereditary groups than in any other kind of group.

Even the close ties among the three organizations that made up the sample in this study were weakened over time, thus illustrating another dimension of the specialization among the women. Crossover memberships among the DAR, the UDC, and the Colonial Dames were examined, as was the prominence of the names in this sample in the affairs of the Atlanta Woman's Club.

The lower rate of activity in the 1930s women over the 1890s group relates to several phenomena: the effect of the Depression, of course, which generally lowered participation rates in women's organizations across the country, was paramount in the drop. However, some of the apparent loss of activity would have to be accounted for by the increased suburbanization of the organizations themselves, especially of the UDC. The women who were officers in all branches of the UDC in this sample might very well have been active in their local suburban areas, in College Park, or East Point, for example, and their activities would not show up in Atlanta per se, but in the organizations localized in those areas—the College Park Woman's Club, or the East Point Woman's Club, respectively. Finally, the numbers of women listed in the Colonial Dames whose names did not appear in any other Atlanta organizations might be attributed to lower rates of organizational participation among the higher levels of society. Here, too, suburbanization is operative, as

FIGURE 2

Crossover Memberships, 1890s and 1930s

1890s (143 women)	Number	Percent
Col. Dames in DAR	39 of 44	89
Col. Dames in UDC	17 of 44	39
Col. Dames in At. W. C.	19 of 44	43
DARs in Atl. Wns. Club	50 of 124	40
UDCs in Atl. Wns. Club	31 of 60	52
UDCs in DAR	47 of 60	78
1930s (total sample-196 women)		
Col. Dames in DAR	20 of 91	21
Col. Dames in UDC	10 of 91	10
Col. Dames in At. W. C.	20 of 91	22
DARs in Atl. Wns. Club	12 of 49	24
UDCs in Atl. Wns. Club	21 of 106	20
UDCs in DAR	38 of 106	36
1930s (actives only-102 women)		
Col. Dames in DAR	20 of 50	45
Col. Dames in UDC	10 of 50	20
Col. Dames in At. W. C.	20 of 50	45
DARs in Atl. Wns. Club	12 of 49	24
UDCs in Atl. Wns. Club	21 of 53	40
UDCs in DAR	38 of 53	72

the Colonial Dames were the most likely to follow the movement of white elite Atlantans toward the northernmost sections of the city and then out of the city entirely where, like the UDC women, they might have participated in a more localized manner—in the Buckhead Women's Club, for example, instead of the Atlanta Woman's Club. In sum, the lessening of ties between the organizations and the lowering rate of activity undoubtedly reflects the social situations just described. The statistics representing only the "active" women (women whose names appeared in more than one organization) are much less drastic in the differences between the 1930s group and the earlier women. Generally speaking, the trends seemed to be these: the ties between the Colonial Dames and the UDC weakened, as did the ties between the Colonial Dames and the DAR, but the ties between the DAR and the UDC remained substantially strong. At the same time that the ties between these seemingly similar organizations were weakened, the prominence of women from these organizations in the Atlanta Woman's Club also dissipated.

A final indicator of the difference between the 1890s women and the 1930s women lay in the predictability of the preeminence of individual women in women's public affairs from the nature of their organizational memberships. Back to the original question: how important were memberships in these hereditary organizations to activity in women's public life? In order to find out, those women whose names appeared in the DAR, the UDC, and the Colonial Dames were taken out and examined. The 1890s group produced sixteen names who showed the joint memberships. At least nine of the sixteen were among the leaders in Atlanta women's affairs, including, of course, Nellie Peters Black. The others included Minnie Hillyer Cassin Cromer, member of at least fourteen organizations; Mrs. William D. Ellis, president of the Atlanta Ladies Memorial Society for over twenty-five years; Mrs. Joseph Madison High, donor of the High Museum, now part of the Atlanta Memorial Arts Center; Mrs. Robert Emory Park, long-time officer in all of the major organizations considered here; Mrs. William P. Patillo, one of the founders of the Atlanta Federation of Women's Clubs; Mrs. William Green Raoul, one of the few in the sample who was an active suffragette; Mrs. John Marshall Slaton, wife of the governor and long-time organization woman; and Mrs. James Osgood Wynn, who had memberships in at least seventeen organizations and a reputation as a painter as well. Importantly, this is a category that the Honorable Rebecca Latimer Felton also belonged to. Others among the sixteen had varying degrees of activity and held official positions in anywhere from two to six organizations.

The 1930s generation included only five women who belonged to all three organizations. Two of these were prominent—Mrs. Frank Mason, probably best known as the sister of the donors of the section of Stone Mountain that was carved into the Stone Mountain Memorial to the Confederacy; Mrs. Joseph C. Mellichamp became, during her active years, the national president of the Service Star Legion. One of the others, Annie Laurie Hill, was better known as a genealogist than as an organization leader.

The momentum of organizational life in the city had passed over to other organizations, and the status of the female community influence no longer depended so much on the lineage implicit in the memberships of these older organizations. The old mold had changed considerably, and the vintage organization woman of the 1890s was succeeded by many varieties, only one of which was that variety that adhered closest to the conservation of racial identities. If one were to look, in the 1930s, for the leaders of the federated women's clubs, of the business and professional women, of the educated women, of the working women, of the women interested in ecumenism and better racial relations, they were not to be found in the ranks of the UDC, the DAR, or the Colonial Dames.

FIVE

In the Public Eye: Patterns of Community Image Making and City Building Among Organization Women

The attempt to capture the qualities of community that the women of this study were consciously trying to build, sustain, or affect, required an examination of their image-producing activities—specifically, writings and cultural artifacts. In order to find appropriate metaphors I searched through southern literature—chiefly, southern women's literature—and through the physical environment itself.

Narrative fiction turned out to be singularly unrevealing: the urban South in general was not a significant aspect of southern fiction for this time, and the city of Atlanta was not the featured locale for more than a handful of works. Furthermore, the urban experience of southern women in the pre-World War II era is noticeably missing from literature, and the specific experience of organization women seems never to have been suitable grist for the literary mill. The almost unrelieved absence of these elements from fictional expression is, however, expressive in itself, and such a negative phenomenon as this bears a little closer examination to determine what it might signify.

If, as Blaine Brownell has suggested, urban consciousness in the South lagged behind the rest of the nation, by some fifty years, until the decade of the Second World War, then there is little reason to expect to find much mindfulness of cities in the South's ethos before that time.[1] After all, the South seemed solid: it was poor, conservative, and rural; it was hardly thought—certainly not in the popular imagination—to be progressive, wealthy, and urban. Even in the 1920s, according to Brownell, the city was a problem for southern writers, because it was seen as a force for change within southern history, not as a buttress of the regional traditions. The crux of the problem, he explains, was this:

> . . . how to demonstrate continuity between a rural region past and a local urban present and yet at the same time give just due to the virtues of the swiftly changing metropolis of which Southern urbanites were generally very proud.[2]

The way the women writers seem to have demonstrated this continuity was to avoid discussing, as much as possible, the modern city, to discuss it, instead, within the context of the past, or to discuss the city not at all.

The lack of focus on urban life probably owes as much to two other attributes of southern literature as to southern urban-rural political dichotomy: 1) the tendency of southern literature to treat the South as "place" in a generalized way rather than in a specific way, so that the region assumes more fictional importance than any identifiable locality,[3] and undoubtedly more important, 2) the Civil War "set" to southern literature that dominated the writing through most of this time period, and that, of course, was not associated with an urban life-style. Where white female authors were concerned, this latter preoccupation was particularly strong, and a direct line would seem to run from Augusta Evans Wilson (*St. Elmo*, 1866) to Atlanta's own Margaret Mitchell (*Gone With the Wind*, 1936). Black writers, too, resisted a southern urban idiom and couched their own dialectic in slightly different terms—pitting southern ruralism against northern urbanism, as Jean Toomer's *Cane* (1923) might aptly illustrate.

The Old South "fix" used by so many southern writers had several aspects that were important to them personally: since it was a popular vein in which to write, publication was relatively easy, and as a result, several of the women writers of plantation literature became financially quite comfortable. Furthermore, if one believes Ellen Glasgow and a host of others, it was therapeutic to write in revolt against the traditions of the Old South while at the same time evoking the spirit of them. "Wherever I was," Glasgow lamented, "whether in the actual world or in the old world of imagination, I was driven, consciously or unconsciously, by my old antagonist, a past from which I was running away." In this connection, *Barren Ground* was a "vehicle of liberation" and a "conversion experience" for Glasgow.[4]

Similar sentiments emanated from the writers of nonfiction as well, for example, Katherine Du Pre Lumpkin, whose autobiography begins with a long section—over a third of the book—about the Lost Cause in which she says she was nurtured and against which she turned. These chapters concern not Katherine Lumpkin at all, but her father, her grandfather, and her great-grandfather. When she finally completes her own story, she affirms, "it took a fresh reading of our past" to account for her own changed convictions about the reality of southern life, which led her toward a belief that white supremacy was not inevitable, immutable, or desirable as she had once been led to believe under the old system.[5]

Those writers who traced fictional chronologies through the past on up into the present managed to explore some more contemporary themes, but in doing so, still seemed to be more at home exploring them in terms of the "land" (its loss, its recapture, its permanence, its value, etc.) than in terms of the man-made environments on the land. Again, Ellen Glasgow is instructive, whose *Barren Ground* is a classic statement of attachment to the earth, as is also Caroline Gordon's *Garden of Adonis*, a Depression era novel centering in the dispossession of all of its characters from the land. The city did not intrude very far into the southern milieu, even in "modern" stories, and if it intruded at all, it did so ambiguously. If southern, the city was old, symbolic, and evocative—as Margaret Mitchell's Atlanta was a symbol of the destruction of the Old South. On the other hand, if the city emerged contemporary, substantial, and vital, it was probably not a southern city at all; in fact, it was probably New York.

It is not the place here to discuss the ramifications of New York City as a major point of reference in southern literature, except to say that the "rejection" of New York—for that is normally how it occurs—is integral to some of the best southern storytelling.[6] Dorinda (*Barren Ground*) fled there, and then returned home to the South; so did Ellen Glasgow herself, who needed New York for literary recognition and inspiration but who found she could actually write her stories only in the South. ("My social history," she explained, "had sprung from a special soil, and it could grow and flower, naturally, in no other air.")[7] A less well-known heroine, the black Helga of *Quicksand*,[8] gave up New York, Chicago, and Copenhagen in turn for the back lands of Alabama to become a preacher's wife. Described by one critic as an unconvincing resolution of her problems, Helga's situation nonetheless reiterates the pattern.[9] Frances Newman's life-style also suggests the same geographic dependencies: Atlanta born, bred, and employed (as a librarian), she was peripatetic as a writer and traveled frequently to New York. Like Ellen Glasgow, she found that she needed the stimulation of the place but could write only in the South. She might lengthen her leash, but she could not unloose it.[10]

Frequently ignored, darkly perceived, and incompletely depicted, the southern city was thus "disembodied" by southern literature during this period, but it was not entirely unpeopled. When town life did appear in fiction, it was used specifically to measure the achievements of the men and to unravel the social relationships of the women, and it is in this context that the female writers become most interesting.

First of all, the southern female writers of this period were almost exclusively domestic in their approach to social relations; they seldom, if ever, depicted female relationships of any significance outside the family. They passed over the female collective experience as part of the whole female experience, as if it never existed. Instead, female protagonists were treated as individuals who solved their problems within the confines of their families—working out their relationships especially in terms of the male members of their families—or who retreated to survive alone on their own terms. The writers left the distinct impression that women do not appear in groups in American life, and if they should happen to, the groups are purported to be as insignificant to the community as the individuals are who make them up.

Positive expressions of what the group or club experience has meant are rare in literature. Only one exceptionally respectable such example was found, and this, in fact, in a novel by a man, and a nonsoutherner to boot. Speaking of Isabelle Lane, the heroine of his novel *Together*, Robert Herrick says:

> Isabelle was too intelligent . . . to believe that a part of the world did not exist outside the social constellation, and an interesting part, too. Some of those outside she touched as time went on. She was one of the board of governors for the Society of Country Homes for Girls, and here and on the Orphanage Board she met energetic and well-bred young married women, who apparently genuinely preferred their charities, the reading clubs, the little country places where they spent the summers, to the glory of Mrs. Anstruthers Leason's opera box or dinner dance.[11]

The distinction he draws between organizational life and "society" is a fine one, and not often made, since the prevailing assumption seems to be that the personae of the one arena are the personae of the other. The complex network of differentiation, as seen in the patterns of crossover memberships here, are glossed over. The picture from female fiction of the organization woman, when it occurs, is simplistic and usually negative. Sometimes, though, it is humorously so, as in this passage from Ellen Glasgow's *Voice of the People*. One of the characters, Sally Burwell, is discussing the "Daughters of Duty," an organization closely identified with another character in the novel, Mrs. Jane Dudley Webb. Mrs. Webb has already been described in the book as an impoverished aristocrat of the antebellum ilk, who "supported an impossible present upon an important past" and who "had once been heard to remark that if she had not something to look back upon she could not live." About the Daughters—to which Sally herself belongs—Sally trifles:

> I'm in it. It seems that our duty is confined to "preserving the antiquities" of Kingsborough—so I began by presenting a jar of pickled cucumbers to Uncle Ish. I trust they won't be the death of him, but he was the only antiquity in sight.[12]

With that, the group, the idea, and the associationalism are flippantly dismissed.

The fictionalized impatience with organizational ties may be elucidated in the biographies of some of the writers, who—to a person—seem to have had unfortunate encounters with women's groups. It was partly a generational problem: the clubs stemmed from their mothers' associations, and they were impatient with their mothers' generation and the social conservatism it represented. For example, Frances Newman's mother was active in the National Society of the Colonial Dames of America and served on the board of the Atlanta Chapter of the DAR in 1899; Frances was thereby eligible for membership in both organizations, but she held no such affiliations. She was a member (through her father) of the elite Piedmont Driving Club, but she made fun of its pretensions. "The Piedmont Driving Club," she wrote in her acerbic style,

> is our [Atlanta's] St. Cecilia, our Assembly, but the requirements for membership are different and years of reflection will not quite reveal what they are. Lineage will do something and money—not so fearfully much money—will do more, but even the two together will not do everything. Fame would doubtless do all, but no one who was famous has ever been put up. It may be

103

that one must contribute something—a genius for dancing will do, but take it all in all, a talent for being fashionable in just the right way and for bounding one's horizon on all four sides by the club's flourishing cedars will do most.[13]

When Frances Newman published *The Hard-Boiled Virgin*, she was twitted by the local clubwomen for her lack of morality—a criticism she did not take too seriously, as she drew a distinction between what she did in her own life and what her character had done in her novel—a distinction the other women seemed not to care to make.[14] Newman was not as severely criticized, however, as was Julia Peterkin, who was ostracized by the society women and publicly censured by organizations throughout the South for a knowledge of interracial behavior "unbecoming" of a lady.[15] Margaret Mitchell is another case: her own outrageous behavior—at least, in the eyes of those who judge such things—was to blame for the denial of her membership in the Atlanta Junior League in 1921. The snub was not forgotten, and, in fact, Mitchell was able to return it in 1939. As the Junior League prepared for *the* gala of the season, in honor of the world premiere of the motion picture version of *Gone With the Wind*, Mitchell respectfully declined to attend their party.[16]

Something more is at stake here, though, than an odd assortment of personal slights and counterslights among women with differing interests. It is a question of both personal identity and social behavior. It is not simply a matter of rejecting outworn values, or of supporting new and competing ones. For example, few of the writers mentioned above were avid suffragists. Frances Newman made a point of mentioning that both she and her mother voted as soon as they were permitted to do so in Georgia (1921), but her name was not prominent among the rolls of the activists, nor was her mother's.[17] As for Ellen Glasgow, she was an ardent suffragist at eighteen, but she became disenchanted with the movement when it "attained respectability." As just another socially acceptable reform movement, it was not exciting to her, though she frankly admitted she was never able to commit herself wholly to the cause anyway.[18]

It is not simply a matter of value differences, old or new, cross- or intragenerational, but it is the collectivity itself that is rejected—artistically and, often, personally. The clearest expression of this rejection among the southern female writers of this period comes from Corra Harris, writer, novelist, journalist, preacher's wife, teacher's wife, and native Georgian. She makes it explicit in her writings that this is an individual and artistic problem, and that it is also a question of female culture conflict.

The instinct for personal liberty has . . . led me to avoid participating in the activities so popular and so ably conducted by the various women's organizations. Place yourself within reach of the executive committee of any up-and-doing group of women, and find out how much time or strength you have left to spend upon your own affairs! If you are a social climber, they will give you prominence in exchange for as much faithful service as you are capable of rendering. If you desire recognition . . . you may have it as a reward for devoting yourself to some department of public service. . . .

If by some fluke of circumstance you have earned distinction, they can use you for the good of half a dozen causes so completely that you will never have another half hour to devote to your own cause. Henceforth you will be identified with their achievements. *You will not have one laurel left on your brow which does not belong to womanhood at large.*

If you belong to that ever-increasing volume of women who crave self-expression, they can provide more ways for you to express yourself than if you were a mere Christian wife and the mother of ten children. They are using up more wasted feminine energy than any other power company known to civilization.[19]

What seems to emerge from this is the expression of the individualistic artistic tradition in a previously unrecognized form: this is the artist against society, but not the society at large, or the society of men, but the artist in revolt against her own, explicitly female society—one created by women, for women, to which she does *not* (by choice, whim, accident, or exclusion) belong. This is an important point, as it appears that the female literary tradition (at least in some of its forms) has evolved in conflict with other female traditions within the American culture. That is to say, not only has it evolved separately (alienated, perhaps) from the female collective experience, it supposes itself to be in actual conflict with that collectivity. Most certainly this conflict appears outside the South and is a widespread cultural phenomenon, but the point should be carefully qualified. The antagonism between the "doers" and the "thinkers" among women may be more a developmental aspect of the female experience than a universal cultural pattern.

For one thing, it relates directly to the increasing professionalism of women as writers and journalists during the time period under study. Those, who in the beginning needed buttressing by the women's groups, at the end of the period would seek female company only with their own (professional) kind. That is, if the writers chose to affiliate with a club or group, it would most likely be a writers club, a press club, or some other professional organization, not a general women's club.

In addition, the pattern for black writers may be different; certainly the careers of Ida B. Wells-Barnett, Frances Ellen Watkins Harper, and Victoria Earle Matthews so indicate. All of these were important organization leaders as well as writers. But, then, black writers had to become group activists to secure their profession, and group activists had to become writers to rally support for their cause. Functioning within organizations was necessary for communication, solidarity, even survival.

Direct racial comparisons are difficult to draw. Barnett, Harper, and Matthews were all chiefly nineteenth-century figures, whereas Newman, Peterkin, Gordon, Mitchell, and Glasgow came to maturity in the twentieth century. Again, the conventions of scholarship diverge: black literary history, like black general history, shifts its focus to the North in this early modern period, toward the Harlem Renaissance; and white literary history, while it shifts its focus south, does not encompass black writers. Consequently, historical criticism of southern black writers (especially female ones) is scarce. Zora Neale Hurston is the single obvious exception to this, but as the solitary example—the only early-twentieth-century, southern, black, female writer of note—she is insufficient evidence to draw a valid comparison from. It is difficult, therefore, to determine whether the same tendency to "dis"-associate occurred among the black writers as seems to have occurred among the white. (Hurston does mention in her autobiography that she was a member of a sorority at Howard University and was accepted into an elite collegiate literary society; she makes no mention of any organizational affiliations taking place after college.)[20]

Simply put, the nineteenth-century white writers were not as far from organizational circles as were their twentieth-century successors. The personal records of some of the most notable female writers of the late nineteenth century—the local colorists such as Kate Chopin—as well as some of the less notable (including Atlantans) suggest that the gulf between the "joiners" and the "literatae" was not as great in the formative years of organizationalism (1890s) as it was a generation or two later. For example, Grace King, who bridges the nineteenth and twentieth centuries, was active in a coed literary club in college, went on to be the vice president of a lecture association, remained active for years in the state historical society, and finally became president of her own version of a French salon in New Orleans.[21] An even better example is Mary Noailles Murfree, who served as state regent of the Tennessee DAR in 1912, a position that presumed leadership, organizational abilities, and long years of prior service in a local chapter.[22]

The very best illustration of increasing professionalism among the female writers and their estrangement from the organizational world can be drawn from the changing relationships between organizations and the press. A certain disenchantment was evident very early on in some quarters, if Josephine Woodward is to be believed. Herself a club reporter, Woodward took women's clubs to task in an 1898 article published in the General Federation magazine. She accused the organizations of being elitist, purposeless, pretentious, and humorless, and metaphorically threw up her hands at their persistence: "The objects of women's clubs bewilder me," she confessed, "and their solemnity appalls me." A woman's club, she concluded tartly, was nothing more than "a body of women banded together for the purpose of meeting together"—harsh words indeed, especially when addressed to the ladies themselves. She very carefully drew a distinction between herself (a working woman) and them, and she excluded herself from their hollow company with these words:

> You must pardon a club reporter if she hasn't much sympathy with theories. She has to practice so much, and she is often so tired that she cannot understand how anybody can even contemplate the doing of anything that involves labor not absolutely necessary to the support of life.[23]

No such lively antagonism broke the surface of Atlanta club affairs, but changes in press relations did occur. The early press relations are evident from Lollie Belle Wylie, poet, playwright, widow, and organization woman, who was also the society "editress" for the *Atlanta Journal* (the first woman to hold that position). Mrs. Wylie founded at least one club herself, the Woman's Press Club of Atlanta, and served as an officer in at least seven others, including the DAR and the UDC (the "right" chapter of each). Furthermore, in her press capacity, she was a member of the all-important Board of Lady Managers of the 1895 Exposition. For her time, she represented a bridge between the best of all female worlds: her name was in the Blue Book; she had a fluid and locally respected pen; she moved in good social circles; and she was as active organizing women's activities as she was writing about them. In its infancy, the Atlanta Woman's Club had a press person within its own ranks, Isma Dooly, who was active in Georgia Federation affairs and well respected in the club world. By contrast, her successors on the newspapers were permitted to have only "associate" member status in the Atlanta Woman's Club, and they had to take their stories from a formal press and publicity committee rather than from the inside. This change had already taken place by 1920. In 1928, a later example of the dissociation between press and club could be found when the Atlanta Federation passed a resolution barring any employees of any daily newspaper from holding elective office.[24]

The reason press relations are illustrative and so important to this discussion is simply this: In the South there is a strong bond between journalism and literature; writers in one field are, as likely as not, writers in the other; hence, it might be said that there is only one literary tradition, which is both journalistic and imaginative. Certainly there are ample cases of this from among the women writers. Corra Harris was both a novelist and a journalist; Frances Newman was a book reviewer for the *Atlanta Constitution* and frequently wrote essays, commentaries, and other pieces for magazines; Margaret Mitchell started her writing career as a stringer for the *Atlanta Journal Sunday Magazine*. Mildred Seydell, who wrote for the conservative Hearst newspaper in Atlanta beginning in the 1920s, was a society columnist who turned feature writer, then novelist. Lollie Belle Wylie has already been mentioned. Thus it is that while press relations may seem a casual feature of the organizational system, it is not, for it may represent the most constant, cohesive interface between two worlds—the active, collective, organizational world and the contemplative, individual, literary world. And the literary/press tradition diverged; it grew up to be separate and outside, even at times antagonistic to, the organizational tradition. By the 1920s, what women's clubs did in this and probably in any community was neither subject for high culture nor material for the front page. And since the press has acted throughout as the most prodigious translator of women's club activities to the general public, the long-term legacy and literary impression have been left that there is ironic and distant respect, but no sympathy, for the women's organizations.

If it is fair to conclude that literary women do not, as a rule, join and lead many organizations, then by the same reasoning, it is fair to conclude that organization women, as a rule, do not write many books; theirs may be a literate tradition, but it is not a literary one. The question then becomes, where does one find their conceptualizations of the community—their ideas and ideals for it—if they don't write about those ideas? What qualities have they projected onto the city, and where are those projections to be found?

They have left documents, of course, which are their fundamental records, but they have also left more dramatic evidence of their concerns and priorities. Everywhere in America there are structures on the landscape that are the result of collective female effort and evidence of what women's organizations think of their communities and their role in those communities—clinics, schools, orphanages, libraries, parks, gardens, social and recreational centers, monuments, clubhouses, headquarters buildings, and other similar institutions. Taken together and in proper sequence, these structural pieces begin to reveal not only some patterns of cultural function and value peculiar to women's organizations, but they also begin to describe a special chronology of city building among American women, which has been long overlooked. Even the small stock of structures in Atlanta, falling into the category of female derivations, suffices to tell the story.

One general observation needs to be made at the outset, and that is that the extant structures in Atlanta are not great architectural masterpieces; as art, they are relatively unimpressive. Most are (or were) recycled, secondhand, domestic structures. Though institutional, few of the structures used or erected in the 1890-1940 period were intended to be commercial; none was intended for industrial use. Of those buildings and monuments that were original creations, most are fairly traditional in appearance; others are intentional imitations of other structures. Some of the edifices and monuments are pretty, but that is all. The architecture of the collective female creation is simply unimportant—certainly it is less important than the single-sexed system that inspired it and the communal expression it implies.[25] It is to the other characteristics of the structures—their location, provenance, comparative size, use, value of property, and so on—that one must look for the interpretation of their meaning.

Three chronological patterns in the construction of the women's institutions give the first clue to their social interpretation. First, there were those buildings and sites erected or used by the women's organizations for their clients' or constituents' purposes (such as day nurseries and schools) that appeared throughout the latter decades of the nineteenth century and in the first two decades of the twentieth. Second, there were those buildings and sites erected or used by the women's organizations for their own purposes (such as chapter houses and headquarters offices) that began appearing about 1910, but that appeared with the greatest frequency in the 1920s. Finally, there were those buildings and sites (mostly monuments) that were erected (or preserved) for general public view and for commemorative purposes. These last appeared throughout the fifty years under study, but in fits and starts, usually rising and falling with the military memories of the community at large, but revealing other interests as well. The broken pattern of commemorative structures is

109

important only in the varying size and subject of the commemorations, as commemoration itself represents a very stable concern during this time period and one that may not have abated among women's groups until after World War II. The more important chronological pattern is the gradual shift from constituent-oriented structures to member-oriented structures.

The structures that might be listed in the first category are almost impossible to document. Of all the early facilities actually operated by women's organizations—the orphanages, settlement houses, clinics, schools, charity institutions, nurseries, kindergartens, old ladies' homes, poorhouses, girls' clubs, etc., founded by Atlanta women between 1880 and about 1920—none is left standing today. Not one structure is intact in its original form on its original site. Several of those old institutions do survive, but they have long since been municipalized, centralized (in the Community Chest, now the United Way) and/or suburbanized, while the stock of historic buildings in central Atlanta has been depleted by natural disaster, decay, and urban development. A few pictures exist of the old facilities, some addresses, and, occasionally, a description of the general location and appearance of the places.

Certainly, decisions to locate any philanthropic institution in the latter part of the nineteenth century had to be governed by the availability of land to build on and money to build with, but there were other important factors to consider, too, communal ones. As charities, the homes and schools that women established had to be inoffensive to the local neighbors in order to be located anywhere at all. Their low status and frequently undesirable tenants meant that the various institutions were placed on the fringes of the good areas or as far removed from the good area as possible. The city directory for 1890, for example, indicates that the Home of the Women's Christian Association (Baptist) was in the vicinity of the Capitol Hill area, but on its far western edge, very close to the railroad tracks, and behind the commercial section. The Home for the Friendless, as listed in the same city directory, was located actually inside the railroad gulch, in a kind of no-man's land. Another telling location would be that of the Home for Incurables. The association itself was founded in 1893, and opened its first facility in 1901 in a rented house in a then commercializing section of the downtown. Within a year the organization expanded to fill two houses on the same block. Then, in 1904, a building was erected for the sole use of the Home for Incurables Association and its patients: $10,000 had been raised by the women, four acres of land had been donated by a local furniture dealer, and a local architect drew up the building plans gratis. The patients then moved into their new quarters, located conveniently, but somewhat morbidly, one block from the cemetery.[26]

Probably no organization in Atlanta had the difficulties in getting located that the Florence Crittenden Home did. It had to move innumerable times and finally settled more or less permanently in 1892 on the old city dump with a ninety-nine-year lease. It was a tenuous beginning: the land had to be cleared by the residents, and the building remained in debt for almost a decade. According to the chronicler of the Florence Crittenden movement, the "fight over the establishment of such a home [in Atlanta] was the most bitter fight in all Florence Crittenden annals."[27] There had been objection to it from every corner: damage from vandals, threats from vigilantes, opposition from some clergy, petitions from "concerned" citizens, and finally, ordinances from the City Council forbidding the home to locate anywhere without explicit council permission. For almost twenty years, from 1881 until 1900, Florence Crittenden in Atlanta was no clear refuge at all.[28]

Some other organizations were more compatible with their neighbors—the settlement houses, for example. Although none of the Atlanta settlement house activities ever achieved the proportions of a Hull House or a Henry Street, they were all effective in a limited way. Each was directed to the needs of a different population group, and each was located in the spot most likely to serve those needs: The Wesley House settlement operated in a mill village called Cabbagetown among the white mill workers and poor rural in-migrants. The Jewish settlement house (the Jewish Educational Alliance) was situated in the heart of a transitional neighborhood where Eastern European Jews, who "needed Americanizing," were settling in next to the German Jews who had been in Atlanta for several generations. And the blacks were served in several neighborhoods on the West and South Sides of the city through the various installations of the Neighborhood Union, while, appropriately enough, the central "office" for the Union was in the midst of the black commercial district.[29]

There is a qualitative difference in the locations of these various settlements. The black and Jewish settlement houses were located in somewhat more heterogeneous neighborhoods than Cabbagetown, which was—and probably always had been—inhabited by poor whites. The other neighborhoods contained a wider diversity of people and institutions within their uniracial (or unireligious) boundaries. The blacks, to be sure, *had* to work in their own neighborhoods, and for them, the Neighborhood Union was a means of self-help and more of a way for them to be "neighborly" than "organizational."[30]

The Jewish settlement house likewise served its own—and in its "own" place, though there were some class and cultural differences between the now socially prominent old German Jews and the newly arrived and lower status Eastern European ones.[31]

In addition, the "colonizing" aspects of the settlement house movement, so intelligently described by John Rousmaniere in relation to Hull House, do not quite fit the Atlanta scene.[32] Even the Wesley House settlement (the Atlanta City Mission in Cabbagetown) does not jibe entirely with his picture: it was a very small effort, consciously missionary more than unconsciously colonial in its intentions, and it could blame some of its limitations on the fact that it was dependent on another, larger organization, namely, the southern Methodist church. In any case, the locations of the houses signify slightly different neighborhood orientations. Those with ghettoized circumstances (the blacks and the Jews) show a stronger relationship between the neighborhood and the voluntary association meant to serve that neighborhood; the members of the voluntary association were not only the servants of the neighborhood but also representative of its "best" (i.e., altruistic, concerned, well-to-do, reform-minded) citizenry.[33] While the Wesley House worker came from "across town" or from somewhere outside Atlanta entirely, the benefactors and beneficiaries of the Jewish and black settlement house affairs were—during the early years, anyway—coexisting within the same residential spaces.

This point is further elaborated when the locations of some other benevolent institutions are considered, especially the orphanages. The best example is the Hebrew Orphan's Home, erected in 1888 in the heart of the Jewish community, situated alongside other welfare establishments and the Jewish residents themselves. Apparently, the orphanage building also served as a community center, for in 1905, the Standard Club was founded there in its "community" room.[34] This is a significant indicator of the nature of the relationship between the community and this institution, for the social upper crust who kept the orphanage going were the same persons who would become members of the fashionable Standard Club, the Jewish equivalent in Atlanta of the Piedmont Driving Club.

Another illustration can be drawn from the Leonard Street Orphanage, which enjoyed a mutually beneficial relationship with Spelman College for many years. As long as Spelman College ran an elementary school and a high school (until 1928), the residents of Leonard Street—just next door—could attend school free and enjoy the "protection of a private school." When the orphanage was closed in 1935, the building was sold back to Spelman. The college continued to use it as a nursery for the neighborhood children at least up until World War II.[35]

The Home for the Friendless went from one no-man's-land to another. In 1900 it perched between predominantly black and predominantly white portions of the same area. Its circumstances improved somewhat in 1930, when it became an official public agency (meaning, for white Protestants only) affiliated with the Family Welfare Association and subsidized by the city of Atlanta and Fulton County and moved to a slightly more affluent section of the city—still, however, not a "preferred" (white) area.[36]

As to the general size and appearance of any of these early institutions, there is little evidence to go on. Most were homes or homelike structures. Logically, they had to depend on whatever resources could be used to create them, and these were limited, so the buildings were seldom very large. The Florence Crittenden Home, said to have had thirty-eight rooms, was probably one of the largest single institutions built by Atlanta women.[37] The first building belonging to the Carrie Steele Logan Orphanage had room for fifty children, and was a three-story brick building with a stone foundation. It was built for $5,000 and was surrounded by a "campus" called both "spacious and most beautiful."[38] The Hebrew Orphans Home could have easily housed forty to fifty children and was also a multistoried brick building.[39] The first Home for Incurables was smaller. Described as a "dingy little weatherbeaten cottage . . . near the very heart" of the city, it held—either at one time or altogether—twenty-seven patients.[40]

The second building to be owned by the Leonard Street Orphanage, which still stands on the campus of Spelman College, was erected in 1916. Although it has been completely remodeled to suit other purposes for the college, it gives the impression from the outside of being an attractive and comfortably sized home. It is not a mansion, neither is it an obvious institutional building (at least, not from the front); the homelike atmosphere of the place was, in fact, a source of considerable early pride.[41]

A "homey" atmosphere was an essential ingredient to these operations, and as time went on drastic steps were taken to try to preserve some semblance of "home." The much overgrown Home for the Friendless, for example, reorganized and rebuilt in 1930 to become "Hillside Cottages." The name alone suggests the direction of change. The president for that year reported that there were now eight cottages to the institution, every one a "home." Each cottage, she affirmed,

> is a complete unit caring for twenty children and two matrons and approximated a simple family home. No servants are employed but all the work done by the matrons and children, each child, thereby learning to become a useful member of his own future home.[42]

Twenty children (almost certainly all of the same sex) and two "mothers" do, however, make a curious home.

If not a home, or homelike, the structure was at least likely to be simple, as the Holy Innocents Mission serves to illustrate. Precursor of the Holy Innocents Episcopal Church in Atlanta, the mission was founded at the turn of the century and is now preserved only in documents. Inspired by Mrs. Nellie Peters Black and reputedly also "designed" by her, it was a simple white frame structure, basically a one-room building with a "tabernacle" roof—the whole of it tucked into the corner of a then sedge field.[43]

The spatial wants of the general women's clubs and the cause-oriented organizations differed somewhat from those of the philanthropic organizations, since these other groups needed space only for themselves—for meeting and "administrating." Some organizations have been accustomed to a small but efficient centralized facility from their inception, though most did not have any permanent headquarters until well into the twentieth century. In 1900, for example, the Atlanta Equal Suffrage Association operated out of the Unitarian Church, while in the same year the Atlanta Woman's Club operated out of the Lowe's Grand Theater/Office Building.[44] (The dissimilarity of locale speaks for itself.) As evidence of its permanence and standing in the community in 1920, the Baptist Woman's Mission Union had offices in the luxurious Candler Building. Ten years later, in 1930, the Baptist Union had offices in the less elaborate (but possibly more spacious) Flatiron building, the Women's Central Committee (the suffrage continuation group) was holding its meetings in the YWCA, and the Atlanta Woman's Club was spending $47,000 on a new chapter house.[45] With some political savvy in the 1920s, the Georgia Federation of Women's Clubs moved its administrative headquarters from the Chamber of Commerce building (which was rent-free to them) to a cubbyhole off the lobby of the Henry Grady Hotel (which was not free, but which was where the legislators stayed during the annual session).[46]

Each facility to some extent reflects the character and personality of that organization. Of all of them, the organization with the greatest demand for facilities and the most complex needs for space was the YWCA. Founded in 1901, the Atlanta YWCA was soon running a combination gymnasium-staff-office-placement center-meeting room-"chapel" out of the (entire) second floor of a downtown commercial building, *plus* two boarding houses—all of this only three years after the association started. In the mid-1920s, the YWCA had two program buildings (one for whites, one for blacks), a boarding house, and a camp in the North Georgia woods. From the very first, the YWCA has had one of the largest investments in property and the largest number of real estate holdings on any women's organization in the city. It is to be regretted that not one brick or board remains of any of its earliest establishments.[47]

The relocation, transformation, and ultimate disappearance of the buildings associated with early city charities speak eloquently of the fundamental changes that occurred in women's public activities at this time—in Atlanta as elsewhere. Not only is the demise—or in some cases the professionalization—of small-scale female philanthropy suggested thereby, so is a quite conspicuous loss of female public visibility. The lady philanthropists, once the ministers of charity themselves, became, instead, the mere supporters of charity—its "gray ladies," its behind-the-scenes fund-raisers and female patrons. Their system of delivering private social welfare had become redundant and dysfunctional, and the women themselves were now unwelcome among large-scale professionalized organizations. As a consequence, the women looked for other outlets. If charity could not begin at home, so to speak, then perhaps it could be dispensed elsewhere: the women continued to build charitable institutions; they simply did not locate them in the cities. In keeping with the "ruralization" of other aspects of their programs, the women began to build a network of rural institutions that would become the very raison d'etre of their activities. If this ruralization represents something of a retreat from the city, so—in part—does the movement to build clubhouses. Together, the rural institutions and the organizational "homes-away-from-home" form the second phase of female city building.

In 1896, a sentiment was heard in the halls of the Georgia legislature, which echoed resoundingly from the women's organizations. Chancellor William E. Boggs of the University of Georgia scolded the legislators for letting "Northern capital come here and build magnificent colleges [for the blacks] . . . without doing anything for the higher education of your own youth."[48] At about the same time, Rebecca Latimer Felton voiced similar concerns before the United Daughters of the Confederacy: the South should take care, she urged, to educate the "neglected children of Confederate veterans in the rural sections, who were growing up in ignorance," for there was a gap—parallel to Boggs's at the university—between the education white girls in the South were getting and what black girls were getting, courtesy of northern philanthropy.[49] The UDC responded by setting up a few scholarships. The Georgia Federation, meanwhile, acted more vigorously. It conducted its own survey of Georgia's educational needs and began to make plans: one resulted in a system of traveling libraries, another in the push for a Training School for Girls (that was finally built in 1913). A third saw the establishment of three model rural schools—one at Cass Station, one at Danielsville, and one at Watters Crossing, where the emphasis was on relevant, vocational training.[50] But the crowning achievement, the federation's educational summit, was the creation of the Tallulah Falls School.

The idea originated in 1905, but the school did not actually open until 1909. From its inception, Tallulah Falls was the pride and joy of the clubwomen, the "light in the mountains and the heart of the Georgia Federation," as it quickly became known.[51] The traveling libraries were transposed into the state's public library system: the Training School was always state-owned; the three model schools were absorbed into their respective county school systems, but Tallulah Falls stayed with the federation. It was then, and is now, the only school owned by a *state* federation of women's clubs in the country, a boast that seems never to have been contested.[52]

The federation was not alone in its efforts to start a mountain school. Georgia's most famous mountain school was founded in 1902 when Martha Berry began to teach Sunday school in a log cabin outside Rome. In about two decades Miss Berry owned a healthy parcel of land at Mt. Berry, where she ran two secondary schools, had plans for a college and model practice school, and could rely on the generous support of every "soft touch" in the country from Henry Ford to local clubwomen everywhere who organized themselves into "Berry Circles" to raise money for the schools. Martha Berry borrowed a lesson from black education, namely from Tuskegee, and won for herself national acclaim and local immortality.[53]

Interest in the Berry School and all of the Appalachian schools was widespread. The Cass Station model school was funded in part by the Massachusetts Federation of Women's Clubs in its infancy. Not to be outdone by any state federation, the National Society of the Daughters of the American Revolution established two mountain schools of their own—Temassee in South Carolina (1919) and Kate Duncan Smith in Alabama (1924)—and began contributing to the maintenance of at least three others—the Hindman Settlement School in Kentucky, Crossnore School in North Carolina, and

Berry School in Georgia.[54] Tallulah Falls came in for special treatment at home in Georgia; everyone seemed to want to support it. The Georgia Federation of Business and Professional Women established a permanent scholarship there; the Atlanta Section of the National Council of Jewish Women were regular contributors to the endowment fund; even some Catholic women's groups sent money and gifts. In 1927, the Young Matrons' Circle for Tallulah Falls School was established with the sole purpose of supporting the school, and by 1971, the Matrons had raised over $750,000.[55]

There are three prominent characteristics about these schools, three images they cast in the public eye. First is their permanence, especially compared with the impermanence of the earlier charitable institutions as women's organizations. The second is the nature of the memorialization involved in their construction and maintenance, which differs in kind, absolutely, from the symbolism of other monuments erected by women's organizations. Third are the reactionary social values in which the schools were conceived.

These schools have *lasted*. They are basically charity institutions, but unlike their predecessors, they have not passed entirely into the public domain. Tennessee land and buildings, for example, are still owned lock, stock, and barrel by the NSDAR, which also pays its residence staff and supports many of its boarding students; but the teachers and the principal are paid by the county and state boards of education. The same is true of Kate Duncan Smith and of Tallulah Falls. Rabun Gap-Nacoochee School, another Georgia school in this tradition (which has become nationally famous through *The Foxfire Book* series), has the same combination of public and private support, complete with "Rabun Gap Nacoochee Guilds"—small bands of women throughout the state who raise money on its behalf.[56]

As long as these schools last, they will be a tribute to the women who created them, a self-conscious memorialization of their own efforts. Unlike other public monuments erected by women's groups—the historic markers, obelisks, bronze plaques, statues, shrines, gardens, and mausoleums built to honor the memories of the sons, husbands, fathers, brothers, and other heroes in the women's eyes—the schools are a living commemoration of the women themselves. They are called "Kate Duncan Smith," for instance, after the state regent of Alabama DAR, and "Berry" after the family name of the founder. They have dormitories called "Fitzpatrick" and scholarships named for "Ottley" and "Brown"—all for women who dedicated years of service to the schools and their parent organizations. At Temassee, every bush and every building is said to bear a plaque, reminding the visitors (and the students) who the

117

benefactresses are. A 1925 itemization of memorials and gifts to Tallulah Falls School contains the names of only a few men, sprinkled among a long list of women: there is the "Mary Ann Lipscomb Fund," the "Mary Ann Lipscomb Cottage," the "Lucy Lester Willet House," "Atlanta Federation Schoolhouse," "Ann Carrington Davis Cottage," "Bessie Branham Art Shop," "Isma Dooly Auditorium," etc., etc., etc. There are scholarships to remember Nellie Peters Black; Celeste Parrish, the educator, a "great and good woman whose influence throughout Georgia . . . grows greater as the years go by"; and even the Atlanta Debutantes of 1925. In the same vein, tribute was paid to Mrs. Passie Fenton Ottley, the president of the Board of Trustees of Tallulah Falls for many years and the force behind its expansion in the 1920s: "Her monument is built upon these hills," it was said, "her name is written in these stones." And three other small endowments were singled out for special citation, as

> much sentiment clusters about [them], which will keep green the memory of three well-beloved Atlanta women. In each case they have been established by an only daughter for a dearly beloved mother.[57]

The honorific lineage could not be clearer, nor the intentions more unmistakable.

The self-congratulations the women indulged in over these schools were genuine and well deserved enough, though they were extreme; as sentiments they were bolstered greatly by feelings of both class and race superiority. The children who attended these schools were not only "deserving" mountain folk, they were also "pure-blood" Americans, *white* Americans. A prominent leader of the Colonial Dames, who was also a trustee of Tallulah Falls, described what the Appalachian mountaineers meant to organization women everywhere (who were in the process at that time of "Americanizing" non-Americans in other parts of the country). They are, she said

> in many respects the most hopeful materials that we have, for these are Americans who have long been settled in the land and who are only waiting an opportunity to make their contribution of value to our national life.[58]

Again and again, the students were referred to as belonging to a "pure strain of English people," as "fine Anglo-Saxon boys and girls," and the like. Martha Berry was not only following a noble vision of helping a poor and dependent people become able and independent, she was also "conserving the native stock and training for some future hour of conflict," according to one admirer.[59]

Along with racism came a sense of paternalism. The women tried to ignore the question of race by setting up schools in places where there simply was no black population. The question of class was also averted. The children were to take the women's gifts and make the most of them, to become better examples of the hard-working, simple people they were supposed to represent; they were not to challenge the status quo, for social equality was not involved. There would be uplift, but no upward mobility. One advocate of Tallulah Falls expressed it this way:

> The sort of equality that demands a division of things—these sturdy mountain folk have too much of a sturdy type of horse-sense to vision such an idea. But equality of opportunity, which they describe as a "chance"—this they ask for and accept quite simply and naturally with quiet gratitude wherever it can be given them.

Their understanding, he elaborated, showed a grasp of the "real significance" of the "declaration of human rights."[60]

At best, the schools were an honest attempt to meet great educational needs in a grossly illiterate part of the country. At worst, they were an exercise in social conservation and an aggressive reinforcement of the status quo. Whatever benefits accrued to the communities the schools served were to remain in the communities and to disrupt the whole order of things as little as possible. Poor whites were to remain on the bottom of the ladder at a respectful, *thankful*, distance from their benefactors; and blacks, of course, were to remain out of the picture entirely.[61] The philosophy of the mountain school, with all of its political conservatism and racial "conservation," was aptly summarized during the dedication ceremonies of "Greater" Tallulah Falls School in 1925. Such a school as theirs, the federation women celebrated,

> is a home school where boys and girls of our blood and breed, shut off in the fastness of the Appalachian Highlands from the opportunities which education acords [sic], are given a chance at life at a school, which beside its academic course, supplies to them instruction in Manual Arts, Horticulture, Hand Crafts, home care and the duty of an American Citizen towards God and home and native land. "Salvaging Americans" is the real significance of the Tallulah Falls Industrial School, Inc.[62]

At the same time the women's organizations were establishing rural educational institutions, they were involved in another form of building, which began to assume epic proportions in the nation in the 1920s. The drive for organizations to establish (own, furnish, and occupy) clubhouses was described by one of the most astute observers of women's affairs in the twentieth century as a "movement" that was both "major" and "modern"—"major" because it commanded a large percentage of organizational energies and attention, and "modern" because it emerged after World War I.[63]

The clubhouses were intended to do more than provide administrative quarters or meeting space; they were to be a real "home," but with a difference. In this home the "wife" was the "guest," as

> costly club houses provide shelter and living conditions that are comfortable and private—where a woman may have "a room of her own," where she may exercise hospitality without the burden of preparation.[64]

In short, they were to imitate the full accommodations commonly found in a gentlemen's club, with facilities for lodging, refreshment, entertainment, and respite. Thousands of them were erected, though it is doubtful that any of them ever quite measured up to the opulence and comfort of the Century Club in New York or the Metropolitan in Washington, D.C.

While the men's clubs served as one model for the women's clubhouses, there was another precedent to follow, among the women's organizations themselves. The first women's organization to have its own quarters—that is, quarters that were more than simply an administrative unit—was probably the National Society of the Daughters of the American Revolution, which began creating Memorial Hall in 1899, when it purchased some swampland in Washington, D.C. Dedicated in 1905, Memorial Hall was not just a place to conduct official business, it was a combination archive and museum for Revolutionary War artifacts, records, and memorabilia.[65]

According to its own testimony, the Atlanta DAR owned the first DAR chapter house outside Washington, D.C.: in 1895 it inherited the Massachusetts State Building from the Cotton States and International Exposition. This building, an imitation of Longfellow's home, "Craigie House" in Cambridge, was used until 1909, at which time it had deteriorated beyond repair. A new "Craigie House" was built in 1911, but records indicate that it was 1915 before the financial and legal matters over the building were finally settled. By then, the last payment had been made, and some necessary remodeling and reroofing had been done.[66]

The Atlanta Woman's Club had its first chapter house, actually a church, in 1908, which it purchased for $12,000. The members occupied this building until 1920, when they sold it for $35,000 and bought, for $47,500, a residence designed by Atlanta architect Walter T. Downing after a French chateau, complete with round rooms and turrets. Much was added to the original structure over time to make it more suitable for club needs and aspirations: a commercial-sized kitchen with banquet hall (infrequently used), a swimming pool (never integrated and now in disuse), and a theater, which went up in 1922 at a cost of $110,000. The theater has been used variously—for classes for club members, for "lectures, moving pictures, garden schools, graduations, concerts, plays, and musicales," and as the permanent home of the Peachtree Playhouse and Theater of the Stars. But while the club was increasing its own facilities with the auditorium, and—it undoubtedly thought—its own revenue-producing capabilities, it was also adding enormously to its financial burdens. The theater required redecorating in 1939, new furnishings in 1956, and constant remortgaging and insuring. Despite continuous financial troubles, however, the Atlanta Woman's Club has clung tenaciously, for more than half a century, to the "Grand Old Lady of Peachtree," its home.[67]

The Atlanta DAR and the Atlanta Woman's Club were not alone. In 1922, the United Daughters of the Confederacy, Atlanta Chapter, bought a house for its headquarters only about seven blocks from the Atlanta Woman's Club building.[68] In the same year, the Joseph Habersham Chapter of the DAR began "Habersham Hall," located less than a block from the other DAR Chapter building.[69] (The UDC no longer owns its building, and the Habersham Hall shares facilities with a quasi-religious organization known as the Foundation of Truth.)

In the boom of the 1920s, an investment in a clubhouse seemed an attractive venture to women's organizations, nationally as well as locally. As if to signal the start for a house movement, the General Federation of Women's Clubs purchased property for a national headquarters in Washington, D.C.[70] Meanwhile, the Georgia Federation began to keep track of the clubs in Georgia that owned their own houses; in fact, one of the first jobs tackled by the state headquarters, once it had opened in 1924, was to do just that. That year the Federation Yearbook recorded the number of "club houses" as well as the number of "clubs" in each district. Although the counting was inconsistent, it showed that new houses were now cropping up in the small towns—Cartersville, Acworth, Kingston, Chatsworth, and Marietta, as well as Austell, Dallas, Cedartown, and Rockmart. The state federation had even taken photos of its "beautiful" clubhouses to exhibit at the national convention that year, and came back with the message that it wished it had had more such pictures to show off.[71] Ten years later, in 1935, the rush to buy and build houses had slowed somewhat; many clubhouses had already been set up, and Depression constraints were affecting the clubs. By then, the figures show—however inexactly—that at least half of the federated women's clubs in the state, not counting the major cities, already had their own clubhouses. Probably many more did.[72]

During this important time, too, many changes were made in the buildings and properties belonging to the Atlanta YWCA. The black branch, Phyllis Wheatley, was formed in 1919, and a building was rented for its use. It was made to serve until the mid-1930s, when the branch moved to a different home. In 1928, the YWCA also acquired Camp Sunshine for Phyllis Wheatley to use. The Central Association, which actually owned the black branch properties, had already acquired and improved Camp Highland for white use, ending up—after improvement—with nineteen bungalows, a swimming pool, tennis courts, a dining room, caretaker's cabin, and an office. (No comparison was made with facilities at Sunshine.)

In 1926, an ambitious building campaign was launched for the Central Association, and $105,000 pledged around the community, of which $30,000 went immediately toward the purchase of the Atlanta Athletic Club. Though not an actual residence like the Atlanta Woman's Club or the UDC building had been, the Y building was a "home" nonetheless, for the club building was "completely renovated, changing it from a man's club to a home essentially feminine and charming." So it was that the Young Women's Christian Association also subscribed to the club-as-home idea.[73]

The Phyllis Wheatley Branch buildings served as combination program centers, offices, and boarding houses. The branch building was not the only meeting place for black women, since they could also meet at numerous fraternal lodges, at schools, churches, and in their own homes, but Phyllis Wheatley was probably the first *exclusively* female meeting place in Atlanta's black community. There were many thoughts in having others. Even the Chautauqua Circle, small as it was, had a dream of someday owning its own home—a "Greek colonial, white-columned" architectural beauty, according to the vision.[74] None of the dreams came true until after World War II, when the Atlanta Federation of Colored Women's Clubs (which included the Chautauquas) bought a piece of property just half a block from the Atlanta University campus. The site was contracted for in 1947 and paid off in 1952. This too was a former residence, though far from an imposing structure. It has since been abandoned, and today the marker to the federation stands before an empty building.[75]

The club buildings suggest many things. The fact that these houses are created as homes is their quintessence: the extension of "home" is an intrinsic and central objective of the system of matronage that created these places. Not only are they homes; for the most part they are also located in residential areas. Their locality reflects the decision making of the organizations in finding environments that are preferred by them for being both advantageous to the members and affordable to the treasury.

The grandeur (or lack of it) speaks of the net worth of the associations as well as some of the tastes involved. There are usually some signs of "gracious living" in the houses, which are furnished to be attractive, or comfortable, or both, and one assumes there has always been a spirited competition among the clubs as to the perfections of any of their decors. Ultimately, they are evidence of the kinds of cultural conservation the clubs come to represent. That is, in their antiques, pictures, paintings, commemorative windows, and the like, in their cast-off and donated furniture and art pieces, in their honor rolls posted on the walls, and other decorations, they reveal those private memories that each club wishes especially to cherish. Sometimes, as is the case with Habersham Hall (which is now on the National Register of Historic Places), they are themselves objects of historical conservation. Usually, however, they are inadvertent objects of preservation, as fluctuating real estate markets and club fortunes have kept many organizations in facilities that are either unsuitable or well past their reparable prime.

While the rural schools and chapter houses are monumental enough, the organization women are much better remembered for other monuments, the ones that they have placed in full public view rather than tucked away inside houses, in residential neighborhoods, or in remote mountain valleys. From 1858—when South Carolinian Ann Pamela Cunningham established the Mt. Vernon Ladies Association of the Union[76]—until the present day, southern women have been deeply involved in all aspects of historic preservation: from the restoration and salvaging of architectural structures, to the collection and preservation of historic documents, to the creation and maintenance of historical clubs and societies, to the reclamation of ancestors, to the erection of every kind of historical marker, statue, memorial, and other enshrinement of the past. As a rule, these activities have paid public tribute to the dead and fallen males of the culture rather than to the females, and the women have been more than a little inventive in the infinitude of channels they have found through which the tributes could be paid. Women have been a constant force—a "primordial force," Mary Beard would say—in the preservation of culture, but in the process, they have managed to magnify and mythologize the past more than they have managed to illuminate it accurately. Actually, several cultures have served in this way—southern, "American," black, white, male, and female cultures. Above all else in the South, white women have paid tribute to the Old South, to the Lost Cause and the Confederacy, but not to that alone. In all the women's efforts, honor to the cause served has outweighed almost every other consideration, and some good intentions and honest efforts have also reflected misguided enthusiasms, excesses, prejudices, racism, and a sense of moral superiority.

In Atlanta women have spearheaded, inspired, financed, or otherwise participated in the erection of a host of monuments, beginning with the Confederate Memorial of 1874, a granite shaft raised in Oakland Cemetery by the Atlanta Ladies Memorial Association. In 1894, the same society added the Lion of Atlanta to the cemetery grounds (a replica of the Lion of Lucerne) to honor the unknown dead buried there.[77] The UDC concentrated its efforts on marking Atlanta's Civil War battlefields and had a special set of bronze markers cast for the Capitol grounds, which encapsulated the city's difficulties during the War.[78] A monument to the women of the 1860s was placed in Piedmont Park by the Pioneer Women of Atlanta in 1938. It is a significant monument for two reasons: it is an open and late recognition of the behavior model that the early generation of women had become for the later generations, and it is one of only two public monuments in the city erected by women's organizations, which honor women.[79]

The DAR was more active in the area of records preservation as they collected and published Revolutionary War records, county records, and genealogies. In addition, the founder of the Joseph Habersham Chapter (also of the Atlanta Chapter, which she left) is generally credited with influencing the establishment of the State Archives in 1912. Since Atlanta did not exist in colonial Georgia, the Atlanta DAR chapters had to support restoration work elsewhere, in Savannah, for example, and Elberton, where the Georgia DAR rebuilt Nancy Hart's cabin.[80]

A few organizational women made grand and occasionally extravagant gestures as individuals to the city: one sold her jewels to buy a statue of Sidney Lanier for Piedmont Park.[81] Another donated her house for the first art gallery in the city and gave a foundation to Peachtree Street in the name of the Atlanta DAR.[82] A third was instrumental in placing the World War I memorial at Pershing Point—a bronze and cement mass that may be chiefly distinguishable for its ugliness.[83] As part of organizations, they all planted trees. Tree planting was a veritable obsession. Thousands of them were put in the ground for every conceivable commemoration. They lined Stone Mountain highway and the Jefferson Davis highway; they were planted in groves in Piedmont Park—to honor mayors and authors—and in schoolyards to do the same. The honored veterans and dead heroes: one was even planted for President McKinley[84]—for once having said in Atlanta:

> Every soldier's grave made during our unfortunate Civil War is a tribute to American valor. . . .[85]

Unmarked, most of the trees have long since blended into their landscape.

Undoubtedly the largest monument is the Stone Mountain Memorial, the idea for which originated simultaneously in several places. One of those places was the Atlanta Chapter of the UDC, where the founder, Mrs. C. Helen Plane, broached the idea to the local daughters and then carried it to the national convention, where it was adopted by the entire federation. The memorial has been plagued by scandal and tragedy; nor was it the UDC's happiest venture: they lost their influence in the project very early on, but they never lost their interest in it, nor stopped their support of it.

The first piece of local architecture to receive organized female attention was the Wren's Nest, the home of author Joel Chandler Harris. The move to preserve his home began immediately after he died, while his widow was still alive. In 1909 the work was turned over to a committee of women by a group of men who were too "busy" with business to carry it out. The fund-raising body, known as the Uncle Remus Association, gained title to the farm in 1913, and—after moving Mrs. Harris out—the society and its successors have run the Nest ever since, not only as a monument "to genius," but also as a monument "to the domestic virtues, a guarantee of the world's respect for faithful married love and for the hearthstones of the world."[86]

Other house museums, ancestral homes, and mausoleums that the women supported were abundant in number and ranged from the Sulgrave Manor in

England (which belonged to George Washington's British forbears)[87] to the Frederick Douglass Home in Washington, D.C. However justifiable this last example is, as compensatory black history, the move to reclaim Cedar Hill was made in a similar spirit as other preservation projects. It was a "great step" toward race pride, the "Mt. Vernon" of the black race, according to one of its most ardent supporters.[88]

Even some of the most "progressive" ventures seemed to have built-in recidivistic tendencies. The Municipal Market, begun as a curb market run by the Atlanta Woman's Club, was finally funded by the City Council in 1924 after some six years of constant lobbying for it by the club. It was an insufficient effort, however symbolic a gesture: a single outlet for truck farming in the city would hardly sustain diversified farming in the state, let alone around Atlanta. The farmers kept leaving their vegetable stalls to go back to tend their cotton.[89]

One final example illustrates beautifully the mix of good intentions and stubborn antiquarianism of some of the women's efforts. The Woodberry School was founded in 1908—a twentieth-century institution—as a female academy—a nineteenth-century educational model. The building constructed for it in 1916 was composed in part from bits and pieces of other, older buildings—a lamp here, a fountain there, and pillars on the veranda. These last happened to be genuine antebellum ionic columns taken from a former Peachtree Street mansion. They may have lent the school historical authenticity, but it had no educational viability. It was superseded by a public school, and in a reversal of the pattern seen so far, this women's building then was turned into a residence.[90]

There are two patterns to be observed here. First, these structures are valid cultural symbols. The memorials, monuments, and clubhouses were all brought into being as creations of the women of the community. Each reflects female identifications and values, loyalties and priorities. They differ from literary creations, which are individualistic and self-conscious, by being collective and more unselfconscious, even naive. They may reflect a variety of societal values from Old South romanticism to New South progressivism; they may do honor to male ancestors or to lady leaders within the collective circle. Whatever the values in each instance, they do all reflect some older female qualities, for they are frozen in time and harken back to the days when the organizations were founded that created them. They reiterate, in the twentieth century, the aspirations and beliefs of the nineteenth century. They speak of duty and sacrifice, of special womanhood and submission to male prerogatives (at least outwardly), of patriotism, pride in culture, love of children, honor to motherhood, piety, and, more than anything else, they speak of the inviolateness of the home. They carry with them the force of united action, and as long as they stand they also carry the authority of permanence.

The second pattern is manifest in the cultural dichotomy these structures represent. They are symbolic in the same way that literature is symbolic, and they illuminate the female experience in an American community just as does one of Ellen Glasgow's novels. At the very least, they should be attended to as much as female literature is, for they symbolize—as a woman's private diary might—the tensions of the female experience.

Where public conventions are the strongest, these structures reflect the larger society; clearly, all the public monuments focus on a historical record that is predominantly male. Where, however, there are fewer conventions—where the women are off on their own—they reflect different feelings. There, the history they write (or build) is personal, more self-aggrandizing, almost feminist—unquestionably female—in its interests. The mountain schools and clubhouses are declarations of self and of autonomous female identity as much as anything could be, just as the monuments to the Civil War are the purest form of female admiration for male endeavor. There are two faces here—a public one that supports a male system and a private one that is declaratively female. Though women's organizations are known to revere the record of men, they may be proudest of their own efforts; not Stone Mountain per se, as much as the amount of money they were able to raise for it; not Joseph Habersham himself, as much as the fact that one DAR chapter did honor to him; and not the State Capitol with its promises of government, but Tallulah Falls—the result of their own handiwork—and its promises of the future in the children.

Notes

EDITOR'S INTRODUCTION

1. Edward T. James, Janet Wilson James, and Paul S. Boyer. eds. *Notable American Women, 1607-1950: A Biographical Dictionary*, 3 vols. (Cambridge: Harvard University Press, 1971); Barbara Sicherman and Carol Hurd Green, eds., *Notable American Women, the Modern Period: A Biographical Dictionary* (Cambridge: Harvard University Press, 1980).
2. New York: R.R. Bowker, 1979.

CHAPTER ONE

1. For a discussion of "distinctive womanhood" and the Victorian idea of womanhood, see the chapter entitled "Love" in Walter E. Houghton, *The Victorian Frame of Mind, 1830-1870* (New Haven: Yale University Press, 1957); "distinctive womanhood" is a Tennyson phrase adopted by Houghton, p. 349. American prescriptions for the female sphere are enumerated in the now classic article by Barbara Welter, "The Cult of True Womanhood," *American Quarterly* 18 (Summer 1966): 151-74.
2. See Aileen Kraditor, *The Ideas of the Woman Suffrage Movement* (New York: Columbia University Press, 1965). For example, she notes that in the 1890s, "the suffragist propaganda began to admit, then to stress, the differences between men and women" (p. 90).
3. Kathryn Kish Sklar, *Catharine Beecher: A Study in American Domesticity* (New Haven: Yale University Press, 1973), chaps. 6, 8, 12.
4. See Jane Addams, "Utilization of Women in City Government," in Alice Rossi, *The Feminist Papers: From Adams to de Beauvoir* (New York: Columbia University Press, 1973), pp. 604-12; Addams's biographer, Allen F. Davis, ventured to suggest that Addams's own image contained an aspect of "feminine mystique," in *American Heroine: The Life and Legend of Jane Addams* (New York: Oxford University Press, 1973), p. 207.
5. Ida M. Tarbell, *The Business of Being a Woman* (New York: Macmillan, 1912), p. 240.
6. Linda Kerber, "The Republican Mother: Women and the Enlightenment—An American Perspective," *American Quarterly* 8 (Summer 1976): 202.

7. Mrs. Josephine S. Yates, quoted by W. E. B. DuBois, in "Efforts for Social Betterment Among Negro Americans," *Atlanta University Publications*, #14, Atlanta University, 1909 (reprinted, New York: Russell and Russell, 1969), p. 47.

8. Carl Degler, *Out of Our Past: The Forces That Shaped Modern America* (New York: Harper & Row, 1959), pp. 343-62; Eleanor Flexner, *Century of Struggle: The Woman's Rights Movement in the United States* (Cambridge: Harvard University Press, 1959), Chapter 2; Merle Curti, *The Growth of American Thought* (New York: Harper & Bros., 1951 [1943]), p. 383-85; J. Stanley Lemons, *The Woman Citizen: Social Feminism in the 1920s* (Urbana, Ill.: University of Illinois Press, 1971).

9. Degler, *Our Past*, p. 361.

10. Belle Kearney, *A Slaveholder's Daughter* (New York: Abbey Press, 1900), p. 118; Anne Firor Scott, *The Southern Lady: From Pedestal to Politics, 1830-1930* (Chicago: University of Chicago Press, 1970).

11. William O'Neill, *Everyone Was Brave: A History of Feminism in America* (New York: Quadrangle Books, 1969), pp. 84-90, 103.

12. Richard Hofstadter, " 'Idealists and Professors and Soreheads': The Genteel Reformers," *Columbia University Forum* (Spring 1962): 7, 8.

13. See William O'Neill, "Feminism as a Radical Ideology," in *Dissent: Explorations in the History of American Radicalism*, ed. Alfred F. Young (DeKalb: Northern Illinois University Press, 1968), p. 276; Lois Banner, *Women in Modern America: A Brief History* (New York: Harcourt Brace Jovanovich, 1974), p. vi.

14. Rossi, *The Feminist Papers*, p. 281. As a sociologist, Rossi has analyzed many aspects of the suffragists and their movement not noted by historians; for another comment on the pitfalls of overemphasizing the "great" women and concentrating on the suffrage movement in professing women's history, see Roberta B. Miller, "Women and American History," *Women's Studies* 2 (1974): 105-13. Italics added.

15. O'Neill, *Everyone Was Brave*, p. 88; Degler, *Our Past*, p. 360; Wright, *Culture on the Moving Frontier* (New York: Harper & Bros., 1961), pp. 224-30; Gerda Lerner, "The Community Leadership of Black Women: The Neighborhood Union of Atlanta, Ga.," presented at the annual meeting of the American Historical Association, New Orleans, La., December 1972; also Lerner, "Early Community Work of Black Women," *Journal of Negro History* 59 (April 1974): 158-67.

The contradiction of images of women on the frontier deserves more serious attention; the popular versions, such as Dee Brown, *The Gentle Tamers: Women of the Old Wild West* (New York: Bantam Books, 1974 [1958]) raise many questions; his "tamers" include such diverse types as Elizabeth Custer, respectable wife of the General, and Belle Starr, an early Bonnie Parker.

16. Arthur M. Schlesinger, *Paths to the Present* (New York: Macmillan, 1949), p. 50.

17. Sara B. Townsend, "The Addition of Women to the University of Georgia," *Georgia Historical Quarterly* 42 (June 1959), pp. 156-69.

18. Described by C. A. Bacote in "James Weldon Johnson and Early Atlanta University," *Phylon* (Winter 1971): 339. A picture from an early Atlanta University circular shows these very eating arrangements.
19. John Cawelti, "America on Display: The World's Fairs of 1876, 1893, and 1933," in Frederick Cople Jaher, ed., *The Age of Industrialism in America: Essays in Social Structure and Cultural Values* (New York: The Free Press, 1968), p. 339.
20. Ibid., p. 340.
21. Frederick Law Olmsted, *Public Parks and the Enlargement of Towns*, read before the American Social Science Association at the Lowell Institute, Boston, February 15, 1870 (Cambridge, Mass.: Riverside Press, 1870), p. 9.
22. Quoted from *Monthly Religious Magazine* (1860), in Arthur W. Calhoun, *A Social History of the American Family*, 3 vols. (New York: Barnes & Noble, 1960 [Cleveland, 1915-1918]), 3: 229.
23. William Bridges, "Family Patterns and Social Values," *American Quarterly* 17 (Spring 1965): 10, passim.
24. Mary I. Wood, *The History of the General Federation of Women's Clubs: For the First Twenty-two Years of Its Organization* (Norwood, Mass.: Norwood Press; New York: History Department, General Federation of Women's Clubs, 1912), p. 312.
25. Quoted in ibid., p. 18.

CHAPTER TWO

1. E. Y. Clarke, *Illustrated History of Atlanta*, facsimile edition (Atlanta: Cherokee Publishing, 1971 [1877]), p. 2.
2. *Pioneer Citizens' History of Atlanta, 1833-1902* (Atlanta: Byrd Printing, 1902), p. 400.
3. Statement by Nathaniel E. Harris, quoted in Raymond B. Nixon, *Henry W. Grady: Spokesman of the New South* (New York: Alfred A. Knopf, 1943), p. 283; Frances Newman, "Atlanta," *The Reviewer* 3 (January 1923), p. 726, the exact quote is "Atlanta, . . . is like the rest of Georgia only in its constantly excavated red clay foundations."
4. For a summary of Atlanta boosterism, especially during the 1920s, see Charles Garofalo, "The Sons of Henry Grady: Atlanta Boosters in the 1920s," *Journal of Southern History* 42 (May 1976), pp. 187-204.
5. A. E. Taylor, "The Origin of the Woman Suffrage Movement in Georgia," *Georgia Historical Quarterly* 28 (June 1944), p. 69.
6. Quoted in Rebecca Latimer Felton, *The Romantic Story of Georgia Women* (Atlanta: *Atlanta Georgian and Sunday American*, 1930), pp. 16-17.
7. Clark, *Illustrated History of Atlanta*, pp. 33, 48; James Michael Russell, "Atlanta, Gate City of the South, 1847-1885," Ph.D. dissertation, Princeton University, 1972, p. 253.

8. Franklin Garrett, *Atlanta and Environs*, 3 vols. (Athens, Ga.: University of Georgia Press, 1969 [1954]), 1: 456-57.

9. Wesleyan College in Macon was the first, founded in 1836, and it still vies for the title of the first women's college in the U.S.

10. Address to the Berkshire Conference on Women's History, Cambridge, Massachusetts, October 1973.

11. Eleanor Boatwright, "The Political and Civil Status of Women in Georgia, 1783-1860," *Georgia Historical Quarterly* 25 (December 1941), pp. 301-24.

12. Valerie Jones of Atlanta University has discovered that among free blacks in antebellum Georgia the largest property owner was a married woman who lived in a county near Savannah; paper delivered to History Department, Atlanta University, February 5, 1976.

13. Boatwright, "Political and Civil Status," p. 311; Felton, *Romantic Story*, p. 24; it was Felton's considered opinion that this was the only recognizable "good" that the Reconstruction carpetbaggers and scalawags did.

14. Dan Durett and Dana F. White, *An-Other Atlanta: The Black Heritage* (Atlanta: The History Group, Inc., 1975), p. 17.

15. Ibid., p. 3.

16. Dana F. White, "Four Cheers for Atlanta," manuscript prepared for the Atlanta Historical Society as text for a permanent slide exhibit of the city, October 1975, quoted from "Cheer #1," p. 5.

17. Emily Hahn, *Once Upon a Pedestal* (New York: Mentor, 1974), p. 167.

18. The works include Bell Wiley, *Confederate Woman* (Westport, Conn.: Greenwood Press, 1975); Scott, *The Southern Lady*; and M. Elizabeth Massey, *Bonnet Brigades: American Women and the Civil War* (New York: Knopf, 1966).

19. Much of this information on Atlanta Confederate life comes from Samuel Carter, III, *The Siege of Atlanta, 1864* (New York: St. Martin's Press, 1973), an exciting narrative of the battles and vivid description of daily life in wartime Atlanta; see also T. Conn Bryan, *Confederate Georgia* (Athens, Ga.: University of Georgia Press, 1953), chapter on "Women's Wartime Activities," and Garrett, *Atlanta and Environs*, 1: 493-700.

20. Wiley, *Confederate Woman*, p. 178.

21. Carter, *Siege*, p. 47.

22. Ibid., p. 61, on the Soldiers' Relief Association; Garrett, *Atlanta and Environs*, 1: 706-7, on the Ladies Memorial Association; Papers, Ladies Memorial Association, Atlanta Historical Society; Eula Turner Kuchler, "Charitable and Philanthropic Activities in Atlanta During Reconstruction," master's thesis, Emory University, 1942, pp. 59-75, author's index cards.

23. *Barnwell's Atlanta City Directory and Stranger's Guide* (Atlanta: V. T. Barnwell, 1867 [printed by the Atlanta Intelligencer Book & Job Office]); *Scholes Directory of the City of Atlanta for 1877* (Atlanta: A. E. Scholes [printed by the Sunny South Publishing House]).

24. Gerda Lerner's *Black Women in White America: A Documentary History* (New York: Pantheon, 1972) is the single most obvious exception, as it uses a great

deal of source material from the South for both modern as well as antebellum periods.

25. T. Lynn Smith, "The Redistribution of the Negro Population of the United States, 1910-1960," *Journal of Negro History* 51 (July 1966): 155-73.

26. Durrett and White, *Black Heritage*, p. 3.

27. For example: "It is characteristic of the South that the power of a single personality . . . could sometimes move mountains. Only in a few Southern communities—notably the cosmopolitan port city of New Orleans—were there to be found the influential clusters of women, volunteers and professionals working together through clubs and other organizations for social welfare goals." Quoted from Edward T. James, Janet Wilson James, and Paul S. Boyer, introduction to *Notable American Women: A Biographical Dictionary* (Cambridge, Mass.: Harvard University Press, 1971), p. xlvi.

28. For more specific information on organizations founded during these years, see Garrett, *Atlanta and Environs*, 1: 827-963, 2: 1-202; Clarke, *Illustrated History*, pp. 73-79, 143-46.

29. M. L. Brittain, ed., *Semi-Centennial History of the Second Baptist Church of Atlanta, Georgia* (Atlanta, n.p., 1904), p. 19.

30. Ibid., pp. 19ff; Mrs. E. L. Connally, *Foundation Stones Upon Which the Baptist Women's Missionary Union of Georgia is Built*, pamphlet (Atlanta?: n.p., 1942), pp. 3-4; "The Story of the Baptist Women's Missionary Union," *The Christian Index* 119 (July 15, 1939): 100; and Alma Hunt, *History of the Women's Missionary Union* (Nashville, Tenn.: Convention Press, 1964), pp. 1-3, 12-26. Hunt also discusses some of the pre-Civil War activities of Southern Baptist women.

31. Mrs. Mary Venable Womble, "Condensed History of the First Methodist Episcopal Church, South, Atlanta, Georgia," *Atlanta Historical Bulletin* 2 (January 1928): 20-28; Mary Culler White, *The Portal of Wonderland: The Life of Alice Culler Cobb* (New York: Fleming H. Revell, 1925), pp. 81, 86, 89. Alice Cobb served as associate secretary of the Women's Board of Foreign Missions, ME Church, South, beginning in 1890.

32. Oswald E. Brown and Anna M. Brown, *Life and Letters of Laura Askew Haygood* (Nashville, Tenn.: Publishing House of the ME Church, South, 1904), p. 69.

33. C. A. Bacote, *The Story of Atlanta University: A Century of Service, 1865-1965* (Atlanta: Atlanta University Press, 1969), p. 206.

34. Rev. E. R. Carter, *The Black Side: A Partial History of the Business, Religious, and Educational Side of the Negro in Atlanta, Georgia* (Atlanta, n.p., 1894), pp. 249, 256, and passim.

35. Durett and White, *The Black Heritage*, pp. 28, 40. The early school-church ties were also sometimes confusing and competitive; see Jerry Thornbery, "Northerners and the Atlanta Freedmen, 1865-69," *Prologue* (Winter 1974): 236-51.

36. Florence Read, *The Story of Spelman College* (Princeton: Princeton University Press, 1961), p. 53.

37. Carter, *Black Side*, p. 34.

38. W. E. B. DuBois, ed., "Some Efforts of American Negroes for Their Own Social Betterment," *Atlanta University Publication No. 3* (Atlanta: Atlanta University, 1898), pp. 3-9.

39. Woman's Christian Temperance Union, *Minutes of the Second Annual Convention of the Georgia WCTU*, Augusta, Georgia, January 24-25, 1884 (Atlanta: Temperance Advocate Printing, 1884), esp. pp. 12-13; H. A. Scomp, *King Alcohol in the Realm of King Cotton: A History of the Liquor Traffic and of the Temperance Movement in Georgia from 1733-1887* (Atlanta?: Blakely Printing, 1888), pp. 679, 683, 694-99; Mrs. J. J. Ansley, *History of the Georgia WCTU, 1883-1907* (Columbus, Ga.: Gilbert Publishing, 1914), pp. 76-78.

40. Carter, *Black Side*, pp. 43-45.

41. Ansley, *Georgia WCTU*, pp. 76-78; Scomp, *King Alcohol*, pp. 694-99.

42. The *Messenger* was Spelman's all-purpose magazine, which carried news of the faculty and alumnae, special features, editorials, poetry and other literary efforts, full coverage of curriculum changes and student activities, and so on. It is still printed today, though in a different format. The *Messenger*, in its entirety, is one of the most important records of female education and student life available for the nineteenth and early twentieth centuries.

43. Eula Aiken, "Women's Issues as Expressed in the *Spelman Messenger*, 1885-1924," seminar paper, Emory University, July 1976, pp. 3-4. In possession of the author.

44. Alpha Delta Pi, *Pledge Book*, 1965 edition, p. 10; also, *Welcome to Alpha Delta Pi Memorial Headquarters*, pamphlet prepared by Carol Dorton Asher, former director of the Executive Office (printed by the sorority, n.d.), pp. 14, 15, and passim. Eunice Thompson, "Ladies Can Learn," *Georgia Review* 1 (Spring 1947): 189-97.

45. Information on early sorority membership of nineteenth-century organization women is very difficult to secure. It is not simply the reluctance of schools and sororities to divulge information on their graduates and members; the matter is made more difficult by the reluctance of members themselves, who in the past would not reveal relationships to organizations considered—quite seriously—to be absolutely secret. For example, see Kate Flournoy Edwards, "A College Girl in War-Time," *Georgia Review* 1 (Summer 1947): 198-206; her mother was president of Philomenthean as a student at Wesleyan, but considered it such a secret affiliation, she would not discuss it even with her daughter.

46. Evidence of the close ties between Wesleyan, specifically, and later Atlanta organizations is often circumstantial. For example, one of the early members of the 19th Century History Class was a relative and close friend of the principal at Wesleyan, Alice Culler Cobb, a prominent educator and leader in women's affairs. Cobb had been a member of Adelphean, the founder of the Atheneum—the first women's study group in Macon, and was otherwise important to women's public activities in the state; see note 31 above and White, *Portal of Wonderland*.

47. Read, *Spelman College*, p. 107; Bacote, *Atlanta University*, pp. 241, 243, 244. The fraternities had gained a rather bad reputation on campus for creating unhealthy competition and an intraclass color line; the most prestigious fraternity also had the lightest-skinned members.

48. Evidence of these early institutions is meager, but founding dates and some discussion of their activities can be found in published local histories, including, of course, Garrett, *Atlanta and Environs*, and Clarke, *Illustrated History*. Also consulted were *Pioneer Citizens' History of Atlanta*; John R. Hornady, *Atlanta Yesterday, Today, and Tomorrow* (Atlanta: Index Publishing, 1922); Walter G. Cooper, *Official History of Fulton Co.* (Fulton Co. Historical Commission, 1934); and Paul Miller, *Atlanta, Capital of the South* (New York: Oliver Durrell, Inc., 1949).

49. Garrett, *Atlanta and Environs*, 2: 389.

50. Cooper, *History of Fulton Co.*, pp. 415-45; see also Cooper, *The Atlanta Cotton States and International Exposition and South, Illustrated* (Atlanta: n.p., 1896), and Garrett, *Atlanta and Environs*, 2: 311-31. See also, Alice Mabel Bacon, "The Negro and the Atlanta Exposition," John F. Slater Fund, *Occasional Papers*, No. 7, 1896.

51. See for example, Scott, *The Southern Lady*, pp. 156-58, and Page Smith, *Daughters of the Promised Land: Women in American History* (Boston: Little, Brown, 1970), pp. 260-64. Female participation in the nineteenth-century fair was already a century old, as documented by Julia Spruill, for example, in *Women's Life and Work in the Southern Colonies*: "Fairs were probably delightful occasions for farmer's wives, for they not only gave the women an opportunity to display their achievements in garden, poultry yards, and kitchens . . ., but they also offered many unusual sights and diversions." (New York: W. W. Norton, 1972 [originally published by the University of North Carolina Press, 1938]), p. 110.

52. Luckhurst draws a distinction between a "fair," where something is sold, and an "exhibition," where something is displayed only, but the overlap between selling and displaying is too great in the U.S. to allow much precision when speaking of individual fairs. See Kenneth W. Luckhurst, *The Story of Exhibitions* (New York: The Studio Publication, 1951), pp. 12-13. "Exhibition" vs. "exposition" seems to be a matter of size and inclusiveness; an exposition requires international or worldwide participation. Here the word *fair* is used generically.

53. Flexner suggests the "earliest rudimentary women's organizations" were church sewing circles of the 1820s; see *Century of Struggle*, p. 41.

54. Garrett, *Atlanta and Environs*, 1: 320.

55. William Quentin Maxwell, *Lincoln's Fifth Wheel: The Political History of the United States Sanitary Commission* (New York: Longmans, Green, 1956), pp. 224-26, 264, 300-301.

56. Dee Brown, *The Year of the Century: 1876* (New York: Charles Scribner's Sons, 1966), p. 22.

57. See John E. Talmadge, *Rebecca Latimer Felton: Nine Stormy Decades* (Athens: University of Georgia Press, 1960), pp. 90ff. Rebecca Latimer Felton, *Country Life in Georgia in the Days of My Youth* (Atlanta: Index Publishing, 1911), pp. 107-115; and Felton, *Romantic Story*, pp. 33-35.

58. Sophonisba Breckinridge, *Women in the Twentieth Century: A Study of Their Political, Social, and Economic Activities* (New York: McGraw-Hill, 1933), pp. 23-24.

59. Atlanta, Section, NCJW, *Yearbook, 1973-74*, p. 5.

60. Cotton States and International Exposition, *Official Programme: Daily Events of the Exposition, September 18-December 31, 1895* (n.p.), passim.

61. NSDAR, *Chapter Histories, Daughters of the American Revolution in Georgia, 1891-1931* (Augusta, Ga.: Ridgely-Tidwell, n.d.), p. xi; NSDAR, Atlanta Chapter, *Atlanta Chapter, DAR, April 15, 1891-April 15, 1921* (n.p., n.d.), p. 7.

62. Garrett, *Atlanta and Environs*, 2: 309-10.

63. C.S.I. Exposition, *Official Programme*, passim.

64. Wood, *General Federation of Woman's Clubs*, p. 74.

65. The exact origins of each woman's club are hazy. Both date from 1895, but there is some indication in each case that organizational activity took place before the exposition. Georgia had a secretary for correspondence (from Atlanta) to the General Federation prior to the formation of the white club, which according to Rebecca Felton was actually formed during the exposition. See ibid., pp. 53-74, and Felton, *Country Life*, p. 111. The black club apparently sent delegates to the Boston Conference of Colored Women held in 1895 prior to the exposition. See Elizabeth Lindsay Davis, *Lifting as They Climb: The National Association of Colored Women* (n.p., printed by the NACW, 1933), p. 11.

66. Quoted in Cooper, *History of Fulton Co.*, p. 428.

67. Augusta Wylie King, "The Woman's Press Club of Georgia," *Atlanta Historical Bulletin* 7 (October 1938): 396-408.

68. Ansley, *The Georgia WCTU*, p. 159.

69. James C. Boykin, "The Cotton States and International Exposition Held in Atlanta, Ga., September 19-December 31, 1895," U.S. Bureau of Education, *Report, 1894-95*, p. 1745.

70. Garrett, *Atlanta and Environs*, 2: 326; NSDAR, *Chapter Histories*, p. xi.

71. Alice Baxter, "Historical Sketch of the Atlanta Chapter, U.D.C." in *History Atlanta Chapter United Daughters of the Confederacy, 1897-1922* (published by the society), unpaginated.

72. Boykin, "The C.S.I Exposition," p. 1739.

73. Cooper, *History of Fulton Co.*, p. 424; Garrett, *Atlanta and Environs*, 2: 324.

74. Historical marker outside headquarters, Atlanta Chapter, DAR, Piedmont Road at 15th Street; NSDAR, *Atlanta Chapter, 1891-1921*, pp. 8, 10-12.

75. The program for the fair in 1900 shows the Department of Women's Work under the management of the Georgia Federation with the president of the federation having offices at the fair headquarters; Southern Inter-state Fair

Associations, *Official Premium List* (Atlanta: printed by the Association, 1900), p. 103.

76. Mrs. J. M. Whitehurst, *Georgia Federation of Women's Clubs, 1896-1971* (Atlanta, Savannah, and Georgia Gas Companies, n.d.), pp. 1-2; the first president of the Atlanta Woman's Club was also the first president of the state federation, Mrs. Rebecca Douglas Lowe.

77. The Southeastern Fair Association, *General Rules and Regulations for the Fair* (Atlanta: printed by the Association, 1916), pp. 5, 95ff; also, Scrapbooks, Nellie Peters Black Papers, University of Georgia.

78. Read, *Spelman College*, p. 134; Boykin, "The C.S.I Exposition," p. 1745.

79. Alice Mabel Bacon, "Negro and the Atlanta Expo," p. 18.

80. The C.S.I. Exposition, *Official Programme*, pp. 137ff.

81. Davis, *Lifting as They Climb*, pp. 24-25, passim.

82. Giles Jackson is a good example of this, who set up the entirely independent Negro Historical and Industrial Exposition at Richmond, Virginia, in 1951; apparently he had "gained experience" in exposition management at the Charleston and Jamestown expositions of 1901 and 1907. See Ruth M. Winton, "Negro Participation in Southern Expositions, 1881-1915," *Journal of Negro Education* 16 (Winter 1947): 34-43.

83. Ibid., p. 39.

84. Ibid.; for the Chicago controversies, see August Meier and Elliott M. Rudwick, "Black Man in the 'White City': Negroes and the Columbian Exposition, 1893," *Phylon* 26 (1965): 354-61.

85. Quoted in Winton, "Negro Participation," p. 37.

86. A disclaimer might be issued for the United Daughters of the Confederacy, which, since open to national membership in local branches anywhere, was a national federation, but it was so strongly identified with the South, and most of its membership came from the South anyway, that it should be considered a regional, not a national, organization at this point.

87. Bacote, *Atlanta University*, p. 128.

88. Louis R. Harlan, *Booker T. Washington: The Making of a Black Leader, 1856-1901* (New York: Oxford University Press, 1972), p. 228.

89. August Meier, *Negro Thought in America, 1880-1915: Racial Ideologies in the Age of Booker T. Washington* (Ann Arbor: University of Michigan Press, 1970), p. 13.

90. From a Pennsylvania newspaper article, undated and unsigned, probably from the *Pittsburgh Press* or the *Pittsburgh Telegraph* in September 1895, in scrapbook of clipping about the exposition, Atlanta Public Library. Italics added.

91. W. E. B. DuBois, "The Work of Negro Women in Society," *The Spelman Messenger*, February 1902, pp. 1-3.

92. "Are We Making Good?" *The Spelman Messenger*, November 1915, pp. 2, 6. Italics added.

93. DuBois, "The Work of Negro Women," p. 1.

94. Felton, *Romantic Story*, p. 35.

CHAPTER THREE

1. The statistical evidence in this chapter is drawn largely from C. A. McMahan, *The People of Atlanta: A Demographic Study of Georgia's Capital City* (Athens: University of Georgia Press, 1950), for population statistics and comparative size see especially pp. 209-11; see also Thomas Deaton, "Atlanta During the Progressive Era," Ph.D. dissertation, University of Georgia, 1969, p. 36.

2. Smith, "The Redistribution of the Negro Population of the United States."

3. McMahan, *People of Atlanta*, p. 57.

4. Richard J. Hopkins, "Patterns of Persistence and Occupational Mobility in a Southern City: Atlanta, 1870-1920," Ph.D. dissertation, Emory University, 1972, pp. 49-50, 64-67.

5. Scott, *The Southern Lady*, p. 106; see also, Marjorie S. Mendenhall, "Southern Women of a Lost Generation," *South Atlantic Quarterly* 33 (October 1934): 334-53. The southern, postwar, so-called matriarchy has been much alluded to by scholars, but not yet much examined, except for Scott.

6. McMahan, *People in Atlanta*, pp. 83-90, 213; see also "Atlanta Has 20,000 More Women Than Men," *Atlanta Journal Magazine*, September 10, 1922, p. 7, for a popular view on the subject.

7. McMahan, *People in Atlanta*, pp. 91-103.

8. Ibid., pp. 127-34, 215-17.

9. See, for example, U.S. Department of Commerce and Labor, Bureau of the Census, *Statistics of Women At Work*, 1907, pp. 306-7, on Atlanta. Of 3,149 white workers, 1,972 were single; of 8,275 blacks, 2,400 single.

10. On this theme, see, for example, James R. McGovern, "The American Woman's Pre-World War I Freedom in Manners and Morals," *Journal of American History* 55 (September 1968): 320; Sigfried Giedion, *Mechanization Takes Command: A Contribution to Anonymous History* (New York: Oxford Press, 1948); and Elizabeth F. Baker, *Technology and Woman's Work* (New York: Columbia University Press, 1964).

11. This description owes much to Leonard Dinnerstein, "Atlanta in the Progressive Era: A Dreyfus Affair in Georgia," [the Leo Frank case], in Jaher, ed., *The Age of Industrialism in America*, p. 131.

12. For varying views of race relations and of the Atlanta Riot in particular, see Walter White, *A Man Called White* (Bloomington: Indiana University Press, 1948), pp. 8-12; Garrett, *Atlanta and Environs* 2: 500-504; Ray Stannard Baker, *Following the Color Line: American Negro Citizenship in the Progressive Era* (New York: Harper Torchbook, 1964 [1908]), pp. 3-26; and Deaton, "Atlanta During the Progressive Era," pp. 186-200.

13. Dinnerstein, "Atlanta in the Progressive Era," pp. 135-36, and Dinnerstein, *The Leo Frank Case* (New York: Columbia University Press, 1968), pp. 32, 62-72, 116-17, 130-32.

14. Deaton, "Atlanta During the Progressive Era," pp. 365-400; City Charter campaign scrapbooks, League of Women Voters Papers, State of Georgia Department of Archives and History.

15. V. O. Key, Jr., *Southern Politics* (New York: Random House, 1949), pp. 106-29; "rule of the rustics" is Key's phrase.

16. First National Bank of Atlanta, *Atlanta Resurgens: The First Hundred Years of a City's Progress, Promise, and Philosophy* (Atlanta: by the bank, 1971), pp. 62-77; Garrett, *Atlanta and Environs*, 2: 775-861; Dana F. White and Timothy J. Crimmins, "How Atlanta Grew: Cool Heads, Hot Air, Hard Work," *Atlanta Economic Review* 38, 1 (January-February 1978), pp. 7-15; George B. Tindall, *The Emergence of the New South, 1913-1945* (Baton Rouge: Louisiana State University Press, 1967), pp. 99-100; Cooper, *History of Fulton Co.*, pp. 802-16.

17. Durett and White, *The Black Heritage*, p. 46.

18. On the CIC, see Edward F. Burrows, "The Commission on Interracial Cooperation: A Case Study in the History of the Interracial Movement in the South," Ph.D. dissertation, University of Wisconsin, 1954; and Wilma Dykeman and James Stokely, *Seeds of Southern Change: The Life of Will Alexander* (Chicago: University Press, 1962).

19. Tindall, *New South*, pp. 181, 187-88, 190-91; Kenneth T. Jackson, *The Ku Klux Klan in the City, 1915-1930* (New York: Oxford University Press, 1967), pp. 29-44.

20. Garrett, *Atlanta and Environs*, 2: 866-1001; White and Crimmins, "How Atlanta Grew," pp. 40-42; Kenneth Coleman, *Georgia History in Outline* (Athens: University of Georgia Press, 1960), pp. 94-117; Tindall, *New South*, pp. 359-60, 457.

21. The modern demography of Atlanta relative to Georgia and the U.S. is described in Everett S. Lee, "Georgia's Population—Its Historical Development," Symposium on Georgia Studies, Department of Archives and History, Atlanta, Georgia, February 6, 1976.

22. The changing southern society today, as the "newest" of the New Souths, is an increasingly popular topic, since the election of Jimmy Carter to the American presidency. Two relevant, but pre-Carter, studies of this phenomenon include Monroe Lee Billington, *The Political South in the Twentieth Century* (New York: Charles Scribner's Sons, 1975), pp. 107-30; and Pat Watters, *The South and the Nation* (New York: Pantheon Books, 1969).

23. William Chafe's contentions in *The American Woman: Her Changing Social, Economic, and Political Roles, 1920-1970* (New York: Oxford University Press, 1972) have not been seriously challenged; see also Eleanor F. Straub, "United States Government Policy Toward Civilian Women During World War II," *Prologue* 5 (Winter 1973): 240-55.

24. Ada Biehl, "Do You Remember?" in Atlanta Woman's Club, *Biennial Report, 1966-68*, pp. 44, 48, 49; *The Atlanta Society Blue Book of Selected Names* (New York: Dau Publishing, 1907), pp. 62-63; Atlanta Woman's Club, *Annual Report, 1932-33*. Georgia Bicentennial Edition, pp. 58-62; Georgia Federation of

Women's Clubs, *Yearbook, 1935-36*, p. 239. Today the club has about 225, judging from dues assessments, as indicated in the *Biennial Report* for 1970-72, pp. 19, 45.

25. Wood, *General Federation of Women's Clubs*, pp. 127, 164; according to Wood, there were six city federations by 1904.

26. Ibid., pp. 127-57, 353; Whitehurst, *Georgia Federation*, pp. 1-3.

27. Mary Savage Anderson, comp., *A History of the Georgia Society of the Colonial Dames of America, from April 1893 to January 1950*, revised from the first edition [1937] (Richmond, Va.: Whittet and Shepperson, n.d.), pp. 7-8, quoted from p. 8; NSCDA, *A Summary of the Histories of the National Society of the Colonial Dames of America and of the Corporate Societies, 1891-1962*, by the National Historic Activities Committee (published by the Society, 1962), pp. 74-79.

28. Savage, *History of Georgia Society*, pp. 8-9; Georgia Society of Colonial Dames of America, *Register of the Georgia Society* (Savannah: Braid and Hutton, Inc., 1926); Georgia Society of Colonial Dames of America, *Directory* (published by the Society, 1927, 1938); the membership statistics were compiled by tabulating the names and dates listed in the 1926 *Register* and the names listed in the two directories.

29. Savage, *History of Georgia Society*, p. 8.

30. Wallace E. Davies, *Patriotism on Parade: The Story of Veterans and Hereditary Organizations in America, 1783-1900* (Cambridge: Harvard University Press, 1955), p. 76.

31. The origins of the Atlanta Chapter and the national association are described, respectively, in [United Daughters of the Confederacy, Atlanta Chapter], *History Atlanta Chapter United Daughters of the Confederacy, 1897-1922* (n.p., n.d, unpaginated), see the section entitled "Historical Sketch of the Atlanta Chapter, U.D.C." by Miss Alice Baxter; and Mary B. Poppenheim et al., *The History of the United Daughters of the Confederacy*, Vol. 1, 1894-1929, Vol. 2, 1930-1955, in one volume (Raleigh, N.C.: Edwards and Broughton, n.d.), pp. 1-12, 28.

32. The membership statistics and the statistics on chapter development given here and in the following paragraphs were tabulated from the listings given in the published minutes of the Georgia Division, UDC, for these years: 1901, 1905, 1907, 1909, 1910, 1911, 1913, 1914, 1915, 1916, 1919, 1923, 1924, 1925, 1926, 1928, 1929, 1930, 1931, 1932, 1933, 1937, 1938, and 1939; from these published Minutes of the annual national convention of the UDC for these years: 1902, 1928, and 1935; and from the *Georgia Division Roster and Ancestry Roll of the United Daughters of the Confederacy* (by the Georgia Division, 1960).

33. In 1960, Atlanta proper had a total of seven UDC chapters: Atlanta Chapter #18 (fd. 1895), Fulton Chapter #1754 (fd. 1921), Rebecca Felton Chapter #1957 (fd. ca. 1928), Crawford Long Chapter #1999 (fd. 1929), Alfred Colquitt Chapter #2018 (fd. 1930), Dorothy B. Lamar Chapter #2104 (fd. 1939), and Adm. Raphael Semmes Chapter #2287 (fd. 1960).

34. Apparently, inattention to accurate membership information is a national phenomenon in the DAR. See especially Peggy Anderson, *The Daughters: An*

Unconventional Look at America's Fan Club—the DAR (New York: St. Martin's Press, 1974), p. 20: "Surprisingly little statistical information is available on the women who make up the DAR. The Daughters have never felt the need to study themselves in any systematic way. They don't really know who their members are, and no one else does, either."

The DAR chapters in Atlanta were probably somewhat smaller than the Woman's Club and the UDC. The Joseph Habersham Chapter, for example, began with a charter membership of fifty, and had just over 300 members by 1920; [Hattie Mae Carmichael], *Seventy-Five Years of the Joseph Habersham Chapter, 1900-1975* (Atlanta: by the society, n.d.), pp. 3, 19.

35. NSCDA, *A Summary of Histories*, p. 16.
36. The essential work on this subject is Roy Lubove, *The Professional Altruist: The Emergence of Social Work as a Career, 1880-1930* (Cambridge: Harvard University Press, 1965); also important is Robert H. Wiebe, *The Search for Order, 1877-1920* (New York: Hill and Wang, 1967).
37. Garrett, *Atlanta and Environs*, 2: 389.
38. Eminie (Mrs. Oscar) Ragland, "The Founding of Atlanta Tuberculosis Association and the Home for Incurables," *Atlanta Historical Bulletin* 4 (October 1939): 256-62.
39. Garrett, *Atlanta and Environs*, 2: 260, 410-11, 562.
40. Ibid., 2: 193-94; Mrs. A. O. Woodward, "Confederate Soldiers' Home of Georgia, Atlanta, Georgia," in *History Atlanta Chapter United Daughters of the Confederacy* (unpaginated).
41. Margaret Richards, comp., "History—Atlanta Y.W.C.A.," typescript (copy in DRR files), pp. 10, 12, 16.
42. This discussion derives from a number of sources. On the Neighborhood Union, see Lerner, *Black Women in White America*, pp. 498-512; Lerner, "The Community Leadership of Black Women"; Lerner, "Early Community Work of Black Women,"; Louie Davis Shivery, "History of Organized Social Work Among Atlanta Negroes, 1890-1935," master's thesis, Atlanta University, 1936; Shivery, "The Neighborhood Union," *Phylon* 3 (1942); and Neighborhood Union Papers, Trevor Arnett Library, Atlanta University.

   On the Urban League, and the relationships of Atlanta University, the School of Social Work, and University Homes, see Durett and White, *The Black Heritage*, pp. 36-38; Clarence A. Bacote, *Atlanta University*, pp. 256-343; Jesse O. Thomas, *My Story in Black and White: The Autobiography of J. O. T.* (New York: Exposition Press, 1967), pp. 97-102, 117-27; and Urban League Papers, Atlanta University.
43. Biehl, "Do You Remember," pp. 47-48; Atlanta Federation of Women's Clubs, *Annual Report, 1927-29*, pp. 20-21; Atlanta Woman's Club, *Annual Report, 1925-26*, p. 37, and *Annual Report, 1932-33*, p. 39.
44. For example, about 1930, the leader of the Atlanta League of Women Voters said, "I believe the specialized voluntary, cultural organizations [i.e., such as the league] are taking the place of the woman's club" in a proposal to reorganize the

league and redirect its energies; see Eleanore Raoul, "The Trend of the League," undated typescript, League of Women Voters Papers.

45. Analyses of women's organizations in the twentieth century have tended to focus primarily—often solely—on their feminist aspects, especially their support of suffrage and other liberal causes, and have missed much of the importance of their purely social characteristics. However, the general story of the development of these new large organizations is told in a variety of sources: the most insightful about the trends of development that were not political is Breckinridge, *Women in the Twentieth Century*; the political involvements of numerous organizations are treated in Martin Gruberg, *Women in American Politics: An Assessment and Sourcebook* (Oshkosh, Wis.: Academic Press, 1968), and Lemons, *The Woman Citizen*; see also Banner, *Women in Modern America*; and Mary Ryan, *Womanhood in America: From Colonial Times to the Present* (New York: Franklin Watts, 1975).

46. E.g., the National Woman's Party had six Atlanta members; see Mildred Seydell Papers, Woodruff Library, Emory University.

47. While the idea of occupational "character" is well developed in sociology, that of organizational character, except of business and governmental organizations, is less well developed or understood, but it certainly applies to matronage: "Organizations develop a sub-culture which has some of the characteristics of a personality that is transmitted from generation to generation of role occupants." So says Kenneth Boulding, *The Organizational Revolution: A Study in the Ethics of Economic Organization* (Chicago: Quadrangle Books, 1968 [1953]), p. ix.

48. There is no scholarly history of the Georgia Federation of Women's Clubs. The descriptions here and the passages that follow are based on an examination of yearbooks from both the Georgia and the Atlanta federations, and other materials, specifically: Georgia yearbooks for the years 1908-1909, 1915-1916, 1925-1926, and 1935-1936; Atlanta federation for the years 1929-31 and 1935-37; Whitehurst, *Georgia Federation*; and several collections of private papers, including as the most important, Nellie Peters Black Papers.

49. Nowadays, the Fifth District has only twenty member clubs, including regular Woman's Clubs and Junior Woman's Clubs. With the single exception of the Fine Arts Forum, no "specialized" organizations belong. (From a 1972-73 membership list provided by the Georgia Federation.)

50. A nearly perfect record of Chautauqua activities exists in five volumes of minutes, unbroken between 1913 and 1956, except for a brief period in the early 1920s. Additional materials—yearbooks and scrapbooks—bring the circle's record up to the present time. For the two debates mentioned above, see Minutes, October 1913 and September 1919, Volume 1.

51. See Eula Aiken, "Women's Issues as Expressed in the *Spelman Messenger*, 1885-1924," seminar paper, Emory University, 1976, Special Collections, Emory University, p. 8; apparently, students at Atlanta University resisted even Susan B. Anthony's exhortations to join the cause; see Aiken; Bacote, *Atlanta University*, p. 247.

52. DuBois supported the suffrage question (all suffrage questions) chiefly through his editorship of *The Crisis*, which had a progressive women's section and ran a series on the woman suffrage debate between 1910 and 1915; Mrs. Booker T. Washington is quoted from "Club Work Among Negro Women," in J. W. Gibson, J. L. Nichols, and W. H. Crogman, eds., *Progress of the Race* (Naperville, Ill.: J. L. Nichols, 1920, reprinted New York: Arno Press, 1969), p. 193.

53. The complexities of black attitudes toward woman suffrage have not received full and fair scholarly treatment, as have not the racial attitudes of the movement in the South. Most works on suffrage in the South tend to avert race as an important factor in the women's arguments and activities, as do the only three scholarly pieces on the movement in Georgia. See A. Elizabeth Taylor, "The Origin of the Woman Suffrage Movement in Georgia," *Georgia Historical Quarterly* 28 (June 1944): 63-79, "The Revival and Development of the Woman Suffrage Movement in Georgia," *Georgia Historical Quarterly* 42 (December 1958): 339-54, and "The Last Phase of the Woman Suffrage Movement in Georgia," *Georgia Historical Quarterly* 43 (March 1959): 11-27.

54. The comments that follow are based on an extensive study of the Chautauqua Circle for its first thirty years of existence and a study of the first thirty years of the Atlanta Chapter of the DAR. Records consulted included the Chautauqua Circle Papers, Atlanta University; [NSDAR, Atlanta Chapter], *Atlanta Chapter D.A.R., April 15, 1891-April 15, 1921* (Atlanta?, n.d.), [DAR], *Proceedings*, Fourth State Conference, 1902, Georgia D.A.R. [in] Atlanta (n.p., n.d.), and Mrs. Samuel Scott (Mary Trammell), "The Atlanta Chapter: A History," *American Monthly* 21 (July-December 1902): 34-37.

55. The most recent assessment of the race relations of the DAR is Anderson, *The Daughters*, which is neither unduly critical nor overly generous, see esp. pp. 109-54.

56. Davies, *Patriotism on Parade*, p. viii.

57. These figures were given by Mrs. Luther L. Watson, State Regent, in an interview with Betty Garner on *Forum*, April 21, 1975, Georgia ETV, Channel 8, in a program entitled "The Modern Day DAR."

58. In the early 1940s, the circle dropped its self-education program in favor of a speakers' series; from then on, members gave an occasional inspirational message to the circle and book reviews, but not papers.

59. The two DAR chapter houses are discussed in more detail in Chapter 5; reference to a Chautauqua house is made in "Prophecy of the Chautauqua Circle," by Claudia White Harreld, on the occasion of the twenty-fifth anniversary of the circle in 1938, p. 8, Chautauqua Circle Papers.

60. From a speech by Mrs. Luke Johnson, quoted in "History of Woman's Work in the CIC," undated, unsigned manuscript, ASWPL Papers, Atlanta University, p. 12.

61. Quoted from Charlotte Hawkins Brown, ibid., p 17; see also, CIC, *Proceedings*, October 8, 1931, Atlanta, Georgia, p. 6, CIC Papers, Atlanta University.

62. The importance of these early personal contacts should not be underestimated, as small circles of interest and influence widened into larger circles. For example, Mary Dickinson was Rosa Lowe's successor in the Atlanta Anti-TB Association; Lowe had first hired black nurses to treat cases of TB, and had enlisted both Mrs. Hope's Neighborhood Union plan and Mrs. Hope herself in carrying much of the organizational burden for the educational campaign among blacks. Both Lowe and Dickinson were present at the formation of the Atlanta School of Social Work, and Dickinson later served on the Women's Committee of the Georgia CIC. See Mary Dickinson, "Report of Race Relationships as Illustrated by the Atlanta Anti-Tuberculosis Association," presented at the conference of the Southern Methodist Church, Memphis, Tennessee, October 6-7, 1920, ASWPL Papers; list, "Local Leaders and Members of the Georgia Committee of 1929," Neighborhood Union Papers; Jesse O. Thomas, *My Story in Black and White* (New York: Exposition Press, 1967), p. 120.

63. The definitive work on the ASWPL is Jacquelyn Dowd Hall, *Revolt Against Chivalry: Jessie Daniel Ames and the Women's Campaign Against Lynching* (Columbia University Press, 1979).

64. Mrs. Ames made a conscious decision to keep the women separated from the men in the CIC; see, for example, Ames to Mrs. J. W. Downs, October 14, 1930 [on the occasion of the appointment of an all-male CIC lynching investigation committee], in which she says, "My long years in public life have brought me to the realization that when there seems no direct contribution to the work in hand that a woman can make, the appointment of her merely as a recognition of her sex is a mockery." The barriers to cooperation between the blacks and whites, of which Mrs. Ames was fully aware, and her belief in the special role white women had to play against lynching that was defended as an extralegal protection of southern white womanhood, are spelled out in ibid., pp. 139-43.

65. The patterns of progression through various organizations is traced by Hall, who, along with Anne Scott in an earlier work, has determined the central importance of the YWCA in the interracial movement among southern women. Research here, for example, shows Mrs. Archibald Davis dropping out of the Atlanta DAR and becoming active in interracial affairs of the Presbyterian church and the YWCA. She was president of the Atlanta Central YWCA during the turbulent days when the Phyllis Wheatley Branch was established. See ibid., pp. 139-143; Scott, "After Suffrage, Southern Women in the Twenties," *Journal of Southern History* 30 (August 1964): 307; Mrs. Davis was traced through DAR records, ASWPL records, and YWCA records.

66. Jessie Daniel Ames, letter to Miss [?] Campbell, July 9, 1930, ASWPL Papers; "Condensed Minutes of the CIC, 1932" [Women's Division], and "Minutes, Membership Committee, CIC, at Atlanta, September 21, 1929," Neighborhood Union Papers, passim.

67. Breckinridge notes the development of adult education among rural women as one of the four major post-World War I movements in women's organizations; though it developed much earlier in the South. See *Women in the Twentieth Century*, p. 43.

68. Mrs. Booker T. Washington, "Club Work Among Negro Women," p. 182; Mrs. A. W. Hunton, "Women's Clubs," *Crisis* 7 (May 1911): 17.
69. Memoranda re John Slater Fund and Jeanes Foundation, correspondence between Mrs. Hope and Mrs. Washington re the Rosenwald Fund, and letter, Booker T. Washington to Mrs. Hope, October 29, 1914, re the Rosenwald Fund's unsuitability for settlement work, in Neighborhood Union Papers.
70. Information compiled from Georgia Federation of Women's Clubs, *Yearbooks, 1925-26*; Georgia Federation, "Program," April 27, 1938, and scrapbooks in Nellie Peters Black Papers; Whitehurst, *Georgia Federation*, pp. 2-14; Georgia Library Club [*Proceedings*], First Annual Meeting, Macon, Georgia, October 28-29, 1897 and Carnegie Library *Bulletin* 1 (November 1902), in Special Collections, Atlanta Public Library.
71. Interview with Mrs. Arthur Merrill by Mildred Seydell, Hearst's *Sunday American*, February 22, 1925.
72. Emily C. McDougald to Clara Savage, Press Chairman, National American Woman's Suffrage Association, January 29, 1915, League of Women Voters Papers.
73. Tom Watson is quoted but unnamed in a typescript entitled "Stories of Agricultural Rallies" in Nellie Peters Black Papers, and copies of his original diatribes in *The Jeffersonian* are pasted in her scrapbooks.
74. Nellie Peters Black, Address to Southern Conference of Education and Industry, Charleston, undated manuscript, Nellie Peters Black Papers.

CHAPTER FOUR

1. There is no full-length biography of Nellie Black, and though she was undoubtedly the most important organizational woman of her time in Georgia, she was not listed in *Notable American Women*; on her life, see Barbara B. Reitt, ed., *Georgia Women: A Celebration* (Atlanta: Atlanta Chapter, AAUW, 1976), pp. 29-29; [Mrs. J. Mac Barber, ed.], *Historic Georgia Mothers, 1776-1976* (Atlanta: Georgia Mothers Association, 1976), pp. 22-23; Nellie Peters Black Papers; Mrs. Black is also listed in Mrs. Collier's *Representative Women of the South*, and several local who's who compilations; on her father, see Garrett, *Atlanta and Environs*, 1 and 2, passim.
2. Georgia Federation of Women's Clubs, *Nellie Peters Black: Pioneer, 1851-1919* (n.p., n.d. [1941], unpaginated), see section entitled "Club Activities and Other Civic Positions."
3. Ella May Thornton, *Georgia Women, 1840-1940: A Record of Achievement* (Atlanta: n.p., 1941), p. 8.
4. Scott, "After Suffrage," p. 300.
5. No biography is available on Mrs. Butler; information here was compiled from various sources where her name appeared; Neighborhood Union Papers, Chautauqua Circle Papers, and ASWPL Papers; "Phyllis Wheatley YWCA, A

Historical Sketch," typescript (copy in Archives, Atlanta University); Carter, *Black Side*, pp. 29-30; Davis, *Lifting as They Climb*, pp. 129-30; Read, *Spelman College*, pp. 90, 108, 121, 132, 161. Her husband is listed in Joseph S. Boris, ed., *Who's Who in Colored America* (New York: Who's Who in Colored America Publishers, 1927). See also, Georgia Congress of the Colored PTA, *Founder, The Georgia Congress* (published by the Congress, 1971), passim; "Through the Years," the 51st Annual Convention (Columbus, Georgia, 1971); and *Golden Anniversary History* (published by the Congress, 1971), pp. 17-18.

6. For example, Mr. Butler had personal property assessed at $4,415 in 1920; this did not include, of course, his medical practice. Information from Timothy J. Crimmins, History Department, Georgia State University.

7. The information on the women was kept on McBee Keysort cards—one card per woman, and a simple coding system was devised to retrieve the information on each one. After all the information had been entered and coded on the cards, and the cards punched, the cards were then hand sorted and the data tallied according to whatever category of information was being sought.

8. The complete breakdown was this: 184 women—one decade, 131 women—two decades, forty-three women—three decades, twenty-two women—four decades, and three women—five decades of service.

9. Names from [NSDAR, Atlanta Chapter], *Atlanta Chapter, D.A.R.*, April 15,1891-April 15, 1921 (n.p., n.d.), passim.

10. Compiled from Programs and Minute Books, Chautauqua Circle Papers.

11. Hearst's *Sunday American*, June 5, 1927.

12. *In Memoriam: Emily Hendree Park, 1848-1910* (Athens, Ga.: The McGregor Co., 1911), pp. 40, 41.

13. Mrs. J. W. Gholston, quoted in Georgia Federation of Women's Clubs, *Yearbook, 1935-36*, p. 38.

14. This was Mrs. Z. I. Fitzpatrick, whose zeal for federation activities carried her all the way to national office; see Georgia Federation of Women's Clubs, *Directory, 1914-1915* (published by the Federation), p. 21.

15. Mary Raoul Millis, *The Family of Raoul: A Memoir* (privately printed, 1943), pp. 101, 118.

16. Interview, Atlanta *Journal*, December 7, 1930.

17. Ruth Reed, "The Negro Woman of Gainesville, Georgia" *Bulletin of the University of Georgia* 22 (December 1921), p. 22.

18. Chautauqua Circle, Minute Book 2, February 19, 1926, p. 110.

19. Ibid., Minute Book 3, November 19, 1937 and August 16, 1940.

20. Information compiled from Chautauqua Circle Papers, from miscellaneous Inquirers Papers, Atlanta University; members' names of the Junior Matrons provided by Mrs. Josephine Dibble Murphy, interview, July 26, 1974; Atlanta University, *General Catalogue, 1867-1929* (Atlanta: Atlanta University Press, 1929), passim; local and black history sources as listed in the bibliography.

21. Chautauqua Circle, Minute Book 2, meeting held September 9, 1932; minutes on loose manuscript placed in the book.

22. The University of Georgia integrated sexually in 1916; Georgia Tech—like Emory—did not integrate until after World War I.
23. All the names were checked in the special Atlanta census of 1896, where some of the ages were undoubtedly understated, but allowing for several years in understatement, the average age would still have fallen in the 40s for the board and in the 20s for the newspaper committee, see Atlanta Census, 1896, microfilm, Emory University.
24. Lee, "Georgia's Population."
25. See Joseph W. Newman, "The Social Origins of Atlanta's Teachers, 1881, 1896, 1922," *Urban Education* 11 (April 1976), pp. 115-22, and Timothy J. Crimmins, "The Crystal Stair: A Study of the Effects of Class, Race, and Ethnicity on Secondary Education in Atlanta, 1872-1925" (Ph.D. dissertation, Emory University, 1972), where the downturn is evident by decreasing numbers of the upper-class students.

CHAPTER FIVE

1. Blaine Brownell, "The Urban Mind in the South: The Growth of Urban Consciousness in Southern Cities, 1920-1927" (Ph.D. dissertation, University of North Carolina, Chapel Hill, 1969), pp. 5, 8, 15.
2. Ibid., p. 189.
3. See H. Blair Rouse, "Time and Place in Southern Fiction," in Louis D. Rubin, Jr., and Robert D. Jacobs, eds., *Southern Renasence: The Literature of the Modern South* (Baltimore: Johns Hopkins Press, 1953), pp. 126-50.
4. Ellen Glasgow, *The Woman Within* (New York: Harcourt, Brace, 1954), p. 195; Ellen Glasgow, *Barren Ground* (New York: Sagamore Press, 1957 [1925]), p. v.
5. Katherine Du Pre Lumpkin, *The Making of a Southerner* (New York: Alfred A. Knopf, 1947), p. 239.
6. And fundamental to its literary theories. For a recent assessment of the complexities of the most famous southern stand against New York and all it represented, see Edward Shapiro, "The Southern Agrarians and the Tennessee Valley Authority," *American Quarterly* 22 (Winter 1970): 791-806.
7. Glasgow, *Woman Within*, p. 195.
8. Nella Larsen, *Quicksand*, published in 1928.
9. Roger Whitlow, *Black American Literature: A Critical History* (Totowa, N.J.: Littlefield, Adams, 1974), pp. 92-96.
10. For example: "You needn't be surprised to see me safely back in Atlanta any day—I don't believe I was born to live in this great city [New York]. But of course if I go back to Atlanta everyone of any consequence will immediately come up here." From a letter to Frank Daniel, New York, Aug. 31, 1925, reprinted in Hansell Baugh, ed., *Letters of Frances Newman*; in a somewhat less personal and less confident tone: ". . . the moment, fatally, that our youths and

maidens [of Atlanta] suspect themselves of being promising, they offer themselves up in the labyrinth of New York and become more or less respectable journalists instead of profiting by the example of those eminent novelists who have remained where they had roots, instead of going away to become intellectual air plants." From "Atlanta," *The Reviewer*, January 1923, p. 733. It would be fascinating to know whom she had in mind.

11. Robert Herrick, *Together* (New York: Fawcett Publications, 1962 [New York: Macmillan, 1908]), p. 155.

12. Ellen Glasgow, *Voice of the People* (Upper Saddle River, N.J.: Literature House/Gregg Press, 1969 [New York: Doubleday, 1904]), pp. 111, 223-24.

13. Needless to say, Newman did not publish these remarks in a local Atlanta newspaper or magazine. Quoted from "Atlanta," *The Reviewer* (January 1923): 727. This article is almost the only self-conscious piece of prose written by a female author about Atlanta during this time. Others, mostly exuding "the Atlanta Spirit" or in other ways self-congratulatory, appear in the newspapers, in published volumes of poetry, and in the historical journal, which began publishing after 1926.

14. See Newman, *Letters*. For example: to A. B. Bernd, Atlanta, February [?] 1925, "I can stand being called no lady much more cheerfully than I can stand being called a fool" (p. 162); and to Mrs. Oscar (Mable) Gieberich, [Atlanta], November 30, [1926], concerning *Hard-Boiled Virgin*, "Atlanta . . . is shocked almost to convulsions over it, and I haven't a particle of character left. Lots of people apparently think I have done everything in it" (p. 229).

15. See Frank Durham, ed., *The Collected Short Stories of Julia Peterkin* (Columbia, S.C.: University of South Carolina Press, 1970). Durham cites several instances of Peterkin being blackballed by women's groups in the introduction to this collection.

16. Finis Farr, *Margaret Mitchell of Atlanta* (New York: Avon Books, 1965), pp. 15, 71, 72. Too much could be read into this incident, for Mitchell's loathing of public view is legendary.

17. Newman, *Letters*, p. 56.

18. Glasgow, *Woman Within*, pp. 42, 187.

19. Corra Harris, *As A Woman Thinks* (Boston: Houghton Mifflin, 1925), pp. 170-71, italics added. It is pertinent to this discussion to add that Corra Harris used Rebecca Latimer Felton as the model for her heroine in *Co-Citizens*, a feminist book of sorts. Felton, who was a politician manquee, a journalist, writer, public speaker, and spokeswoman on many issues, was never a good clubwoman. She associated with many groups, but did not hold offices. In this respect she represents more the individualistic position Harris is touting than the collective experience of the organizational types.

20. See Zora Neale Hurston, *Dust Tracks on the Road* (Philadelphia: J. B. Lippincott, 1942), p. 175 and passim.

21. Grace King, *Memoirs of a Southern Woman of Letters* (Freeport, N.Y.: Books for Libraries, 1971), pp. 56, 190, 211, 386.

22. James, *Notable American Women*, 2: 603.

23. Josephine Woodward, "Woman's Clubs from a Reporter's Point of View," *The Club Woman* 3 (December 1898), reprinted in William L. O'Neill, *The Woman Movement: Feminism in the United States and England* (Chicago: Quadrangle Press, 1971), pp. 146, 147.

24. Atlanta Woman's Club, Bulletin, 1920; Atlanta Federation of Woman's Clubs, *Annual Report*, 1927-29, p. 19.

25. This point was first discussed in Darlene Roth-White, "Atlanta Is a Female Noun: Evidence of City-Building Among Women," paper and tour given at the annual meeting of the American Historical Association, December 1975, in Atlanta, Georgia.

   Questions of women's relationships to environment, space, and architecture are new concerns in women's studies and not well defined. One rising authority in the field, Gwendolyn Wright, has made several observations that are relevant here. First: for whatever reason, women have apparently been more functional in their approach to the architectural profession itself—less ostentatious, more user-oriented than artist-oriented. This approach, existing at all levels of the practice of the craft, might help to explain the apparent lack of artistic concerns in some of the structures studied here. Second: female architects have often developed themselves professionally by cultivating women's groups as their special clients. Unfortunately, there are not enough records to make this case in Atlanta. The only instance of a female architect being used self-consciously by a women's group was for the design of the Woman's Building at the 1895 Exposition. Wright's comments on functionalist approaches seem to pertain, but the involvement with female architects may not. See G. Wright, "On the Fringe of the Profession: Women in American Architecture," (1975), xerox of typescript in possession of the author.

26. Garrett, *Atlanta and Environs*, 2: 410-11.

27. Otto Wilson with Robert Waller Barrett, *Fifty Years Work With Girls, 1883-1933: A Story of the Florence Crittenden Home* (Alexandria, Va.: by the Crittenden Association, 1933), p. 207.

28. Ibid., pp. 207-11, 162-65. It is probably more than an "oversight" that the Florence Crittenden Home was not listed in the early city directories. It was listed in 1910, but not 1900 or 1890.

29. Still the best, and for some purposes the only, source on settlement houses in Atlanta is Anne Lavinia Branch, "Atlanta and the American Settlement House Movement" (master's thesis, Emory University, 1966). Addresses for all of the organizations listed here were traced through Atlanta city directories.

30. "Neighborliness" was given as the intent of the Neighborhood Union's activities by one of its former members in an interview with Vivian Washington, student at Atlanta University; see Washington, "The Activities of Black Women as Seen in the Atlanta *Daily World* and Other Related Sources, 1931-1933" (seminar paper), p. 17; the point about self-help is emphasized in Lerner, "Community Work of Black Club Women."

31. On the Jews in Atlanta, see Solomon Sutker, "The Jews of America: Their Social Structure and Leadership Patterns" (Ph.D. dissertation, University of North

Carolina at Chapel Hill, 1950); Sutker has described the use of leadership positions in the Jewish welfare and community organizations actually to draw social distinctions and to create a strategic elite in the community; see "The Jewish Organizational Elite in Atlanta," *Social Forces* 31 (December 1952): 136-43.

32. John P. Rousmaniere, "Cultural Hybrid in the Slums: The College Woman and the Settlement House, 1889-1894," *American Quarterly* 22 (Spring 1970): 45-66.

33. This close and complex relationship is discussed by Donald I. Warren, who also concludes that close neighborhood linkage is one essential difference between the voluntary associationalism of whites and of blacks, except for white females between the ages of thirty and fifty-nine, whose ratio is fairly consistent with that of black females in the same age group. This is a contemporary analysis of neighborhood linkage, but the research here indicates some lines of historical validity to these conclusions. See Donald I. Warren, "The Linkage between Neighborhood and Voluntary Association Patterns: A Comparison of Black and White Urban Populations," *The Journal of Voluntary Action Research* 3 (April 1974): 1-14.

34. Garrett, *Atlanta and Environs*, 2: 481-82. The Hebrew Orphanage was not a woman's organization, so it might be disqualified from discussion here. It was a community group with a mixed staff and an all-male board. However, there was no orphanage run exclusively by the women, and this one received much support from the Jewish women's clubs.

35. Read, *Spelman College*, pp. 214, 274.

36. Atlanta city directories, 1890, 1900, 1930; Garrett, *Atlanta and Environs*, 2: 632; Miller, *Atlanta*, p. 83; Atlanta Federation of Women's Clubs, [*Yearbook*], 1929-31, pp. 30, 52.

37. Wilson, *Fifty Years*, p. 165.

38. Carter, *Black Side*, pp. 35-37.

39. "The City," *Atlanta* 12 (January 1973): 26, 28, 30, describes the Our Lady of Perpetual Help Free Cancer Home, run by the Hawthorne Dominican Sisters, which occupied the Hebrew Orphans Home building from 1939 until it was demolished to make way for a modern facility (ca. 1974). According to this article, the Free Cancer Home had forty beds.

40. Ragland (Mrs. Oscar), "The Atlanta Tuberculosis Association," p. 258.

41. Read, *Spelman College*, p. 274, "Miss [Amy C.] Chadwick [the director] made the orphanage truly a home for the Negro girls admitted to her care—a home to which they returned for visits and advice and encouragement long after they had jobs or homes of their own."

42. Atlanta Federation of Women's Clubs, [*Yearbook*], 1929-31, p. 30.

43. Louise Black MacDougald, "Holy Innocents Mission," *Atlanta Historical Bulletin* 4 (July 1939): 170; photograph of the mission, Nellie Peters Black Papers.

44. Atlanta *City Directory*, 1900.

45. Atlanta City Directories, 1900, 1910, 1920; early meeting notice and roster, League of Women Voters Papers. Darlene R. Roth-White, "Atlanta Is a Female

Noun," paper presented at the American Historical Association meeting, December 1975, pp. 4-5.

46. Whitehurst, *Georgia Federation*, pp. 10, 12.

47. Atlanta City Directories, 1900-1930; Darlene Roth-White, "The Atlanta YWCA: An Inquiry and A Commemoration," copy of typescript in DRR files. The "oldest" extant YWCA building still standing in its original form and location is the Phyllis Wheatley Branch building, which dates from 1950.

48. Quoted in Clarence A. Bacote, "Some Aspects of Negro Life in Georgia, 1880-1908," *Journal of Negro History* 43 (July 1958): 203.

49. Talmadge, *Rebecca Latimer Felton*, p. 111; [United Daughters of the Confederacy, Atlanta Chapter], *History Atlanta Chapter United Daughters of the Confederacy 1897-1922* (n.p., n.d.), unpaginated, see section entitled "Gift Scholarships."

50. Whitehurst, *Georgia Federation*, pp. 2, 4-5; Carnegie Library, *Bulletin* 1 (November 1902): 11.

51. [Mrs. Arch Brantley], "Tallulah Falls School Report, 1923-1924" (published by the Georgia Federation of Women's Clubs), passim.

52. See, for example, Mildred Marshall Scouller, *Women Who Man Our Clubs* (Philadelphia: John C. Winston, 1934), pp. 87-89; the entry describing Mrs. Z. I. Fitzpatrick of Georgia is an open invitation to "sister" federations to share in the Tallulah Falls work.

53. Harnett Kane, *Miracle in the Mountains: The Story of Martha Berry* (Garden City, N.Y.: Doubleday, 1956); Anne Firor Scott, "Martha Berry," *Notable American Women*, 1: 137-38.

54. All of the discussion here pertaining to the National Society of the Daughters of the American Revolution owes much to Anderson, *The DAR*, esp. pp. 187-224.

55. Leita Thompson, *A History of the Georgia Federation of Business and Professional Women's Clubs, Inc., May 1919-May 1956, Inclusive* (n.p., [1957]), p. 4; Atlanta Federation of Women's Clubs, [*Yearbook*], 1929-31, pp. 22-23; Georgia Federation of Women's Clubs, *Yearbook*, 1925-26, passim; Young Matrons' Circle for Tallulah Falls School, *Yearbook*, 1971-72, passim.

56. Anderson, *The DAR*, pp. 199-200; Georgia Federation, *Yearbook*, 1925-26, pp. 111-14; conversation with Eliot Wigginton, editor of *Foxfire*, April 13, 1976.

57. Anderson, *The DAR*, pp. 199, 203; Georgia Federation, *Yearbook*, 1925-26, pp. 49, 78, passim. The year 1925-26 was the jubilee year of the federation, and the annual convention took place on the grounds of the Tallulah Falls School, so the school was very much in evidence in all of the proceedings that year. In addition, the expansion program of the school, which more than doubled its facilities, had just been finished. The women were celebrating quite a bit that year.

58. Clarinda Pendleton Lamar, *A History of the National Society of Colonial Dames of America from 1891 to 1933* (Atlanta: Walter W. Brown, 1934), p. 30.

59. Lucian Lamar Knight, Foreword to Mrs. Bryan Wells Collier, *Biographies of Representative Women of the South* (n.p., [1928?]), Volume 4 (1861-1927), p. 17.

60. Lamar Trotti, " 'The Light in the Mountains': Tallulah Falls School for Mountain Children, Tallulah Falls, Georgia: An S.O.S. Call From Americans to Americans for Americans," printed in Georgia Federation, *Yearbook*, 1925-26, p. 3.

61. While black women were not permitted to be a part of the support system for the mountain schools, they were themselves keenly aware of the deteriorating conditions for blacks in rural areas of the South and concerned about rural-urban cooperation in their club programs. Certainly, Charlotte Hawkins Brown's Palmer Institute, founded on the "farm life" idea, might be considered an institutional response to those problems that was similar in some ways to what the other women were doing. See International Library of Negro Life and History, *Historical Negro Biographies* (New York: Publishers Co., 1967), p. 167.

62. [Mrs. Arch Brantley?], "Dedication Exercises," Georgia Federation of Women's Clubs, *Yearbook*, 1925-26, p. 14.

63. Breckinridge, *Women in the Twentieth Century*, pp. 43, 82.

64. Ibid., p. 11.

65. Margaret Gibbs, *The DAR* (New York: Holt, Rinehart, and Winston, 1969), pp. 63-66.

66. "The Atlanta Chapter," NSDAR, *Chapter Histories*; NSDAR, *Atlanta Chapter, D.A.R.*, pp. 8-12.

67. Atlanta Woman's Club, *Yearbook*, 1970-1972, pp. 13, 15; Ada Biehl, "Do You Remember," *Biennial Report*, 1966-68, *Officers*, 1968-70 (Atlanta Woman's Club), pp. 44-51; Hornady, *Atlanta*, p. 367; Elizabeth M. Sawyer and Jane Foster Matthews, *The Old in New Atlanta* (Atlanta: JEMS Publications, 1976), p. 6.

68. *History Atlanta Chapter, UDC*, unpaginated, about page 5 of the narrative; city directories, 1930, 1940, 1960.

69. Carmichael, *Daughters of the American Revolution*, pp. 9, 20-22.

70. Ida Clyde Clarke, ed., *Women of 1924, International* (New York: Women's News Service, 1924), p. 6; Clarke estimated that there were already more than 2,500 clubhouses in the country at that time.

71. Georgia Federation of Women's Clubs, *Yearbook*, 1924-25, pp. 78-81, 87, 91, 179, 194, and passim.

72. A total of seventy-nine of 156 clubs listed were counted as having clubhouses; Ibid., 1935-36, pp. 46, 50, 61, 68, 74-75, 86, 96, 103, and passim.

73. Location was not the only problem for the branch; see YWCA records, Neighborhood Union Papers; on Y properties, see Margaret Richards, "History—Atlanta Y.W.C.A.," [1932], copy of typescript in DRR files, pp. 9-13.

74. Mrs. Kemper Herreld, "Address," on the occasion of the 25th anniversary of the Chautauqua Circle, 1938, Chautauqua Circle Papers.

75. Historic marker lists Mrs. Geneva Haugabrooks, Chairman, Executive Board, and these local clubs as supporters of the house: Friendly Neighborhood Garden Club, Blue Bird Circle, Bonton Civic Club, Federated Girls Clubs, Local Graduate Nurses, Chautauqua Circle, Twelve Travelers, Business and Professional Women, Loyal Workers, Pittman Savings Club, L.C.B., For Get Me Not, High Pride Floral Club, and The Religion Committee.

76. The Mt. Vernon Ladies Association of the Union, "Mt. Vernon, Virginia," circular issued at the site, [1964]; Clifford Lord, *Keepers of the Past* (Chapel Hill: University of North Carolina Press, 1965), pp. 193-202; historic preservation seems to be following the pattern of the early charities; it is being expanded and professionalized while amateur efforts, such as the early ones, are discouraged, left behind, and/or go unrecorded.

77. Garrett, *Atlanta and Environs*, 1: 903, 2: 905; Atlanta Ladies Memorial Association Papers, Atlanta Historical Society.

78. *History Atlanta UDC*, passim.

79. The other monument is a marble drinking fountain in the State Capitol, placed there by the Georgia Equal Suffrage Association and the WCTU in honor of the "Mother of Suffrage" in Georgia, Mary Latimer McLendon.

80. NSDAR, *Chapter Histories*, passim; NSDAR, *Atlanta Chapter*, pp. 8-11, 15, 21-23; James B. Nevin, ed., *Prominent Women of Georgia* (Atlanta: National Biographical Publishers, n.d.), entry for Mrs. William Lawson Peel; Lewis Barrington, *Historic Restorations of the Daughters of the American Revolution* (New York: Richard Smith, 1941), site #142; Nancy Hart reportedly entertained a British pillaging party during the war with "turkey, drinks, and buckshot," capturing the whole party in the process.

81. Hornady, *Atlanta*, p. 388; Ruth Blair, "Atlanta's Monuments," *Atlanta Historical Bulletin* 5 (October 1940): 275; the woman was Mrs. Livingston Mims, also responsible for introducing Christian Scientism to Atlanta.

82. Mrs. Joseph Madison High; see Garrett, *Atlanta and Environs*, 2: 480; NSDAR, *Chapter Histories*, p. 19; NSDAR, *Atlanta Chapter*, p. 13; the High Museum became the nucleus of the combination of cultural outlets now known as the Atlanta Memorial Arts Center, located on the same spot where Mrs. High's home stood.

83. Mrs. Samuel Dews Jones, president of the Service Star Legion in 1920 when the monument was erected; she is responsible for its presence, probably not for its ugliness. See Thornton, *Georgia Women*, p. 15.

84. Atlanta Federation of Women's Clubs, *Annual Report*, "President's Address," 1927-1929," p. 15, AFWC, [*Yearbook*], 1929-1931, p. 19, Mary B. Coppenheim, et al., *The History of the United Daughters of the Confederacy* (Raleigh, N.C.: Edwards & Broughton, n.d.), pp. 79ff; Augusta Wylie King, "The Atlanta Writers Club," *Atlanta Historical Bulletin* 6 (October 1941): 287-91; even the Girl Scouts got involved, see Hornady, *Atlanta*, p. 376.

85. Marker on tree in Piedmont Park, near the Peace Monument; the tree was planted in 1922 by the Atlanta Writers Club under the auspices of Chapter 18 of the UDC (Atlanta Chapter), the J. B. Gordon Camp of the Confederate Veterans, and the Lee/Roosevelt Spanish War Veterans.

86. Garrett, *Atlanta and Environs*, 2: 444, 533-34, 762; see also "The Winning of the Wren's Nest," appended to Julia Collier Harris, *The Life and Letters of Joel Chandler Harris* (Boston: Houghton Mifflin, 1918), p. 601.

87. Sulgrave Manor was the long-term project of the Colonial Dames; see Lamar, *History of NSCDA*, p. 144.
88. Mrs. Booker T. Washington in *Progress of the Race*, ed. Gibson et al. (Naperville, Ill., 1920), pp. 177-209, esp. p. 181: Cedar Hill is "now the property of the NACW and it will be used as a memorial to the memory of Mr. Douglass in the same sense, and with the same veneration as is true of Mt. Vernon, set aside by the national government to George Washington, the father of our country."
89. Atlanta Woman's Club, *Biennial Report*, 1966-68, pp. 46-48.
90. Roth-White, "Atlanta Is a Female Noun," p. 7; Garrett, *Atlanta and Environs*, 2: 901; see listing for Rosa Woodberry in Collier, *Representative Women*, Vol. 6.

Bibliography

AUTHOR'S NOTE

It has been more than twenty years since I started research for this project, more than a dozen since I taught my last course in women's history. The field of women's history has changed in many respects in these years, an intellectual and political movement that I have not been a part of for more than a decade. Though I see evidence of "matronage" around me in the organizations I now serve, the scene is very much changed professionally and academically. The vacuum that existed in repositories where women's manuscripts now reside has been filled; universities teach courses and have majors in the subject which was in those days suspect; and, important publications have emerged to fill a void on Atlanta topics. This bibliography represents the state of the art at the time this study was begun; it is still useful for the irreplaceable rare and fugitive women's organization material; it cannot be considered the last word on recent interpretive studies.

Darlene Rebecca Roth
Director of Programs and Collections,
Atlanta History Center
April 1994

PRIMARY SOURCES

Manuscript and Special Collections

Anderson, Constance Spalding (Mrs. Albert), Papers. Atlanta Historical Society.

Arkwright, Dorothy Colquitt (Mrs. Preston S.), Scrapbook. Atlanta Historical Society.

Association of Southern Women for the Prevention of Lynching Papers. Trevor Arnett Library, Atlanta University.

Atlanta Federation of Women's Clubs Collection. Atlanta Historical Society.

Atlanta Kindergarten Alumnae Club Collection. Atlanta Historical Society.

Atlanta Pioneer Women's Society Collection. Atlanta Historical Society.

Black, Nellie Peters (Mrs. George R.), Papers. Idah D. Little Library, Special Collections, University of Georgia.

_____. Letters. Manuscripts Division, Georgia Department of Archives and History.

_____. Papers. Atlanta Historical Society.

Brown, Harriett Johnson (Mrs. Elijah A.), Papers, Atlanta Historical Society.

Chautauqua Circle Papers. Trevor Arnett Library, Atlanta University.

Commission on Interracial Cooperation [Women's Division] Papers. Trevor Arnett Library, Atlanta University.

Cox College Papers. Manuscripts Division, Georgia Department of Archives and History.

Cox, Mrs. D. Mitchell, Scrapbooks. Atlanta Historical Society.

Equal Suffrage Party of Georgia Collection. Atlanta Historical Society.

Felton, Rebecca Latimer (Mrs. William H.), Papers. Idah D. Little Library, Special Collections, University of Georgia.

Genealogy Collections. Atlanta Public Library.

Georgia Collection. Atlanta Public Library.

Georgia Federation of Women's Clubs Collection. Atlanta Historical Society.

Girls' High School Collection. Atlanta Historical Society.

Harwood-Arrowood, Bertha, Collection. Atlanta Historical Society.

History Class of 1884 Collection. Atlanta Historical Society.

Huff, Sarah, Collection. Atlanta Historical Society.

The Inquirers, Miscellaneous Papers. Trevor Arnett Library, Atlanta University.

Junior League Records. Atlanta Historical Society.

Junior Matrons, Miscellaneous Records. [In private hands.]

Ladies Memorial Association Records, Atlanta Historical Society.

Lamar, Clarinda Pendleton (Mrs. Joseph R.), Collection. Atlanta Historical Society.

League of Women Voters Papers. Manuscripts Division, Georgia Department of Archives and History.

Mims, Sue Harper (Mrs. Livingston), Scrapbook. Atlanta Historical Society.
Needlework Guild Scrapbook. Atlanta Historical Society.
Neighborhood Union Papers. Trevor Arnett Library, Atlanta University.
Nineteenth Century Class Records. Atlanta Historical Society.
1900 Study Club Records. Atlanta Historical Society.
1908 History Class Collection. Atlanta Historical Society.
Paul, Emma V., Scrapbook. Atlanta Historical Society.
Rabun Gap-Nacoochee School Collection. Atlanta Historical Society.
Raoul Family Papers. Atlanta Historical Society.
Seydell, Mildred (Mrs. Paul), Papers. Special Collections, Woodruff Library, Emory University.
Spalding, Mary Connally (Mrs. John), Scrapbooks. Atlanta Historical Society.
United Daughters of the Confederacy Collection. Atlanta Historical Society.
Washington Seminary Collection. Atlanta Historical Society.
Williams Collection. Atlanta Public Library.
Wylie, Lollie Belle (Mrs. Hart), Collection. Atlanta Historical Society.
Young Matrons Circle for Tallulah Falls School Collection. Atlanta Historical Society.

Printed, Published, and Other Sources

Allen, Ivan. *Rotary in Atlanta: The First Twenty-Five Years, 1905-1939.* Atlanta: Darby Printing Co., n.d.
Alpha Delta Pi. *Pledge Book.* Published by the Sorority, 1965.
Alpha Delta Pi. *Welcome to Alpha Delta Pi Memorial Headquarters.* [Prepared by Carol Dorton (Mrs. William) Asher.] Published by the Sorority, n.d.
Ames, Jessie Daniel. *Southern Women and Lynching.* Revised and reprinted. Atlanta: Association of Southern Women for the Prevention of Lynching, October 1936.
Anderson, Mary Savage, comp. *A History of the Georgia Society of the Colonial Dames of America, from April 1893 to January 1950.* Revised from the first edition, published in 1937. Richmond, Va.: Whittet and Shepperson, n.d.
Annual Report of the Teachers and Pupils of the Capital Female College, 1892-1893. Atlanta: Franklin Printing and Publishing Co., 1894.
Ansley, Lula Barnes (Mrs. J. J.). *History of the Georgia W.C.T.U., 1883-1907.* Columbus, Ga.: Gilbert Publishing Co., 1914.

Atlanta Centennial Yearbook, 1837-1937. Atlanta: Gregg Murphy, 1937.

Atlanta City Directories. [*Williams Atlanta Directory, City Guide and Business Mirror, 1859-1860*] Atlanta: M. Lynch, 1859. [*Barnwell's Atlanta City Directory and Stranger's Guide.*] Atlanta: V. T. Barnwell (printed, Atlanta Intelligencer Book and Job Office), 1867, [*Hanleiter's Atlanta City Directory for 1870.*] Atlanta: William R. Hanleiter, Publisher, 1870. [*Beasley's Atlanta Directory for 1875.*] Atlanta: James W. Beasley, published by Southern Publishing Co., 1875. [*Sholes Directory of the City of Atlanta for 1877.*] *Atlanta City Directory.* Atlanta: R. L. Polk and Co., 1890. Atlanta: Foote and Davies Co., 1900. Atlanta: Atlanta City Directory Co., 1910, 1921, 1927, 1930, 1940.

Atlanta, City of. City Council and Chamber of Commerce. *Handbook of the City of Atlanta: A Comprehensive Review of the City's Commercial, Industrial, and Residential Conditions.* Atlanta: Southern Industrial Publishing Co., 1898 [?].

_____. Education Department. *Census*, 1896. Manuscript, Microfilm Division, Woodruff Library, Emory University.

_____. Education Department. *History of Girls' High, 1873-1938.* Atlanta: n.p., n.d.

Atlanta City Federation of Women's Clubs. *Announcement, 1908-1909.* Atlanta: Foote and Davies Co.

_____. *Calendar, 1916.* Atlanta: n.p.

_____. *Calendar, 1919-1920.* Decatur: Dennis Lindsey Printing Co.

_____. *Yearbook, 1920-1922.* Atlanta: n.p.

_____. *Yearbook, 1925-1927.* Atlanta: n.p.

_____. *Yearbook, May 1927-May 1929.* Atlanta: n.p.

_____. *Yearbook, May 1929-May 1931.* Atlanta: Keelin Press.

_____. *Yearbook, 1931-1933.* Atlanta: Ruralist Press, Inc.

_____. *Yearbook, May 1935-May 1937.* East Point, Ga.: Martin-Johnson Printing Co.

Atlanta Community Chest Agencies Statements of Organization and Purpose. Atlanta: Community Chest, November 1934. Typescript, Atlanta Public Library.

"Atlanta Has 20,000 More Women Than Men," *Atlanta Journal Magazine,* September 10, 1922, 7.

Atlanta Historical Society, "Roster of Membership, May 1, 1945." Typescript, Atlanta Public Library.

Atlanta Public Forum, arr. *An Introduction to Social Service Agencies in Atlanta*, 1938. Mimeograph, Atlanta Public Library.

Bischoff, Lillian M. "Jane van de Vrede, 1880-1972." Atlanta?: n.p., 1973. Xerox of pamphlet.

Blair, Ruth. *Georgia Women of 1926*. Atlanta: Georgia Department of Archives and History, 1926.

_____. "Rhodes Memorial Hall," *Atlanta Historical Bulletin* 6 (May 1930), 3-4.

_____. "Atlanta's Monuments," *Atlanta Historical Bulletin* 5 (October 1940), 273-77.

Blalock, Jess. "Social, Political and Economic Aspects of Race Relations in Atlanta, 1890-1908." Master's thesis, Atlanta University, 1969.

The Blue Book: A Social Register of Atlanta, Ga. Atlanta: B. G. Allen, 1932-1933.

Board of Commissioners Representing the State of New York. *Report of the Board at the Cotton States and International Exposition, Atlanta, Georgia.* New York: Wynkoop Hallnbeck Crawford Co., 1896.

Boatwright, Eleanor. "The Political and Civil Status of Women in Georgia, 1783-1860," *Georgia Historical Quarterly* 25 (December 1941), 301-24.

Bowlby, Elizabeth Catherine. "The Role of Atlanta During the Civil War." Master's thesis, Emory University, 1939.

Boykin, James C. "The Cotton States and International Exposition Held in Atlanta, Ga., September 19-December 31, 1895," *Education Report, 1894-95.* Washington, D.C.: U.S. Bureau of Education. Pp. 1735-56.

Boylston, Elise Reid. *Atlanta: Its Lore, Legends, and Laughter.* Doraville, Ga.: Foote and Davies, 1968.

Branch, Anne Lavinia. "Atlanta and the American Settlement House Movement." Master's thesis, Emory University, 1966.

Brittain, M. L., ed. *Semi-Centennial History of the Second Baptist Church of Atlanta, Georgia.* Atlanta: n.p., 1904.

Brown, Oswald Eugene and Anna Muse. *The Life and Letters of Laura Askew Haygood.* Nashville, Tenn.: Publishing House of the Methodist Episcopal Church, South, 1904.

Bryan, T. Conn. *Confederate Georgia.* Athens, Ga.: University of Georgia Press, 1953.

Business and Professional Women of Georgia. Atlanta: F. E. Johnson Publishing Co., 1931.

Caldwell, A. B., ed. *History of the American Negro, Georgia Edition*. Atlanta: A. B. Caldwell Publishing Co., 1920.

Candler, Allen D., and Clement A. Evans, eds. *Cyclopedia of Georgia*. Vol I: A-E. Vol. II: F-N. Vol. III: O-Z. Spartanburg, S.C.: The Reprint Co., 1972. (Atlanta: State Historical Association, 1906.)

Carmichael, Hattie Mae, ed. *Seventy-Five Years of the Joseph Habersham Chapter* [National Society Daughters of the American Revolution] *1900-1975*. Atlanta: published by the Society, n.d.

Carnegie Library. *Bulletin* 1 (November 1902).

Carter, Rev. E. R. *The Black Side: A Partial History of the Business, Religious, and Educational Side of the Negro in Atlanta, Ga.* Atlanta, Ga.: n.p., 1894.

Carter, Samuel, III. *The Siege of Atlanta, 1864*. New York: St. Martin's, 1973.

Chidsey, John N. "Statistical Study of Negro Churches in Georgia." Master's thesis, Emory University, 1932.

Clarke, E. Y. *Illustrated History of Atlanta*. Facsimile edition. Atlanta: Cherokee Publishing Co., 1971 [1877].

Cobb, Carolyn, C. S. G. "Sue Harper Mims, C. S. B.," *Atlanta Historical Bulletin* 14 (April 1939), 77-89.

Comments on the Cotton States and International Exposition, Atlanta, Georgia. 3 vols. Clipping scrapbooks of Pennsylvania news clippings. Atlanta Public Library.

Connally, Mrs. E. L. *Foundation Stones Upon Which the Baptist Women's Missionary Union of Georgia Is Built, Found in the Old Second Baptist Church of Atlanta, Georgia*. Atlanta: n.p., [1942].

Cooper, Walter G. *The Atlanta Cotton States and International Exposition and South, Illustrated*. Atlanta: n.p., 1896.

_____. *Official History of Fulton County*. Fulton County, Ga.: Historical Commission, 1934.

_____. *The Story of Georgia*. Biographical volume. New York: American History Society, Inc., 1938.

Copeland, Edna Arnold. *Nancy Hart: The War Woman*. Elberton, Ga.: Published by the author, 1950.

Cotton States and International Exposition. New York: New York *Observer* [Supplement], June 27, 1895.

Coulter, E. Merton. *A Short History of Georgia*. Chapel Hill: University of North Carolina Press, 1937.

Crimmins, Timothy J. "The Crystal Stair: A Study of the Effects of Class, Race, and Ethnicity on Secondary Education in Atlanta, 1872-1925." Ph.D. dissertation, Emory University, 1972.

Davis, Mary Roberts. "The Atlanta Industrial Expositions of 1881 and 1895." Master's thesis, Emory University, 1952.

Deaton, Thomas Mashburn. "Atlanta During the Progressive Era." Ph.D. dissertation, University of Georgia, 1969.

Dinnerstein, Leonard. "Atlanta in the Progressive Era: A Dreyfus Affair in Georgia," in Jaher, Frederic Cople, ed. *The Age of Industrialism in America: Essays in Social Structure and Cultural Values*. New York: The Free Press, 1968.

_____. *The Leo Frank Case*. New York: Columbia University Press, 1968.

Dodd, Rebecca F. "History of East Point, Georgia." Master's thesis, Georgia State University, 1971.

DuBois, W. E. B., ed. *Atlanta University Publications*. Vol. I: 1896-1901. Vol. II: 1902-1906. New York: Octagon Press, 1968. [Atlanta: Atlanta University Press, 1896-1906.]

Durett, Dan, and Dana F. White. *An-Other Atlanta: The Black Heritage*. Atlanta, The History Group, Inc., 1975.

Eaton, Clement. "Breaking a Path for the Liberation of Women in the South," *The Georgia Review* 28 (Summer 1974), 187-99.

Edwards, Kate Flournoy. "A College Girl in War-Time," *The Georgia Review* 1 (Summer 1947), 198-206.

English, Thomas H. *Emory University, 1915-1965: A Semi-Centennial History*. Atlanta: Emory University, 1966.

Fargason, Mrs. Leroy. [Formerly President, Atlanta Woman's Club.] Interview. May 23, 1973.

Farr, Finis. *Margaret Mitchell of Atlanta*. New York: Avon Books, 1965.

Fede, Frank J. "Urbanization in Georgia, 1860-1900." Master's thesis, Emory University, 1941.

Felton, Rebecca Latimer. *Country Life in Georgia in the Days of My Youth*. Atlanta: Index Publishing Co., 1911.

_____. *The Romantic Story of Georgia Women*. Atlanta: *Atlanta Georgian and Sunday American*, 1930.

First National Bank of Atlanta. *Atlanta Resurgens: The First Hundred Years of a City's Progress, Promise, and Philosophy*. Atlanta: First National Bank, 1971.

Flanagan, Herbert Livingston, Jr. "The Cotton States and International Exposition, 1895." Master's thesis, University of Georgia, 1950.

Frank, Thomas E. "Voluntary Associations and Urban Change: A History of Race Relations in the Atlanta Young Women's Christian Association." Seminary paper, Emory University, June 1975. In private hands.

Frazier, E. Franklin. "The Neighborhood Union in Atlanta," *Social Work* 52 (1923), 437-42.

Gaines, F. H. *The Story of Agnes Scott College, 1889-1921*. Atlanta?: n.p., n.d.

Garofalo, Charles. "Business Ideals in Atlanta, 1916-135." Ph.D. dissertation, Emory University, 1972.

Garrett, Franklin. *Atlanta and Environs*. 3 vols. Athens, Ga.: University of Georgia Press, 1969 [1954].

Georgia Congress of Colored Parents and Teachers. "Through the Years," Fifty-first Annual Convention, Columbus, Georgia, March 18-19, 1971. Published by the Congress.

_____. *Founder*. Published by the Congress, 1971.

_____. *Golden Anniversary History*. Published by the Congress, 1971.

Georgia Federation of Women's Clubs. [*Program*] First Annual Convention, Rome, Georgia, 1897. N.p., n.d.

_____. *Yearbook, 1908-1909*. Published by the Federation.

_____. *Directory, 1914-1915*.

_____. *Bulletin*, Nos. 1-3, Published by the Federation, 1917-1918.

_____. *Tallulah Falls School: Report, 1923-1924*. Published by the Federation.

_____. *Yearbook, 1924-1925*. Atlanta: Lester Book and Stationery Co.

_____. *Yearbook, 1925-1926*. [First Biennial Council and Jubilee Meeting, June 9-12, 1925, Tallulah Falls, Ga.] Published by the Federation.

_____. [*Program*, Thirty-first Annual Convention], Valdosta, Ga., 1934.

_____. *Yearbook, 1935-1936*. Atlanta: Lyon-Young Printing Co.

_____. *Directory*, 1921-1926; 1929-1943. Atlanta: The Federation.

_____. Student Aid Foundation. [Report], 1940-1941. Atlanta: By the Federation.

_____. *Yearbook, 1938-1939*; *1940-1941*. Atlanta: By the Federation.

_____. *Nellie Peters Black: Pioneer, 1851-1919*. N.p., [1941].

_____. "How to Organize Women's Clubs and How to Join." N.p., n.d. Pamphlet.

Georgia Historical Markers. Valdosta, Ga.: Bay Tree Grove Publishers, 1973.

Georgia Library Association. *Program of the 8th Annual Meeting*, Atlanta, Georgia, March 30-31, 1910.

Georgia Library Club. [*Proceedings*], First Annual Meeting, Macon, Georgia, October 28-29, 1897.

Georgia Press Reference Association. *Women of Georgia*. Atlanta: Byrd Publishing Co., 1927.

Georgia, State of. Department of Archives and History. *Georgia's Official Register*. Compiled by Ruth Blair. Atlanta: Stein Printers, State Printers, 1927.

_____. Secretary of State. Docket of Legislative Appearance. Vol. I: 1912; Vol. II: 1912, 1913-14, 1918, 1919, 1920, 1922, 1923, 1924, 1927, 1929. Handwritten, bound volumes.

_____. Board of Visitors, State College for Women. *Reports*, 1893, 1896, 1904, 1907, 1912, 1914.

Gordon, George Arthur. "Eleanor Kinzie Gordon: A Sketch," *Georgia Historical Quarterly* 1-2 (1917-1918), 179-97.

Hall, Jacquelyn Dowd. *Revolt Against Chivalry: Jessie Daniel Ames and the Women's Campaign Against Lynching*. New York: Columbia University Press, 1979.

_____. "Root of Bitterness: The Dynamic of Private Experience and Public Activity in the Life of Jessie Daniel Ames." Paper read before the Texas Historical Society, 1975.

Harris, Corra. *My Book and Heart*. Boston: Houghton Mifflin Co., 1924.

_____. *As A Woman Thinks*. Boston: Houghton Mifflin Co., 1925.

Harris, Julia Collier. *The Life and Letters of Joel Chandler Harris*. Boston: Houghton Mifflin Co., 1918.

Harris, Nathaniel. *Autobiography: The Story of an Old Man's Life and Reminiscences of Seventy-Five Years*. Macon, Ga.: The J. W. Burke Co., 1925.

[Harrison, Emily, comp.] *In Memoriam, Emily Hendree Park, 1848-1910*. Athens, Ga.: The McGregor Co., 1911.

Hebrew Orphan's Home Annual Report, 1929-1930. Atlanta: By the Association.

Herndon, Emmett. "Grady Hospital and New Directions in Health Care Delivery." Seminar paper, Emory University, June 1974.

Hill, Mozell C., and Bevode C. McCall. "Social Stratification in a Georgia Town," *American Sociological Review* 15 (December 1950).

Hills, Habersham. "Atlanta's Clubs and Club Life," *City Builder* 15 (September 1930).

Hollinshed, Leon. "Political, Educational, and Economic Aspects of the Atlanta Negro, 1880-1895." Master's thesis, Atlanta University, 1971.

Hopkins, Richard J. "Patterns of Persistence and Occupational Mobility in a Southern City: Atlanta, 1870-1920." Ph.D. dissertation, Emory University, 1972.

_____. "Status, Mobility, and the Dimensions of Change in a Southern City: Atlanta, 1870-1910," in Kenneth T. Jackson and Stanley K. Schultz, eds., *Cities in American History*. New York: Alfred A. Knopf, 1972.

Hornady, John R. *Atlanta Yesterday, Today, and Tomorrow*. Atlanta: Index Publishing Co., 1922.

Huff, Sarah. *My Eighty Years in Atlanta*. Atlanta, 1937.

Jeanes Supervision in Georgia Schools, A Guiding Light in Education: A History of the Program from 1908-1975. [Atlanta]: Georgia Association of Jeanes Curriculum Directors in cooperation with the Southern Education Foundation, 1975.

Jennings, M. Kent. *Community Influentials: The Elites of Atlanta*. London: 1964.

Johnson, Amanda. *Georgia As Colony and State*. Atlanta: Walter W. Brown Publishing Co., 1938.

Johnson, Irene. "Some Factors Related to Participation in Voluntary Associations." Master's thesis, Atlanta University, 1952.

Jones, Charles Edgeworth. *Education in Georgia*. Washington, D.C.: U.S. Bureau of Education, 1889.

Jones, Eula. "Voluntary Associations in the Atlanta Community." Master's thesis, Atlanta University, 1952.

Jones, Mabel Maxwell. "Georgia and the P.T.A.," *The Georgia Review* 4 (Winter 1950), 346-52.

Junior League of Atlanta, Inc. *Cultural Atlanta at a Glance*. Atlanta: Foote and Davies, n.d.

_____. *Yearbook, 1972-1973*, 56th Annual Report. Atlanta: n.p.

Kane, Harnett T., with Inez Henry. *Miracle in the Mountains: The Story of Martha Berry*. Garden City: Doubleday and Co., Inc., 1956.

King, Augusta Wylie. "International Cotton Exposition, 1881," *Atlanta Historical Bulletin* 4 (1939), 181-98.

_____. "The Atlanta Writers Club," *Atlanta Historical Bulletin* 6 (October 1941), 287-91.

_____. "The Woman's Press Club of Georgia," *Atlanta Historical Bulletin* 7 (October 1938), 296-308.

Kuchler, Eula Turner. "Charitable and Philanthropic Activities in Atlanta During Reconstruction." Master's thesis, Emory University, 1942.

Knight, Lucian Lamar. *A Standard History of Georgia and Georgians.* Chicago: The Lewis Publishing Co., 1917.

Lamar, Clarinda Pendleton (Mrs. Joseph R.). *A History of the National Society of the Colonial Dames of America from 1891 to 1933.* Atlanta: Walter W. Brown Publishing Co., 1934.

Lamar, Dolly Blount. *When All Is Said and Done.* Athens: University of Georgia, 1952.

Lamar, Grace (Mrs. Walter D.). *The Vulnerability of the White Primary.* Macon, Ga.: Georgia Association Opposed to Woman Suffrage, n.d.

Lane, Mills. *The People of Georgia: An Illustrated Social History.* Savannah, Ga.: Beehive Press, ca. 1975.

Lerner, Gerda. "Early Community Work of Black Women," *Journal of Negro History* 59 (April 1974), 158-67.

List Committee of the Town and Country Foundation, comp., ed. *The Atlanta Civic, Social, and Cultural Register.* Atlanta: by the Foundation, 1957.

Lockerman, Doris. "Why They Remember Fiery Mrs. Peters," *Atlanta Journal Constitution Magazine*, February 19, 1967, p. 14.

Logan, M. G. "A Developmental History of the Gate City Day Nursery Association." Master's thesis, Atlanta University, 1955.

Lyon, Elizabeth Anne Mack. "Business Buildings in Atlanta: A Study in Urban Growth and Form." Ph.D. dissertation, Emory University, 1971.

MacDougald, Louise Black. "Holy Innocents Mission," *Atlanta Historical Bulletin* 4 (July 1939), 166-74.

_____. "A Trip Down Peachtree Street in 1886," *Atlanta Historical Bulletin* 5 (April 1940), 134-45.

Maddox, Dorothy. "Y.W.C.A. History." [1901-1955]. Mimeographed.

Malone, Alberta. "Churches on Peachtree Street in Atlanta, Georgia." 1957. Typewritten.

_____. "Location of Atlanta Churches." Undated. Typewritten.

Martin, Thomas H. *Atlanta and Its Builders: A Comprehensive History of the Gate City of the South.* 2 vols. Atlanta? Century Memorial Publishing Co., 1902.

Matthews, Antoinette Johnson. *Oakdale Road, Atlanta Georgia, Its History and Its People*. Atlanta: Atlanta Historical Society, 1972.

McBride, R. B., and R. S. McDonald, comps. *Atlanta of Today*. Atlanta: Review Publishing Co., 1897.

McCallie, Elizabeth H. "A Grand Ladies Fair," *Atlanta Historical Bulletin* 1 (February 1939), 35-41.

_____. "School Days in the 80s," *Atlanta Historical Bulletin* 1 (February 1939), 35-41.

McMahon, C. A. *The People of Atlanta: A Demographic Study of Georgia's Capital City*. Athens, Ga.: University of Georgia Press, 1950.

Meier, August, and David Lewis. "History of the Negro Upper Class in Atlanta, Georgia, 1890-1958," *Journal of Negro Education* 28 (Spring 1959), 128-39.

Mell, Mrs. Anthony White. "Obstacles to DAR Work in the South," *American Monthly* 11 (October 1897), 369.

Middleton, Merlissie Ross. "Residential Distribution of Members of an Urban Church." Unpublished Master's thesis, Atlanta University, 1953.

Miller, Paul W., ed. *Atlanta Capital of the South*. New York: Oliver Durrell, Inc., 1949.

Millican, Haviland Houston. Interview. February 14, 1974.

Millis, Mary Raoul. *The Family of Raoul: A Memoir*. Privately printed, 1943.

Mims, Gloria G. "A Biographical Account of a Black Atlanta: Carrie Steele Logan, Founder of the Carrie Steele Orphanage." 1974. Typescript, Atlanta University.

Mitchell, Gordon. "The Saturday Night Club, Founded 1893," *Atlanta Historical Bulletin* 6 (October 1941), 276-86.

Moseley, J. Edward. *Disciples of Christ in Georgia*. St. Louis, Mo.: The Bethany Press, 1954.

Mullins, Mildred Gregory. "Homefront Activities of Atlanta Women During World War I." Master's thesis, Emory University, 1947.

Murphy, Mrs. Josephine Dibble. Interview. July 20, 1973.

National Council of Jewish Women, Atlanta Section. *Yearbook, 1973-1974*. Atlanta: AAA Printing.

National Society, Colonial Dames of America [Georgia Society]. *Directory, 1927; 1938*. N.p.

_____. *Register of the Georgia Society, Colonial Dames of America*. Savannah, Ga.: Braid and Hutton, Inc., 1926.

_____. The National Historic Activities Committee. *A Summary of the Histories of the National Society of the Colonial Dames of America and of the Corporate Societies, 1891-1962*. By the Society, 1962.

National Society, Daughters of the American Revolution. Georgia DAR. *Proceedings*, Fourth State Conference, 1902, Atlanta. N.p.

_____. *Chapter Histories: Daughters of the American Revolution in Georgia, 1891-1931*. Augusta, Ga.: Ridgely-Tidwell, n.d.

_____. Atlanta Chapter. *Atlanta Chapter, D.A.R., April 14, 1891-April 14, 1921*. N.p., n.d.

_____. Joseph Habersham Chapter. *Golden Anniversary Book of Records*. N.p., n.d.

The Negro Business Directory and Commercial Guide of Atlanta. Atlanta: Atlanta Ad Agency, 1911.

Nevin, James B., ed. *Prominent Women of Georgia*. Atlanta: National Biographical Publishers, n.d.

Newman, Frances. "Atlanta," *The Reviewer* 3 (January 1923), 725-34.

Newman, J. W. "The Social Origins of Atlanta's Teachers," *Urban Education* 11 (April 1976), 115-22.

Nixon, Raymond B. *Henry W. Grady: Spokesman of the New South*. New York: Alfred A. Knopf, 1943.

Official Programme: Daily Events of the [Cotton States and International] Exposition, September 19-December 31, 1895. N.p.

Orr, Dorothy. *History of Education in Georgia*. Chapel Hill: University of North Carolina Press, 1950.

Partridge, Croom. "Mrs. E. L. Connally," *Atlanta Historical Bulletin* 6 (1942), 220-22.

Pattison, Mrs. Frank A. "The Relationship of the Woman's Club to the American City," *American City* (November 1909), 129-30.

Payne, J. C. "Atlanta Art Association," *City Builder* 12 (February 1928), 3-4.

Pierce, Alfred M. *A History of Methodism in Georgia: February 5, 1736-June 24, 1955*. Atlanta: The North Georgia Conference Historical Society, 1956.

Pioneer Citizens Society of Atlanta. *Pioneer Citizens' History of Atlanta, 1833-1902*. Atlanta: Byrd Printing Co., 1902.

Pradd, Tommie L. "A Study of Neighborhood Clubs of the Atlanta Urban League." Master's thesis, Atlanta University, 1939.

Ragland, Erminie (Mrs. Oscar). "The Founding of Atlanta Tuberculosis Association and the Home for Incurables," *Atlanta Historical Bulletin* 4 (October 1939), 256-62.

Ragsdale, Barton W. *The Story of Georgia Baptists*. Atlanta: Georgia Baptist Convention and Foote and Davies, 1932.

Read, Florence M. *The Story of Spelman College*. Princeton: Princeton University Press, 1961.

Read, John Shelton. "An Evaluation of an Anti-Lynching Organization," *Social Problems* 16 (Fall 1968), 172-82.

Reed, Ruth. "The Negro Women of Gainesville, Georgia," *Bulletin of the University of Georgia* 22 (December 1921). Phelps-Stokes Fellowship Studies, No. 6.

Reed, Wallace P., ed. *History of Atlanta, Georgia*. Syracuse, N.Y.: D. Mason and Co., 1889.

Reitt, Barbara B., ed. *Georgia Women: A Celebration*. Atlanta: American Association of University Women, 1976.

Richards, Margaret. "History—Atlanta Y.W.C.A." [1901-1955] Mimeographed.

Roberts, Mrs. McCord. "Atlanta Women's Club Featured as Model Club in National Magazine," *City Builder* 8 (August 1923), 52-54.

Romare, Mrs. Paul. "Women Who Once Labored in St. Phillips," *Atlanta Historical Bulletin* 6 (December 1930), 14-15.

Rothschild, Janice O. *As But A Day: The First Hundred Years, 1867-1967*. Atlanta: The Hebrew Benevolent Congregation, The Temple, 1967.

Roth-White, Darlene R. "Atlanta Is a Female Noun: Evidence of City-Building Among Women." Prepared for the meeting of the American Historical Association, December 1975.

_____. "Lifestyles In a 'New South' City." Prepared for the meeting of the Organization of American Historians, April 1977.

Russell, James Michael. "Atlanta, Gate City of the South, 1847 to 1885." Ph.D. dissertation, Princeton University, 1972.

Sawyer, Elizabeth M., and Jane Foster Matthews. *The Old in New Atlanta*. Atlanta: JEMS Publications, 1976.

Schultz, Gladys Denny, and Daisy Gordon Lawrence. *Lady from Savannah: The Life of Juliette Low*. Philadelphia: J. B. Lippincott Co., 1958. Produced and distributed by the Girl Scouts.

Scomp, H. A. *King Alcohol in the Realm of King Cotton: A History of the Liquor Traffic and of the Temperance Movement in Georgia from 1773 to 1887*. Atlanta?: The Blakely Printing Co., 1888.

Scott, Mrs. Samuel (Mary Trammell). "The Atlanta Chapter: A History," *American Monthly* 21 (July-December 1902), 34-37.

Shivery, Louie D. "History of Organized Social Work Among Atlanta Negroes, 1890-1935." Master's thesis, Atlanta University, 1936.

———. "The Neighborhood Union," *Phylon* 3 (1942), 149-62.

Slade, Dorothy. "The Evolution of Negro Areas in Atlanta." Master's thesis, Atlanta University, 1946.

Southeastern Council of the General Federation of Women's Clubs. *Program of 13th Annual Meeting.* N.p., 1935.

The Southeastern Fair Association, *General Rules and Regulations for the Fair.* Atlanta: N.p., 1916.

Southeastern Federation of Colored Women's Clubs. *Southern Negro Women and Race Cooperation.* Atlanta: The Federation, 1921.

The Southern Interstate Fair Association. *Official Premium List.* Atlanta: 1900.

Souvenir Album of the Cotton States and International Exposition. Atlanta: 1895.

Spaulding, Jack. "History of the Piedmont Driving Club." Manuscript, Atlanta Historical Society.

Stacy, James. *A History of the Presbyterian Church in Georgia.* Elberton, Ga.: Press of the Star, 1912.

Stafford, Martha. "Interracial Progress as Illustrated by the Work of the Atlanta TB Association." Master's thesis, Atlanta University, 1939.

Steed, Hal. "Atlanta," *The Georgia Review* 2 (Spring 1948), 98-108.

"Supersalesman," [Martha Berry], *Entrepreneur Spirit* 2 (August 1, 1974), 49-52.

Sutker, Solomon. "The Jews of Atlanta: Their Social Structure and Leadership Patterns." Ph.D. dissertation, University of North Carolina, 1950.

———. "The Jewish Organizational Elite in Atlanta," *Social Forces* 31 (December 1952), 136-43.

Tallulah Falls School, *Annual Report*, Fiscal Year Ending June 30, 1972. Tallulah Falls School, Inc., 1971.

Talmadge, Franklin C. *The Story of the Presbytery of Atlanta.* Atlanta: Foote and Davies, 1960.

———. *Corra Harris: Lady of Purpose.* Athens: University of Georgia Press, 1960.

Tarver, James I. *Population Trends of Georgia Towns and Cities.* University of Georgia, College of Agriculture Experimental Station, Research Report #43, 1969.

Taylor, A. Elizabeth. "The Origin of the Woman Suffrage Movement in Georgia," *Georgia Historical Quarterly* 28 (June 1944), 63-79.

_____. "The Revival and Development of the Woman Suffrage Movement in Georgia," *Georgia Historical Quarterly* 42 (December 1958), 339-54.

_____. "The Last Phase of the Woman Suffrage Movement in Georgia," *Georgia Historical Quarterly* 43 (March 1959), 11-27.

Temple, Sarah B. G. "Life Today in Buckhead," *Atlanta Journal Magazine*, December 29, 1935, 1-2.

Thomas, Jesse O. *My Story in Black and White: The Autobiography of Jesse O. Thomas*. New York: Exposition Press, 1967.

Thompson, James R. "The Forward Atlanta Movement." Master's thesis, Emory University, 1948.

Thompson, Leita. *A History of the Georgia Federation of Business and Professional Women's Clubs, Inc., May 1919-May 1956, Inclusive*. Atlanta: n.p., 1941.

Thornton, Ella May. *Georgia Women, 1840-1940: A Record of Achievement*. Atlanta: n.p., 1941.

Torrance, Ridgely. *The Story of John Hope*. New York: Macmillan, 1948.

Townsend, Marie. *One Hundred Years of the First Christian Church, Atlanta, Georgia*. Atlanta: Cullum and Ghertner, 1951.

Townsend, Sara Bertha. "The Addition of Women to the University of Georgia," *Georgia Historical Quarterly* 42 (June 1959), 159-69.

Traylor, Leatrice. "Leaders in Voluntary Associations." Master's thesis, Atlanta University, 1952.

Troup, Cornelius. *Distinguished Negro Georgians*. Dallas: Royal Publishing Co., 1962.

[United Daughters of the Confederacy, Atlanta Chapter.] *History, Atlanta Chapter, United Daughters of the Confederacy, 1897-1922*. N.p., n.d.

_____. Georgia Division. *Minutes of the Annual Convention*. New Orleans, 1902; Columbus, Ga., 1901; West Point, Ga., 1909; Macon, Ga., 1905; Cartersville, Ga., 1910; Augusta, Ga., 1907; Griffin, Ga., 1911; Moultrie, Ga., 1913; Eastman, Ga., 1914; Thomasville, Ga., 1915; Dublin, Ga., 1916; Valdosta, Ga., 1919; Augusta, Ga., 1923; Quitman, Ga., 1924; Sandersville, Ga., 1925; Statesboro, Ga., 1926; Atlanta, 1928; Moultrie, 1929; Albany, Ga., 1930; Dublin, 1931; Athens, Ga., 1933; Bainbridge, Ga., 1932; Macon, Ga., 1937; Atlanta, 1939. Published by the UDC.

_____. *Georgia Division Roster and Ancestry Roll of the United Daughters of the Confederacy*. N.p., 1960.

Wall, Mabelle S., ed. "Artistic Atlanta, Featuring Music, Drama, Dance, sponsored by the Rabun Gap-Nacoochee Guild, and Georgia Piano Ensemble," [program]. October 4, 1935. Atlanta, n.p.

Washington Seminary, Atlanta. *Catalogue*, 1893-94.

White, Dana F., and Timothy J. Crimmins. "Urban Structure, Atlanta," *Journal of Urban History* 2 (February 1976), 231-51.

White, Gayle. "White-Ribboned Birthday," [Georgia W.C.T.U.], *Atlanta Journal Constitution Magazine*, January 19, 1975.

White, Mary Culler. *The Portal of Wonderland: The Life and Story of Alice Culler Cobb*. New York: Fleming H. Revell Co., 1925.

White, Walter. *A Man Called White*. Bloomington: Indiana University Press, 1948.

[Whitehurst, Mrs. J. M.] *Georgia Federation of Women's Clubs, 1896-1971*. Atlanta, Savannah, and Georgia Gas Companies.

Wilson, Dr. Stainback. "Atlanta As It Is," *Atlanta Historical Bulletin* 6 (January 1941, April 1941), entire issue.

Womble, Mrs. Mary Venable. "Condensed History of the First Methodist Episcopal Church, South, Atlanta, Georgia," *Atlanta Historical Bulletin* 2 (January 1928), 20-28.

Women's Christian Temperance Union, Georgia Division. *Report of the 91st Anniversary Convention*, Savannah, Georgia, October 20-21, 1972. N.p.

_____. *Minutes of the Second Annual Conference*, Augusta, Georgia, January 24-25, 1884. Atlanta: Temperance Advocate Printing, 1884.

_____. *Bulletin*, 1930-1938.

Woodberry, Rosa. *Pioneer Notes on the Foundation Period of the Georgia Federation*. Savannah: Women's Federation, 1921.

Works Progress Administration, Georgia. *The Social and Economic Pattern of Atlanta, Georgia*: A Statistical Study of Certain Aspects of the Social and Economic Pattern of the City of Atlanta, Georgia. Official Project No: 465-34-3-4, 1939.

Wright, Wade H. *History of the Georgia Power Company, 1855-1956*. Atlanta: Georgia Power Co., ca. 1957.

Young Matrons Circle for Tallulah Falls School. *Yearbook, 1971-1972*. N.p.

Yohan, Walter. "The Presbyterians and Social Class in the Atlanta Metro Area." Ph.D. dissertation, Emory University, 1967.

SECONDARY SOURCES

Acker, Joan. "Woman and Social Stratification: A Case of Intellectual Sexism," *American Journal of Sociology* 78 (January 1973), 936-45.

All Colors, A Study Outline of Women's Part in Race Relations. New York: Women's Press and Associated Press, 1926.

Allen, Robert L. *Reluctant Reformers: Racism and Social Reform Movements in the U.S.* New York: Doubleday, 1975.

Almanzor, Angelina C. "Volunteer and Staff Participation in a Voluntary Social Welfare Association in the United States: A Study of the National YWCA." D.S.W. dissertation, Columbia University, 1961.

Anderson, Mary. *Woman's Place in Industry in Ten Southern States.* Washington, D.C.: GPO, 1931.

Anderson, Peggy. *The Daughters: An Unconventional Look at America's Fan Club—The DAR.* New York: St. Martin's Press, 1974.

Argyle, Michael. *The Social Psychology of Work.* New York: Taplinger Publishing Co., 1972.

Axelrod, Morris "Urban Structure and Social Participation," *American Sociological Review* 21 (February 1956), 13-18.

Babchuk, Nicholas, and Ralph V. Thompson. "The Voluntary Associations of Negroes," *American Sociological Review* 27 (October 1962), 647-55.

Bailey, Hugh C. *Liberalism in the New South: Southern Social Reformers and the Progressive Movement.* Coral Gables, Fla.: University of Miami, 1969.

Bailey, Kenneth K. *Southern White Protestantism in the Twentieth Century.* New York: Harper and Row, 1964.

Baker, Elizabeth F. *Technology and Woman's Work.* New York: Columbia University Press, 1964.

Baker, Paul. *Negro-White Adjustments.* New York: Association Press, 1934.

Banner, Lois W. *Women in Modern America: A Brief History.* New York: Harcourt Brace Jovanovich, Inc., 1974.

Banton, Michael. *Roles: An Introduction to the Study of Social Relations.* London: Tavistock Publications, Ltd., 1965.

Barber, Virginia, and Merrill M. Skaggs. *The Mother Person.* Indianapolis: Bobbs-Merrill, 1975.

Baro, Gene, ed. *After Appomatox: The Image of the South in Its Fiction, 1865-1900.* New York: Corinth Books, Inc., 1963.

Barrington, Lewis. *Historic Restorations of the D.A.R.* New York: Richard Smith, 1941.

Beard, Charles A., and Mary R. Beard. *The Rise of American Civilization*. New York: Macmillan, 1930.

Beard, Mary R. *Woman's Work in Municipalities*. New York: D. Appleton Co., 1915.

_____. *America Through Women's Eyes*. New York: Macmillan, 1934.

_____. *Women as Force in History*. New York: Macmillan, 1946.

Bell, Juliet O., and Helen J. Wilkins. *Interracial Practices in Community YWCAs*. New York: The Women's Press, 1944.

Benedict, Mary K. "The Higher Education of Women in the Southern States," in *The South in the Building of the Nation*, Vol. 10, 260-71. Richmond, Va.: The Southern Historical and Publication Society, 1909.

Berger, Bennett M. "Suburbia and the American Dream," *The Public Interest* 1 (Winter 1966), 80-91.

Bernard, Jessie. *The Future of Motherhood*. New York: The Dial Press, 1974.

Berne, Eric. *The Structure and Dynamics of Organizations and Groups*. New York: J. P. Lippincott, 1963.

Billington, Monroe Lee. *The Political South in the Twentieth Century*. New York: Charles Scribner's Sons, 1975.

The Biographical Cyclopaedia of American Women. 3 vols. Compiled by Mabel Ward Cameron. New York: Halvord Publishing Co., 1924.

Birmingham, Stephen. *Certain People: America's Black Elite*. Boston: Little, Brown and Co., 1977.

Blau, Peter M., and William R. Scott. "Formal Organizations," *American Journal of Sociology* 43 (July 1957), 58-69.

Bliss, Kathleen. *The Service and Status of Women in the Churches*. London: S.C.M. Press, Ltd., 1952.

Boris, Joseph J., ed. *Who's Who in Colored America: A Biographical Dictionary of Notable Living Persons of Negro Descent in America*. New York: Who's Who in Colored America Corp., Publishers, 1927.

Bott, Elizabeth. *Family and Social Network: Roles, Norms, and External Relationships in Ordinary Urban Families*. New York: The Free Press, 1971.

Boulding, Elise M. "The Effects of Industrialization on the Participation of Women in Society." Ph.D. dissertation, University of Michigan, 1969.

Boulding, Kenneth E. *The Organizational Revolution: A Study of the Ethics of Economic Organization*. Chicago: Quadrangle Books, 1968.

Bowers, Raymond V., ed. *Studies on Behavior in Organizations: A Research Symposium*. Athens: University of Georgia Press, 1966.

Bradbury, Harriet Bowker. *Civilization and Womanhood*. Boston: Richard G. Badger, 1916.

Breckinridge, Mary. *Wide Neighborhoods: A Story of the Frontier Nursing Service*. New York: Harper & Bros., 1952.

Breckinridge, Sophonisba D. *Madeline McDowell Breckinridge, A Leader in the New South*. Chicago: University of Chicago Press, 1921.

_____. *Women in the Twentieth Century: A Study of their Political, Social, and Economic Activities*. New York: McGraw-Hill, 1933.

_____. "Women's Organizations," and "The Activities of Women Outside the Home," in Vol. 1 of *Recent Trends in the U.S.: Report of the President's Committee on Social Trends*. New York: McGraw-Hill, 1933.

Bridges, William E. "Family Patterns and Social Values in America, 1825-1875," *American Quarterly* 17 (Spring 1965), 3-11.

Briffault, Robert. *The Mothers: A Study of the Origins of Sentiments and Institutions*. New York: Macmillan, 1927.

Brown, Dee. *The Year of the Century: 1876*. New York: Charles Scribner's Sons, 1966.

Brown, Hallie Quinn. *Homespun Heroines and Other Women of Distinction*. Xenia, Ohio: The Aldine Publishing Co., 1926.

Brownell, Blaine. "The Urban Mind in the South: The Growth of Urban Consciousness in Southern Cities, 1920-1927." Ph.D. dissertation, University of North Carolina, 1969.

Buckman, Rilma O. "Interaction Between Women's Clubs and Institutions in Greater Lafayette, Indiana." Ph.D. dissertation, University of Chicago, 1953.

Burdett-Coutts, Baroness Angela Georgina, ed. *Woman's Mission: A Series of Congress Papers on the Philanthropic Work of Women*. New York: Charles Scribner's Sons, 1893.

Burrows, Edward Flud. "The Commission on Interracial Cooperation: A Case Study in the History of the Interracial Movement in the South." Ph.D. dissertation, University of Wisconsin, 1954.

Burton, Margaret E. *Mabel Cratty: Leader in the Art of Leadership*. New York: The Woman's Press, 1929.

Calhoun, Arthur Wallace. *A Social History of the American Family from Colonial Times to the Present*. Cleveland: Arthur H. Clarke Co., 1917-1919.

Cash, W. J. *The Mind of the South*. Garden City, N.Y.: Doubleday and Co., Inc., 1956.

Castle, Cora S. *Statistical Study of Eminent Women*. New York: The Science Press, 1913.

Cawelti, John G. "America on Display: The World's Fairs of 1876, 1893, 1933," in Frederick Cople Jaher, ed., *The Age of Industrialism in America: Essays in Social Structure and Cultural Values*. New York: The Free Press, 1968.

Chafe, William H. *The American Woman, Her Changing Social, Economic, and Political Roles, 1920-1970*. New York: Oxford, 1972.

Chapin, F. Stuart, and John Isouderos. "The Formalization Process in Voluntary Organizations," *Social Forces* 34 (May 1956), 342-44.

Clark, Peter B., and James Q. Wilson. "Incentive System: A Theory of Organization," *Administrative Science* 6 (June 1961), 223-37.

Clarke, Ida Clyde, ed. *Women of 1924, International*. New York: Women's News Service, Inc., 1924.

_____. *Uncle Sam Needs A Wife*. Philadelphia: John C. Winston Co., 1925.

Cleveland, Grover. "Woman's Mission and Woman's Clubs," *Ladies Home Journal* 22 (May 1905), 7-8.

Cole, Doris. *From Tipi to Skyscraper: A History of Women in Architecture*. Boston: i press inc., 1973.

Coll, Blanche. *Perspectives in Public Welfare: A History*. Washington, D.C.: U.S. Dept. of Health, Education and Welfare, 1969.

Collier, Mrs. Bryan Wells (Margaret Wooten). *Biographies of Representative Women of the South*. Vol. I: 1861-1920; Vol. II: 1861-1923; Vol. III: 1861-1925; Vol. IV: 1861-1927; Vol. V: 1861-1929; Vol. VI: 1831-1938. Published by the author.

Cooper, Anna Julia. *A Voice from the South: By a Black Woman of the South*. New York Negro Universities Press, 1969 [1892].

Couch, W. T., ed. *Culture in the South*. Chapel Hill: University of North Carolina Press, 1934.

Cox, Oliver. *Caste, Class and Race: A Study in Social Dynamics*. New York: Doubleday and Co., 1948.

Croly, Mrs. J. C. (Jennie June). *The History of the Woman's Club Movement in America*. New York: H. G. Allen, 1898.

Culver, Elsie Thomas. *Women in the World of Religion: From Pagan Priestesses to Ecumenical Delegates*. Garden City, N.Y.: Doubleday and Co., 1967.

Cumming, Kate. *Gleanings from the Southland*. Birmingham, Ala.: Roberts and Son, 1895.

Curti, Merle. "The Changing Pattern of Certain Humanitarian Organizations," *Annals of the American Association of Political and Social Sciences* 179 (May 1935), 59-67.

_____. *The Growth of American Thought*. New York: Harper and Bros., 1951.

Dabney, Virginius. *Liberalism in the South*. Chapel Hill: University of North Carolina Press, 1932.

Daniel, Sadie Iola. *Women Builders*. Washington, D.C.: Associated Publishers, Inc., 1931.

Dannett, Sylvia G. L. *Profile of Negro Womanhood*. 2 vols. Negro Heritage Library. Yonkers, N.Y.: Educational Heritage, Inc., 1964-1966.

Davies, Wallace Evan. *Patriotism on Parade: The Story of Veterans and Hereditary Organizations in America, 1783-1900*. Cambridge, Mass.: Harvard University Press, 1955.

Davis, Allen F. *American Heroine: The Life and Legend of Jane Addams*. New York: Oxford, 1973.

Davis, Allen F., and Mary Lynn McCree, eds. *Eighty Years at Hull House*. Chicago: Quadrangle Books, 1969.

Davis, Allison, Burleigh B. Gardner, and Mary R. Gardner. *Deep South: A Social Anthropological Study of Caste and Class*. Chicago: University of Chicago, 1941.

Davis, Elizabeth Lindsay. *Lifting as They Climb: The National Association of Colored Women*. Published by the Association, 1933.

Davis, Lenwood G. *Black Women in the Cities, 1872-1972*. Monticello, Ill.: Council of Planning Librarians, 1972.

Degler, Carl N. *Out of Our Past: The Forces That Shaped Modern America*. New York: Harper & Row, 1959.

_____. "What Ought to be and What Was: Women's Sexuality in the 19th Century," *American Historical Review* 79 (December 1974), 1467-90.

Dobriner, William M. *Class in Suburbia*. Englewood Cliffs, N.J.: Prentice-Hall, 1963.

Dollard, John. *Caste and Class in a Southern Town*. New Haven: Yale University Press, 1937.

Douglass, H. Paul, and Edmund DeS. Brunner. *The Protestant Church As a Social Institution*. New York: Harper & Bros., 1935.

Doyle, Bertram. *The Etiquette of Race Relations*. New York: Schocken Books, 1971 [1937].

Drake, Richard B. "The American Missionary Association and the Southern Negro, 1861-1888." Ph.D. dissertation, Emory University, 1957.

Drake, St. Clair. *Churches and Voluntary Associations in a Negro Community.* Chicago: Works Progress Administration, 1940.

DuBois, W. E. B. "Race Relations in the United States, 1917-1949," *Phylon* 9 (1948), 234-47.

Durr, Virginia Foster. "The Emancipation of Southern, Pure, White Womanhood," *New South* 26 (Winter 1971), 46-54.

Duster, Alfreda M., ed. *Crusade for Justice: The Autobiography of Ida B. Wells.* Chicago: University of Chicago Press, 1970.

Dykeman, Wilma, and James Stokely. *Seeds of Southern Change: The Life of Will Alexander.* Chicago: University of Chicago Press, 1962.

Dynes, Russell. "The Consequences of Sectarianism for Social Participation," *Social Forces* 35 (May 1957), 331-34.

Evans, Eli N. *The Provincials: A Personal History of Jews in the South.* New York: Atheneum, 1973.

Fisher, Dorothy Canfield. *Why Stop Learning?* New York: Harcourt, Brace, and Co., 1927.

Fletty, Valborg Esther. "Public Services of Women's Organizations." Ph.D. dissertation, Syracuse University, 1952.

Flexner, Eleanor. *Century of Struggle: The Woman's Rights Movement in the United States.* Cambridge: Harvard University Press, 1959.

Franklin, John Hope. *From Slavery to Freedom.* New York: Alfred Knopf, Inc., 1947.

Furer, Howard B. "The American City: A Catalyst for the Woman's Rights Movement," *Wisconsin Magazine of History* 52 (Summer 1969), 285-306.

Gage, Matilda Joslyn. *Women, Church, and State.* New York: Arno Press, 1972.

Gaston, Paul M. *The New South Creed: A Study in Southern Mythmaking.* New York: Alfred A. Knopf, 1970.

Gibbs, Margaret. *The D.A.R.* New York: Holt, Rinehart, & Winston, 1969.

Giedion, Sigfried. *Mechanization Takes Command: A Contribution to Anonymous History.* New York: Oxford University Press, 1948.

Giele, Janet Z. "Social Change in the Feminine Role: A Comparison of Woman's Suffrage and Woman's Temperance, 1870-1920." Ph.D. dissertation, Radcliffe College, 1961.

Gillette, John M. "Community Concepts," *Social Forces* 4 (1926), 677-89.

Glasgow, Ellen. *The Deliverance.* New York: Doubleday Page & Co., 1904.

_____. *Voice of the People*. New York: Doubleday, 1904.

_____. *Barren Ground*. New York: Sagamore Press, Inc., 1957 [1925].

_____. *The Woman Within*. New York: Harcourt, Brace, and Co., 1954.

Goldhammer, Herbert. "Voluntary Associations in the United States," *Third Year Readings in Contemporary Sociology*. Chicago, 1935.

Gordon, Milton M. *Social Class in American Sociology*. New York: McGraw-Hill Co., Inc., 1950.

Gossett, Thomas J. *Race: The History of an Idea in America*. Dallas: Southern Methodist University Press, 1963.

Gouldner, Alvin. *Studies in Leadership: Leadership and Democratic Action*. New York: Harper and Co., 1950.

Gouldner, Helen Beem. "The Organization Woman: Patterns of Friendship and Organizational Commitment." Ph.D. dissertation, UCLA, 1960.

Grantham, Dewey, ed. *The South and the Sectional Image: The Sectional Theme Since Reconstruction*. New York: Harper, 1967.

Green, Elizabeth. "I Resign from Female Politics," *New Republic* 42 (April 22, 1925), 233-35.

Green, Fletcher. "Women of the Confederacy in War Times," *Southern Magazine* 2 (1935), 16-20, 47-48. Address before the Agnes Lee Chapter, UDC.

Grimes, Alan P. *The Puritan Ethic and Woman Suffrage*. New York: Oxford, 1967.

Groves, Ernest Rutherford. *The American Woman: the Feminine Side of a Masculine Civilization*. New York: Arno Press, 1972 [1944].

Gruberg, Martin. *Women in American Politics: An Assessment and Sourcebook*. Oshkosh, Wis.: Academia Press, 1968.

Gully, William H. "Relative Effectiveness in Negro and White Voluntary Associations," *Phylon* 24 (1963), 192-73.

Gusfield, Joseph. "The Problem of Generations in an Organizational Structure," *Social Forces* 35 (May 1957), 323-30.

_____. *Symbolic Crusade: Status Politics and the American Temperance Movement*. Chicago: University of Illinois Press, 1969.

Haas, J. Eugene, Richard N. Hall, and Norman J. Johnson. "Toward an Empirically Derived Taxonomy of Organizations," in Raymond V. Bowers, ed., *Studies on Behavior in Organizations*, 157-80.

Hacker, Helen Mayer. "Women As a Minority Group," *Social Forces* 30 (October 1951), 60-69.

Hall, Mary Ross, and Helen Firman Sweet. *Women in the Y.M.C.A. Record.* New York: Association Press, 1947.

Hall, Richard H., ed. *The Formal Organization.* New York: Basic Books, 1972.

Hammond, Mrs. Lily Hardy. *In Black and White.* New York: Fleming H. Revell Co., 1914.

Harkness, Georgia. *Women in Church and Society: A Historical and Theological Inquiry.* Nashville: Abingdon Press, 1972.

Harris, Frederic. "Christian Associations and the Community," *Social Forces* 4 (June 1926), 776-80.

Herman, Sondra R. "Loving Courtship or the Marriage Market? The Ideal and Its Critics," *American Quarterly* 25 (May 1973), 235-52.

Herrick, Robert. *Together.* New York: Macmillan Co., 1908.

Hobson, Mrs. E. C., and Mrs. C. E. Hopkins. "A Report Concerning the Colored Women of the South," *Occasional Papers*, No. 9. Baltimore: John F. Slater Fund, 1896.

Hofstadter, Richard. " 'Idealists and Professors and Soreheads': The Genteel Reformers," *Columbia University Forum* (Spring 1962), 4-11.

Holt, Rackham. *Mary McLeod Bethune: A Biography.* Garden City, N.Y.: Doubleday & Co., 1964.

Houghton, Walter E. *The Victorian Frame of Mind, 1830-1870.* New Haven: Yale University Press, 1957.

Howell, Mabel Kate. *Women and the Kingdom: Fifty Years of Kingdom Building by the Women of the Methodist Episcopal Church South, 1878-1928.* Nashville: Cokesbury Press, 1928.

Howes, Durand, ed. *American Women: The Official Who's Who Among the Women of the Nation, 1935-36.* Los Angeles: Richard Blank Publishing Co., 1935.

Huber, Joan, ed. *Changing Women in a Changing Society.* Chicago: University of Chicago Press, 1973.

Hunt, Alma. *History of the Woman's Missionary Union.* Nashville, Tenn.: Convention Press, 1964.

Hunt, Charles L. "Female Occupational Roles and Urban Sex Ratios," *Social Forces* 43 (March 1965), 407-17.

Hunton, Mrs. W. A. "Women's Clubs," *The Crisis* 7 (May 1911), 17.

_____. "Caring for the Children," *The Crisis* 7 (July 1911), 78-79.

_____. "Caring for the Young Woman," *The Crisis* 7 (July 1911), 121-22.

Hurston, Zora Neale. *Dust Tracks on the Road: An Autobiography.* Philadelphia: J. B. Lippincott Co., 1942.

International Library of Negro Life and History. *Historical Negro Biographies.* New York: Publishers Co., Inc., 1967.

Jackson, Kenneth T. *The Ku Klux Klan in the City, 1915-1930.* New York: Oxford, 1967.

James, Edward T., Janet Wilson James, and Paul S. Boyer. *Notable American Women, 1607-1950: A Biographical Dictionary.* 3 vols. Cambridge, Mass.: Belknap Press of Harvard University Press, 1971.

Jennings, Eugene E. *An Anatomy of Leadership: Princes, Heroes, and Supermen.* New York: McGraw-Hill Book Co., 1960.

Jessup, Josephine Lurie. *The Faith of Our Feminists: A Study in the Novels of Edith Wharton, Ellen Glasgow, and Willa Cather.* New York: R. R. Smith, 1950.

Johnson, Dorothy E. "Organized Women as Lobbyists in the 1920s," *Capitol Studies* 6, 41-58.

Jones, Katharine, ed. *Heroines of Dixie.* Indianapolis: Bobbs-Merrill Press, 1955.

Jones, Lance G. E. *The Jeanes Teacher in the U.S., 1908-1933: An Account of 25 Years of Experience in the Supervision of Negro Rural Schools.* Chapel Hill: University of North Carolina Press, 1937.

Kearney, Belle. *A Slaveholder's Daughter.* New York: Abbey Press, 1900.

Keller, Suzanne. *Beyond the Ruling Class: Strategic Elites in Modern Society.* New York: Random House, 1963.

Kerber, Linda. "The Republican Mother and the Enlightenment—An American Perspective," *American Quarterly* 8 (Summer 1976), 187-205.

Key, Ellen Karolina Sofia. *The Renaissance of Motherhood.* New York: Source Book Press, 1970.

Key, V. O., Jr. *Southern Politics.* New York: Random House, 1949.

Killian, Lewis M. *White Southerners.* New York: Random House, 1970.

King, Grace. *Memories of a Southern Woman of Letters.* Freeport, N.Y.: Books for Libraries Press, 1971 [1932].

King, Peggy Cameron. *Ladies, Please Come to Order!* New York: Grosset and Dunlap, 1968.

Kohut, Rebekah Bettelheim. "Jewish Women's Organizations in the U.S.," *Jewish Year Book* 33 (1931-32), 165-201.

Komarovsky, Mirra. "A Comparative Study of Voluntary Organizations," *American Sociological Review* 27 (May 1933).

———. "Cultural Contradictions and Sex Roles," *American Journal of Sociology* 3 (November 1946), 184-90.

———. "The Voluntary Associations of Urban Dwellers," *American Sociological Review* 2 (December 1946), 686-98.

Kovel, Joel. *White Racism: A Psychohistory*. New York: Random House, 1970.

Kraditor, Aileen. *The Ideas of the Woman Suffrage Movement*. New York: Columbia University Press, 1965.

LaGanke, Lucile E. "The NSDAR: Its History, Policies, and Influence, 1890-1949." Ph.D. dissertation, Case-Western University, 1951.

Lasch, Christopher. *The New Radicalism in America, 1889-1962: The Intellectual as a Social Type*. New York: Alfred A. Knopf, 1965.

Lauman, Edward O. *Prestige and Association in an Urban Community: An Analysis of an Urban Stratification System*. New York: Bobbs-Merrill Co., 1966.

Laurence, Margaret. *The School of Femininity: A Book About Women As They Are Interpreted Through Feminine Writers of Yesterday and Today*. Port Washington, N.Y.: Kennikat Press, 1936.

Lemons, J. Stanley. *The Woman Citizen: Social Feminism in the 1920s*. Urbana: University of Illinois, 1973.

Lerner, Gerda. *Black Women in White America: A Documentary History*. New York: Pantheon Books, 1972.

Litterer, Joseph A. *Organizations: Structure and Behavior*. 2d ed. New York: John Wiley and Sons, Inc., 1969.

Lollis, Lorraine. *The Shape of Adam's Rib: A Lively History of Women's Work in the Christian Church*. St. Louis, Mo.: Bethany Press, 1970.

Lord, Clifford L. *Keepers of the Past*. Chapel Hill: University of North Carolina Press, 1965.

Lubove, Roy. *The Professional Altruist: The Emergence of Social Work as a Career, 1880-1930*. Cambridge, Mass.: Harvard University Press, 1965.

Luckhurst, Kenneth W. *The Story of Exhibitions*. London: The Studio Publication, 1951.

Lumpkin, Katherine Du Pre. *The Making of a Southerner*. New York: Alfred A. Knopf, 1947.

Lundberg, Georg A., Mirra Komarovsky, and Mary A. McInery. *Leisure: A Suburban Study*. New York: Columbia University Press, 1934.

Lyman, Stanford M. *The Black American in Sociological Thought: A Failure of Perspective*. New York: G. P. Putnam's Sons, 1972.

MacDougal, G. Elise (Johnson). "The Double Task: The Struggle of Negro Women for Sex and Race Emancipation," *Survey* 53 (March 1, 1925), 689-91.

Majors, M. A. *Noted Negro Women: Their Triumphs and Activities*. Chicago: Donohue and Henneberry, 1893.

Marden, Charles F. *Rotary and Its Brothers: An Analysis and Interpretation of the Men's Service Club*. Princeton: University Press, 1935.

Martin, George Madden. "The American Woman and Representative Government," *Atlantic Monthly* 135 (March 1925), 363-71.

Massa, Ann. "Black Women in the 'White City.' " *American Studies* 8, 319-37.

Massey, Mary Elizabeth. *Bonnet Brigades: American Women and the Civil War*. New York: Alfred A. Knopf, 1966.

Mayfield, Sara. *The Constant Circle: H. L. Mencken and His Friends*. New York: Dell Publishing Co., 1968.

Mayo, Amory Dwight. *Southern Women in the Recent Educational Movement in the South*. Washington, D.C.: Bureau of Education. Circular No. 1, 1892.

McClintock, Charles G. "The Behavior of Leaders, Non-Leaders, Non-Joiners, and Non-Leader-Joiners Under Conditions of Group Support and Non-Support," in Raymond V. Bowers, ed., *Studies on Behavior in Organizations*, 181-210.

McDonald, Thomas C. *Free Masonry and Its Progress in Atlanta and Fulton Co*. Atlanta: n.p., 1925.

McGovern, James R. "The American Woman's Pre-World War I Freedom in Manners and Morals," *Journal of American History* 55 (September 1968), 315-33.

Meier, August. *Negro Thought in America, 1880-1915*. Ann Arbor: University of Michigan Press, 1970.

Meier, August, and E. M. Rudwick. "Black Man in the 'White City': Negroes and the Columbian Exposition, 1893," *Phylon* 26 (1965), 354-61.

_____. *From Plantation to Ghetto: An Interpretive History of American Negroes*. New York: Hill and Wang, 1966.

Mendenhall, Marjorie. "Southern Women of a Lost Generation," *South Atlantic Quarterly* 33 (October 1934), 334-53.

Merton, Robert K. *Social Theory and Social Structure*. Glencoe, Ill.: Free Press, 1957.

Meyerand, Gladys. "Women's Organizations," *Encyclopedia of the Social Sciences*, Vol. 15, 460-65. New York: Macmillan, 1935.

Milholland, Mrs. J. E. "Talks About Women," *The Crisis* 1 (January-June, 1910).

Moffat, Adalene. "Views of a Southern Woman," *The Crisis* 2 (August 1911), 160-62.

Moore, Joan W. "Patterns of Women's Participation in Voluntary Associations," *American Journal of Sociology* 61 (May 1961), 598-607.

Mossell, N. F. *The Work of the Afro-American Women*. Philadelphia: George S. Ferguson Co., 1908.

Munford, Mrs. B. B. "Woman's Part in the Educational Progress of the South," in *The South in the Building of the Nation*, 10, 638-44.

Myrdal, Gunnar. *An American Dilemma: The Negro Problem and Modern Democracy*. New York: Harper & Bros., 1944.

Nathan, Maud. "Women Who Work and Women Who Spend," *Annals of the American Association of Political and Social Science* 27 (September 1906), 646-50.

National Society, Colonial Dames of America. *Directory 1900*. Manchester, N.H.: John B. Clarke Co., 1901.

Nearing, Scott. *Women and Social Progress: A Discussion of the Biological, Domestic, Industrial, and Social Possibilities of American Women*. New York: Macmillan, 1917.

[Newman, Frances]. *The Letters of Frances Newman*, ed. Hansell Baugh. New York: Horace Liveright, 1929.

Noble, Jeane L. *The Negro Woman's College Education*. New York: Bureau of Publications, Teachers College, Columbia University, 1956.

O'Neill, William. *Everyone Was Brave: A History of Feminism in America*. New York: Quadrangle Books, 1969.

_____. *The Woman Movement: Feminism in the United States and England*. Chicago: Quadrangle, 1971.

Overton, Grant Martin. *The Women Who Make Our Novels*. New York: Moffat, Yard, and Co., 1918.

Palmer, D. H. "Moving North: Negro Migration During World War I," *Phylon* 28 (1967), 52-62.

Palmer, Edward N. "Negro Secret Societies," *Social Forces* 23 (December 1944), 207-12.

Parker, Alice N. "Kindergarten in the South," in *The South in the Building of the Nation* 10, 381-86.

Penn, I. Garland. *The Afro-American Press and Its Editors*. New York: Arno Press, 1969.

Peterkin, Julia. *The Collected Short Stories of Julia Peterkin*, edited and with an introduction by Frank Durham. Columbia: University of South Carolina Press, 1970.

Pierce, Bessie Louise. "The Political Pattern of Some Women's Organizations," *Social Forces* 174 (May 1935), 50-58.

Poppenheim, Louisa B. "Woman's Work in the South," in *The South in the Building of the Nation* 10, 623-37.

Presthus, Robert. *The Organizational Society: An Analysis and A Theory*. New York: Random House, 1962.

Price, Margaret Nell. "The Development of Leadership by Southern Women through Clubs and Organizations." Master's thesis, University of North Carolina, 1968.

Pruett, Lorine. *Women and Leisure: A Study of Social Waste*. New York: E. P. Dutton and Co., 1924.

Reeves, Nancy. *Womankind: Beyond the Stereotypes*. Chicago: Aldine Atherton, 1971.

Reissman, Leonard. "Class, Leisure and Social Participation," *American Sociological Review* 19 (February 1954), 76-84.

Rich, Adrienne. *Of Woman Born: Motherhood as Experience and Institution*. New York: W. W. Norton, 1976.

Riegel, Robert E. *American Women: A Story of Social Change*. Teaneck, N.J.: Farleigh Dickinson University Press, 1970.

Ripley, Katharine Ball. *Sand Dollars*. New York: Harcourt, Brace, and Co., 1933.

Rose, Arnold M. "The Adequacy of Women's Expectations for Adult Roles," *Social Forces* 30 (October 1951), 69-77.

Rosenberg, Charles E. "Sexuality, Class, and Role in 19th Century America," *American Quarterly* 25 (May 1973), 131-53.

Ross, Aileen. "Control and Leadership in Women's Groups: An Analysis of Philanthropic Money-raising Activity," *Social Forces* 37 (October 1958), 124-31.

Ross, Elizabeth Dale. *The Kindergarten Crusade: The Establishment of Preschool Education in the United States*. Athens: Ohio University Press, 1976.

Ross, Ishbel. *Sons of Adam, Daughters of Eve: The Role of Women in American History*. New York: Harper & Row, 1969.

Rossi, Alice. *The Feminist Papers: From Adams to de Beauvoir.* New York: Columbia University Press, 1973.

Rousmaniere, John P. "Cultural Hybrid in the Slums: The College Woman and the Settlement House, 1889-1894," *American Quarterly* 22 (Spring 1970), 45-66.

Rubin, Louis D., and Robert D. Jacobs, eds. *Southern Renascence: The Literature of the Modern South.* Baltimore: Johns Hopkins Press, 1953.

Rushbrooke, Rev. J. H., ed. *Official Report of the Sixth Baptist World Congress, Atlanta, Georgia, July 22-28, 1939.* Atlanta: Published by the Alliance, 1939.

Russell, Charles Edward. "Is Woman Suffrage a Failure?" *Century* 107 (March 1924), 724-30.

Ryan, Mary P. *Womanhood in America: From Colonial Times to the Present.* New York: Franklin Watts, 1975.

Schlesinger, Arthur M. *Learning How to Behave: A Study of American Etiquette.* New York: Macmillan, 1946.

_____. *Paths to the Present.* New York: Macmillan, 1949.

Scott, Anne Firor. "After Suffrage, Southern Women in the Twenties," *Journal of Southern History* 30 (August 1964), 298-318.

_____. "The Study of Southern Urbanization," *Urban Affairs Quarterly* 6 (March 1966), 5-14.

_____. *The Southern Lady: From Pedestal to Politics, 1830-1930.* Chicago: University of Chicago Press, 1970.

_____. "Making the Invisible Woman Visible: An Essay Review," *Journal of American History* 38 (November 1972), 629-38.

Scott, W. Richard. "Theory of Organizations," Chapter 14, Robert E. L. Faris, ed., *Handbook of Modern Sociology.* Chicago: Rand McNally and Co., 1964.

Scouller, Mildred Marshall. *Women Who Man Our Clubs.* Philadelphia: John C. Winston Co., 1934.

Scruggs, L. C. *Women of Distinction.* Raleigh, N.C.: By the author, 1893.

Sebald, Hans. *Momism: The Silent Disease of America.* Chicago: Nelson Hall, 1976.

Seeley, John R., Alexander R. Sim, and Elizabeth W. Loosley. *Creswood Heights: A Study of the Culture of Suburban Life.* New York: Basic Books, Inc., 1956.

Sellers, Charles Grier, Jr., ed. *The Southerner as American.* New York: Basic Books, Inc., 1956.

Seyersted, Per. *Kate Chopin: A Critical Biography*. Baton Rouge: Louisiana State University Press, 1969.

Sills, David. "Voluntary Associations: Sociological Aspects," *International Encyclopedia of the Social Sciences*, Vol. 16, 362-79. New York: Free Press, 1968.

Sinclair, Andrew. *The Emancipation of the American Woman*. New York: Harper & Row, 1965.

Sirjamaki, John. *The Sociology of Cities*. New York: Random House, 1964.

Sklar, Kathryn Kish. *Catharine Beecher: A Study in American Domesticity*. New Haven: Yale University Press, 1973.

Slater, Carol. "Class Differences in Definition of Role and Membership in Voluntary Associations Among Urban Married Women," *American Journal of Sociology* 65 (May 1960), 616-19.

Smith, David H. "The Importance of Formal Voluntary Organizations for Society," *Sociology and Social Research* 50 (July 1966), 483-94.

Smith, Lillian. *Killers of the Dream*. Garden City: Doubleday and Co., 1963.

Smith, Nellie May. *The Three Gifts of Life: A Girl's Responsibility for Race Progress*. New York: Dodd, Mead and Co., 1919.

Smith, Page. *Daughters of the Promised Land: Women in American History*. Boston: Little, Brown and Co., 1970.

Smith, T. Lynn. "The Redistribution of the Negro Population of the United States, 1910-1960," *Journal of Negro History* 51 (July 1966), 155-73.

Smith-Rosenberg, Carroll. "Beauty, the Beast, and the Militant Woman: A Case Study in Sex Roles and Social Stress in Jacksonian America," *American Quarterly* 23 (October 1971), 562-84.

The South in the Building of the Nation. 13 vols. Richmond, Va.: The Southern Historical Publication Society, 1909-1913.

Spencer, Anna Garlin. *Women's Share in Social Culture*. Philadelphia: J. B. Lippincott, 1925.

Spruill, Julia Cherry. *Women's Life and Work in the Southern Colonies*. Chapel Hill: University of North Carolina Press, 1938.

Stampp, Kenneth M. *The Era of Reconstruction, 1865-1877*. New York: Alfred A. Knopf, 1965.

Stanton, Elizabeth Cady et al., *History of Woman Suffrage*. 6 vols. New York: Source Book Press, 1970 [1882-1922].

Stein, Maurice R. *The Eclipse of Community: An Interpretation of American Studies*. New York: Harper & Row, 1964.

Sterling, Dorothy, and Benjamin Quarles. *Lift Every Voice: The Lives of Booker T. Washington, W. E. B. Du Bois, Mary Church Terrell, and James Weldon Johnson.* Garden City: Doubleday and Co., Inc., 1965.

Stern, Madeleine B. *We the Women: Career Firsts of 19th-Century America.* New York: Schulte Publishing Co., 1963.

Straub, Eleanor. "Government Policy Toward Civilian Women During World War II." Ph.D. dissertation, Emory University, 1973.

Strayer, Martha. *The D.A.R.: An Informal History.* Washington, D.C.: Public Affairs Press, 1958.

Svalastoga, Kaare. *Social Differentiation.* New York: David McKay Co., 1965.

Tarbell, Ida. *The Business of Being a Woman.* New York: Macmillan, 1912.

_____. *The Ways of Woman.* New York: Macmillan, 1915.

Tardy, Mary S. *The Living Female Writers of the South.* Philadelphia: Claxton, Romsen, and Haffelfinger, 1872.

Tillett, Wilbur Fisk. "Southern Womanhood as Affected by the War," *Century* 43 (November 1891), 9-14.

Tindall, George B. *The Emergence of the New South, 1913-1945.* Baton Rouge: Louisiana State University Press, 1967.

Todd, Helga C. "Women's Organizations in the United States—their Development and Present Status." Ph.D. dissertation, American University, 1925.

Tompkins, Jean Beattie. "Reference Groups and Status Values as Determinants of Behavior: A Study of Women's Voluntary Association Behavior." Ph.D. dissertation, State University of Iowa, 1955.

Twelve Southerners. *I'll Take My Stand: The South and the Agrarian Tradition.* New York: Harper & Bros., 1930.

Tyler, Helen E. *Where Prayer and Purpose Meet: The W.C.T.U., 1874-1949.* Evanston: The W.C.T.U., n.d.

Van Auken, Sheldon. "The Southern Historical Novel in the Early Twentieth Century," *Journal of Southern History* 14 (1948), 157-91.

Vance, Rupert, and Nicholas Demerath. *The Urban South.* Chapel Hill: University of North Carolina Press, 1954.

Wald, Lillian. "Organization Amongst Working Women," *Annals of the American Association of Political and Social Sciences* 174 (May 1935), 638-45.

Washington, Mrs. Booker T. "Club Work Among Negro Women," in J. W. Gibson, J. L. Nichols, and W. H. Crogman, eds., *Progress of the Race.* Naperville, Ill.: J. L. Nichols Co., 1920.

Washington, Mary Helen, ed. *Black-Eyed Susans: Classic Stories By and About Black Women.* Garden City: Doubleday, 1975.

Watters, Pat. *The South and the Nation.* New York: Pantheon Books, 1969.

White, Martha E. C. "Work of the Woman's Club," *Atlantic Monthly* 93 (May 1904). Reprinted in O'Neill, *The Woman Movement.*

Whitehurst, Sara A. *The Twentieth Century Clubwoman: A Handbook for Organization Leaders.* N.p., 1947.

Whiting, Elizabeth G. *The American Woman's Primer: Her Role in War, Peace—Social Action Pamphlet.* New York: Council for Social Action of Congregational Churches, 1943.

Whitlow, Roger. *Black American Literature: A Critical History.* Totowa, N.J.: Littlefield, Adams, and Co., 1974.

Wiebe, Robert H. *The Search for Order, 1877-1920.* New York: Hill and Wang, 1967.

_____. *The Segmented Society: An Introduction to the Meaning of America.* New York: Oxford, 1975.

Wiley, Bell. "Women of the Lost Cause," *American History, Illustrated* 13 (December 1973), 10-23.

_____. *Confederate Women.* Westport, Conn.: Greenwood Press, 1975.

Willard, Frances, and Mary A. Livermore. *A Woman of the Century.* Detroit: Gale, 1967 [1893].

Williams, Fannie Barrier. *Present Status and Intellectual Progress of Colored Women.* Chicago: Exposition Press, 1893.

Williams, Ona. *American Black Women in the Arts and Social Sciences.* New York: Scarecrow Press, 1973.

Wilson, Margery. *The New Etiquette.* New York: Frederick A. Stokes, 1937.

Wilson, Otto, with Robert Waller Barrett. *Fifty Years Work with Girls, 1883-1933: A Story of the Florence Crittenden Home.* Alexandria, Va.: F. Crittenden Assn., 1933.

Winter, Alice Ames. *The Business of Being a Club Woman.* New York: Century Co., 1925.

Winton, Ruth M. "Negro Participation in Southern Expositions, 1881-1915," *Journal of Negro Education* 16 (Winter 1947), 34-43.

Wish, Harvey. *Society and Thought in Modern America: A Social and Intellectual History of the American People from 1865.* New York: Longmans, Green, and Co., 1952.

Wixen, Burton N. *Children of the Rich.* New York: Crown Publishers, 1973.

Womack, Margaret Anne. "Mildred Lewis Rutherford." Master's thesis, University of Georgia, 1946.

Wood, Mary I. *The History of the General Federation of Women's Clubs: For the First Twenty-two Years of its Organization*. Norwood, Mass.: Norwood Press; New York: History Department, General Federation, 1912.

Woodward, C. Vann. *Origins of the New South, 1877-1913*. Baton Rouge: Louisiana State University Press, 1951.

Woodward, Josephine. "Woman's Clubs from a Reporter's Point of View," *The Club Woman* 3 (December 1898), reprinted in William O'Neill, ed., *The Woman Movement*.

Woody, Thomas. *A History of Women's Education in the United States*. New York: Octagon Books, 1966 [1922].

Wright, Charles R., and Herbert H. Heyman. "Voluntary Association Membership of American Adults: Evidence from National Sample Surveys," *American Sociological Review* 23 (June 1958), 284-94.

Wright, Louis B. *Culture on the Moving Frontier*. New York: Harper & Bros., 1961.

Young, Alfred. *Dissent: Explorations in the History of American Radicalism*. DeKalb, Ill.: Northern Illinois University Press, 1968.

Zald, Mayer N. *Organizational Change: The Political Economy of the Y.M.C.A.* Chicago: University of Chicago Press, 1970.

Zald, Mayer N., and Roberta Ash. "Social Movement Organizations: Growth, Decay, and Change," *Social Forces* 44 (March 1966), 327-40.

Index

Date Due